WHAT READERS ARE SAYING....

There are not many teacher educators who really can work from their course participants' agenda. And only some of these professionals would be able to describe articulately and helpfully what they do. On the other hand, there is a real need for demystifying participant-oriented training in terms of nuts and bolts as well as sound principle.
We find this book manages to do just that. Rod Bolitho and Tony Wright draw on years of experience in many countries and educational contexts in order to make visible the thinking, processes and practices that, together, constitute good training. At the same time the authors offer a fascinating glimpse into their own development as trainers. It is this rare mix which will make the book a source of inspiration and guidance for teacher trainers around the world.

Margit Szesztay and Uwe Pohl,
Centre for English Teacher Training (CETT), Budapest, Hungary

At last – a book to help negotiate the transition from teaching to training. This superb exposition of the skills, knowledge and attitudes required for successful teacher education is a must read for any practitioner interested in facilitating the professional development of trainees and colleagues alike.

Andrew Morris and Julietta Schonmann
AJ International

This is the book I have been waiting for. The authors show 'trainers of trainers' how to create finely-tuned experiential spaces in which 'real content' is developed and fashioned through inquiry reflection, experiment and practice, enabling would-be trainers to find their own authentic training voice.
Even course leaders using this manual will find their own training styles transformed as they explore new ways of working with diversity, self-direction, life-enhancing learning, and the aims of teacher training.

Adrian Underhill
Training Consultant

TRAINER DEVELOPMENT

Tony Wright
&
Rod Bolitho

Copyright © 2007 Tony Wright and Rod Bolitho

First published in 2007

ISBN 978-1-84753-232-9

All rights reserved. No part of this publication may be reproduced or transmitted in any form or by any means, electronically or mechanically, including photocopying, recording or any information storage or retrieval system, without prior permission in writing from the authors.

Type set in 8/12 point Garamond.

CONTENTS

Introduction		1
Chapter 1	Inside A Training Course 1	3
Chapter 2	A Framework For Training	21
Chapter 3	Working With Groups In Training	34
Chapter 4	Working With Participants' Experience	64
Chapter 5	New and Shared Experiences In Training	83
Chapter 6	The Awareness-raising Process and Its Consequences	95
Chapter 7	Talk In Training Courses	111
Chapter 8	Creating Meaning: New Learning	128
Chapter 9	Planning For Action	158
Chapter 10	Feedback, Assessment and Evaluation in Training	173
Chapter 11	Inside A Training Course 2	192
Chapter 12	Developing As A Trainer	224
Resources For Trainers		236
Appendices		242

Acknowledgements

We would like to express our gratitude to the following people who knowingly and unknowingly contributed so much to this book:

To all the many professionals from over 70 countries worldwide who have participated in our training programmes and courses over the years, and who have contributed so much to the evolution of our practice through their contributions and feedback to us.

To those professionals from whose writing we have quoted in this book.

To our colleagues in the School of International Education at Marjon for their support, and their input into our thinking and practice on numerous courses in so many contexts.

To Paul Gentle, for his unstinting support in helping us bring this project to a successful conclusion, despite many setbacks

To Mersedes Farjad at Marjon, for her timely contribution to the preparation of the print copy of the book.

To Adrian Underhill, for getting us started on this project.

INTRODUCTION

A key moment in our courses for trainers, whether short, intensive or one-year, is towards the end, when groups of participants present a major piece of work they have undertaken collaboratively. This is their opportunity to display publicly the full extent of their personal and professional learning over the course. In one sense, it is a moment of reckoning, but it is also a time for reflection. What has happened to the group and its members while they have been on the course? What have they learned - about training, about learning, about themselves, about each other? What has the course meant for them, and how have they experienced it?

This book sets out to answer these questions, and to crystallise our thoughts about the journey, or the process, that participants experience in training. Each group's journey and every individual's journey is different, but as trainers, we are responsible for guiding them through it. The book endeavours to explore the principles that inform us in this task. These derive from a broadly shared and evolving set of beliefs about the nature of professional learning and the role of training in this process.

We shall also discuss some of the difficult issues which can arise (and have arisen for us) on training courses. The interactions between participants on a course, our own roles as trainers, the role of group processes, conflicts - all of these are a part of the seldom straightforward story of a training course. We also attempt in our account to describe our own professional learning. We are richer, for example, from acknowledging the contribution of difficulties to our own learning, as well as to that of the participants. This is one of our central beliefs. We also believe in taking risks in our training work, though we are aware that they usually have unpredictable outcomes, and we acknowledge that we have to take responsibility for anything that goes wrong. We thus continue to learn about the process of training and about being trainers, and believe very strongly that our knowledge and expertise will always be incomplete. What we can offer here is a window into our work in training, how and why we work in the ways we do, and how we learn from the experience of training.

The book begins by introducing readers to a training process (developed from a learning cycle - Kolb 1984) as it works through a particular training experience led by Rod. From this account, we develop a set of basic training principles which inform much that follows in the book, in particular training activities, procedures, issues and processes. For example, we explore at length the all-important early group-forming and agenda-setting phases of a course. We also discuss the issue of relationships between members of a training group, including trainers. We believe passionately in the importance of 'unwrapping' the interpersonal aspects of the learning experience. The role of talk in training, and the contribution of 'theory' to the process of professional learning are also discussed in connection with making meaning from experience. We look at the role of 'action planning' in participants' learning, and finally we examine the difficult issue of assessment in process-driven courses. Each chapter explores and illustrates a particular training area, either through an actual training activity or a personal account by a participant, and contains a discussion of the principles underpinning our practice.

This is followed by a second illustrative account of a specific course run by Tony, this time making direct reference to many of the areas explored in the middle chapters. We close with a review of the main principles and beliefs which support our practice, and talk about how we continue to develop as trainers.

This is neither a traditional resource book nor a recipe book. It is simply an attempt to put three-dimensional, lived experience down in words, and to unpick some of the issues underlying the experience. It is offered in the belief that the sharing of practice is a key element in professional learning. We hope that readers will engage with it critically and wholeheartedly, just as we have done in our own professional reading, and that it will in some small way make a difference.

CHAPTER 1
INSIDE A TRAINING COURSE

In this chapter we shall take our first glimpse at the way we conduct training courses and also outline our understanding of what happens during training courses and why. Rod describes in some detail a sequence of training activities he followed when working with a group of teacher trainers, including his reflections on the process at each stage. Each stage of this sequence is followed by a commentary which discusses some of the principles that inform our practices.

The Zambian Trainers' Course: *Classroom Observation and Supervision*

In 1992, our College ran a 3-month course on 'Approaches to Teacher Training' for a group of Zambian College of Education lecturers from institutions throughout Zambia. The programme was a part of a British Council managed project aimed at upgrading the quality of English teaching throughout the Zambian system. The course covered various aspects of training methodology and course design for pre-service programmes in ELT. Another key component of the course focused on the practicum, as there was considerable debate in Zambia about the procedures used for supervising and assessing student teachers on school practice. Rod describes the early sessions in this component in some detail. (N.B. Rod's descriptions and comments are in italics.)

Session 1 (1 hour) Exploring Group Concerns

Advance briefing about this group from the British project officer in Lusaka was extremely comprehensive, but I had not yet visited Zambia, and felt the need to consult participants personally before drawing up and agreeing upon an outline for the component. At this first meeting, this is what I did, and the following concerns emerged:

- *the ratio of students to lecturers was very unfavourable, which made it impossible to take a long-term formative approach to supervision; when school visits were made, they were made for the purposes of assessment of the student teachers*
- *there was no standardisation of assessment criteria or observation procedures, either within or between colleges*
- *the lecturers felt uncomfortable in the role of assessor mainly because of the tension engendered in trainees by their visits, which were regarded as 'swoops' from on high*

3

- they also felt it was unfair to assess practice when trainees had no real opportunity to learn from their mistakes
- there was no established link between methodology 'input' sessions in colleges, and school practice - indeed there was no guarantee that English classes would be observed and assessed by specialist lecturers

A sense of dissatisfaction was palpable right from the start, and the group was keen to learn about alternative approaches to supervising and assessing school practice. Furthermore, they wanted to 'work on themselves', having begun to realise that some of their concerns arose from their dissatisfaction with their own practices.

Commentary 1: 'Starting From Where They're At'

We believe that the participants themselves are the preferred starting point in training courses. They come to courses with **experience**. They also possess a system of **beliefs, attitudes and values** about teaching and learning, and about how people relate to each other in a variety of contexts. They also come with **expectations**. We believe that it is imperative that a course begins with an exploration of all these elements, in any order that seems appropriate to the group in question.

The decision to help participants discuss their current concerns in the first session contributed directly to the relevance both of the particular session and of the course as a whole. It revealed participants' personal and professional concerns and also provided an initial means for Rod to assess the group's needs. This procedure enables us to be reactive as well as proactive on courses we run, in addition to starting off the process of enabling participants to invest personally in the course by making it relevant to their own pressing concerns.

Reflections and Forward Planning 1

Having reflected on the group's concerns, and also being aware that time for this component of the programme was limited to 36 hours, I decided on the following sequence of activity and shared it with the group at the beginning of the next session:

1. *Examine own experiences in classrooms, and establish beliefs and values underlying current practice*

2. *On the basis of a clearer understanding of existing practices, beliefs and values, consider some alternatives to see what they might have to offer in the Zambian experience.*

3. *Attempt to reach a measure of consensus within the group about possible (realistic) ways forward.*

4. *Draft action plans, including any necessary documentation, for implementation on return to Zambia*

The group appeared content to follow this sequence through. In particular, it met with the approval of the Ministry of Education representative who was one of the participants. By now it was clear that the group enjoyed discussion and most group members were happy to work collaboratively.

Session 2 *(2 hours):* **Opening Up Participants' Previous Experience and Ideas**

I chose to open up previous experience and underlying ideas through a series of questions for individual contemplation and subsequent group discussion. The first three of these were covered in a very animated session.

i. What exactly is a classroom? Give a definition or a metaphorical image to answer this question.

ii. Think about your answer to the first question. Is it easy or difficult to understand what happens in classrooms? Give reasons for your answer.

*iii. In what roles do **you** know classrooms? Which role dominates in terms of time, and which in terms of your own impressions?*

One of the participants acted as secretary, and produced the following set of notes summarizing responses to the questions. For each question, the same sequence was followed:

- quiet, individual time to consider the question and make notes on responses
- small group discussion (4 in each group)
- reports back from small group to plenary

Session 2 Summary
Question 1
A classroom is .....
..... a laboratory..... a prison   ..... a merry-go-round
..... a cafeteria..... a market   ..... a warehouse
..... a workshop.... a beer party   .....a playground
..... a clinic..... a newspaper printing house

Question 2
It's not easy to understand what happened in classrooms because:
- what is taught may not be learned
- it is not easy to choose from the 'menu' on offer
- there are so many variables
- a classroom contains so many social groups
- so much goes on that we can't see or hear

> - any observer carries in his/her preconceived ideas.
>
> **Question 3**
> Experience of a classroom as a trainer is different from that of a teacher and different again from that of a pupil. Some problems experienced by observers in Zambian classrooms:
> - good lesson preparation but poor implementation
> - how to follow up observation, to help trainee overcome failure
> - awarding grades
> - dealing with trainees' emotional upsets
> - observer as 'executioner' or judge
> - lack of time for individual guidance
> - trainees 'drying up'
> - observing what goes on in group work
>
> ***Thinking Question:*** Can you sort out these problems into categories?

The summary was copied and handed out to the group at the beginning of the next session. I had also added the 'thinking question' in italics at the foot of the handout.

Commentary 2: Working On Previous Experience and Ideas

We believe that participants need to reach into their past experience and into their current ideas and beliefs through **shared** experiences in training room activities. These take place in the immediate or 'current' training situation.

The questions in the training sequence in Session 2 illustrate how it is possible to enable participants to explore experience and beliefs in the training room. We often make use of metaphor-based activities to help participants articulate and describe their experience. This is particularly valuable when we are reaching into unconscious or subconscious dimensions of experience.

We feel that participants need to have the opportunity to examine their existing knowledge and beliefs as a prelude to developing new knowledge and skills. Very often experienced participants require a period in training courses for 'review' of their existing constructs - it is an opportunity for both the cognitive and affective domains to be explored. The latter is particularly relevant for experienced participants, for whom ideas are inevitably tinged with the emotion of the experiences which helped to form them. Unravelling current ideas can be a risky undertaking - the decision to begin with current concerns in the first session, followed by metaphor work and questions on existing beliefs is a particularly helpful means of lessening the emotional load of such sessions, for all present. The choice of these activities was intended to reflect the depth and complexity to which they needed to reach in order to begin to address their concerns constructively and practically.

Reflection and Forward Planning 2
The group's responses to the questions indicated a number of useful and interesting points.

In answering question 1, all the group members went for metaphors rather than definitions. Images ranged from the ordered and purposeful (laboratory, workshop, clinic) to the disorganised, almost chaotic (beer party, playground); from the repressive (prison) to the open, consumer-oriented (cafeteria, warehouse, market); from controlled enjoyment (merry-go-round) to the production line (newspaper printing house). Participants shared my surprise at this wide range of images, all based on experience of Zambian classrooms. We followed up in plenary, by imagining roles for teachers and learners in each image (jailer and inmates; doctor and patients; stallholder and customers; host and guests etc.). The discussion remained light-hearted but thoughtful, and I chose not to push for further interpretation at this stage.

Responses to question 2 revealed slightly more depth of thought, with some participants still plainly feeding off the metaphors. The plenary discussion quickly moved from the intended focus on differing perspectives to participants' own preoccupation with the role of observer. I allowed this to take its course, hoping that I would gain further insights into the concerns which had been expressed in fairly general terms in the opening session. The notes show that this hope was fulfilled to some extent.

Session 3 *(2 hours)* *Reflecting and Exploring*
At the beginning of the next session, the group considered the thinking question and came up with the following categories:
- problems relating to assessment
- problems relating to the relationship between the trainer and the trainee
- problems in the trainees' heads
- observers' problems of perception
They also returned briefly to the question of differing perspectives and wanted to record the following note:

Most trainers know the classroom as learners (often a long time ago!) as teachers and as supervisors. Each role gives a different perspective. It is very important for supervisors not to forget what it was like to be a teacher or a learner.

I had planned to go on immediately to explore participants' notions of good teaching, but one of them raised a different question on behalf of the

7

group. They had begun to be bothered by terminology and wanted to be clear about the overlap and boundaries between **observation, supervision, assessment** and **appraisal**. *Again, I chose to follow the group's priorities and to spend time exploring this question, although I did have reservations about the potential for 'waffle' and abstraction at the expense of the concreteness which had characterised the exchanges up to this point. This was done in plenary, and a Venn diagram was built up on the board as a result of an interactive discussion punctuated by summaries and short inputs from me. All of this was recorded by 2 participants. (See Session 5 Summary on page 9)*

Commentary 3: Exploring Concepts - An Emerging Need

Session 3 illustrates how the sequence of activities encourages participants to develop new ideas on areas of concern, and also to begin to conceptualise their thoughts on the issues arising. The creation of an opportunity for the participants to make their notes on the process so far in this session illustrates how the overall approach is flexible enough to allow for participants' emerging thinking to be captured.

The collective need to deal with terminology, and the ensuing discussion are also illustrations of how a trainer can seize an opportunity to shape the emergent discussion and to assist in the clarification of concepts as well as the development of a common language among participants. It is also an opportunity to provide an alternative perspective to that offered by the participants. The notes reflect a combination of trainer's and participants' ideas on the terminology.

The planned sequence of activity was not followed - what had seemed neat and tidy at the outset of the session was not in fact the case. The participants felt the urge to explore particular terms. The trainer felt it important to do so, and shelve some of the planned activities. All of this points to the need for trainer and participants to actively process the emerging ideas and concepts both in sessions and after sessions. A group is often unable to 'move on' until they have actively processed and discussed material which activities have triggered. The role of talk in the processing of ideas is pivotal, and the generous allocation of time allowed for focused discussion of issues is crucial.

Inside A Training Course

Session 3 Summary — TERMINOLOGY

There was a discussion about the relationship between the often-confused terms *appraisal, assessment, observation* and *supervision*.

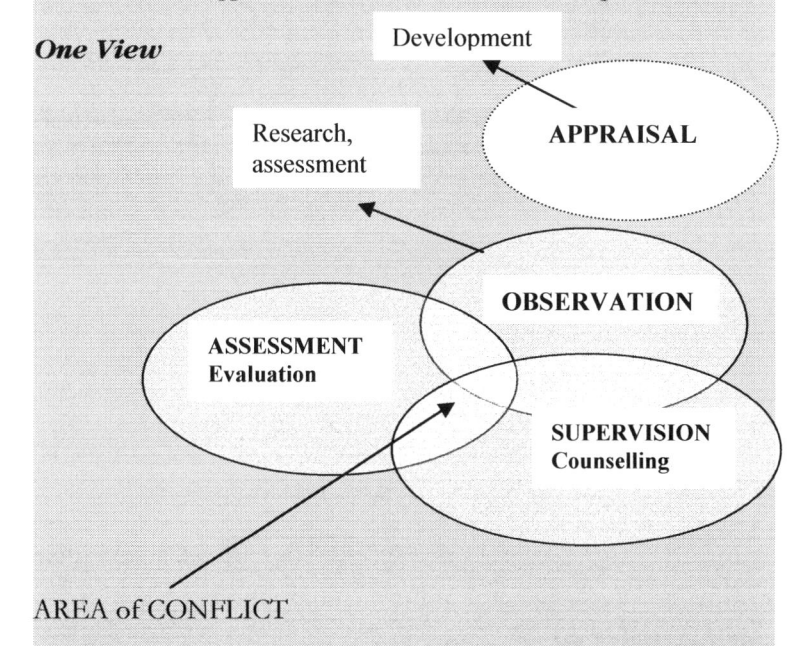

One View

[Diagram: Overlapping ellipses labelled APPRAISAL, OBSERVATION, ASSESSMENT (Evaluation), and SUPERVISION (Counselling). Arrows point from APPRAISAL to "Development" and to "Research, assessment". An arrow points to the overlap area labelled "AREA of CONFLICT".]

Observation is seen as an essentially neutral term, describing the process of looking at what goes on in a classroom. One purpose of observation is to carry out **_research_**. Another purpose is to **_assess_** trainee teachers or teachers in service. **Appraisal** is a process by which professional **_development_** in an individual is discussed and assessed. It may or may not involve observation. The process of **supervision** usually extends to pre-practice support and post-practice feedback, and is usually dependent on observation of a lesson or lessons. An area of conflict arises when the **_supervisor_** is asked/expected to be an **_assessor_**, too. It is difficult to reconcile these two roles. Supervision involves close one-to-one work, and may draw on the related field of **_counselling_**.

Reflection and Forward Planning 3

As a follow-up to this discussion I advised participants to read Chapter 7 of Wallace's Training Foreign Language Teachers. *Although I was not totally happy with the outcome of the discussion on terminology expressed in the summary, I realized that it had removed a barrier to progress (terminology can block people's thinking if it is not clarified) and it had also helped to identify more closely a key problem area: the conflict between supervision and assessment. For participants, it was also a step towards articulating objectives. They stated a desire to produce some kind of standardised observation instrument to support the process of assessment and to find out much more about supervision - the processes involved and the skills they needed to work on in themselves. This led me to reframe the task I had planned on 'A Good Lesson' (see below). However, I still felt a need to find out more about participants' experience of classrooms, thereby coming a little closer to their reality. So I set them the following written assignment, to be handed in at the next session:*

> In no more than 500 words, describe a lesson you have observed, taught or taken part in as a learner, and which has, for some reason, stayed in your mind.

I responded to them later with the following group handout in addition to notes and questions to each individual participant.

Handout
ACCOUNTS OF CLASSROOM EXPERIENCE

I enjoyed reading these accounts. Not surprisingly, 11 of them were written from an observer's point of view, one from a lecturer's viewpoint and one from the perspective of a trainee/learner.

Of the eleven, one gave an account of a multiple-perspective observation with 5 supervisors involved; four described lessons in which things had gone wrong and which left them with questions unanswered; the remaining six were, to a greater or lesser extent, success stories.

Your accounts raised the following questions for me:
1. Why, in some cases, do trainees seem to learn from methodology classes and in other cases not?
2. Are practical models likely to have a stronger impact on trainees than theoretical input? Why/why not?
3. Why do some trainees seem to benefit more from feedback sessions than others?
4. What are the most effective strategies for raising trainees' self-awareness?
5. What are the links between language awareness and classroom practice?

> 6. Is linguistic knowledge an absolute prerequisite for successful English teaching?
>
> By the way, why not read each other's accounts?

Discussion of my six questions was, for the group, a way of reflecting more deeply on the classroom experiences which they had described, leading them to question some of their ideas and practices.

Session 4 *(2 hours)* ***Further Exploration of Existing Ideas***

In the next session the process of exploration continued with an activity sequence intended to reveal participants' notions of a "good lesson", as a lead-in to the design of observation instruments to be trialled and eventually adopted back home in Zambia.

The procedure for the "Good Lesson" activity is given in full here.

Activity: A GOOD LESSON
1. Group sits in a circle without tables. 6 or 7 slips of paper are given to each group member. Participants are then asked to write, clearly and boldly one key characteristic of a good lesson on each slip of paper. No conferring at this stage.
2. Participants then seek to sort slips into priority order. Still no discussion.
3. Group facilitator then asks each participant in turn to call out her/his top priority characteristic and to place the slip on the floor in the middle. Participants are asked to place slips <u>near</u> others with apparently similar characteristics, but <u>further away</u> from slips with obviously different characteristics. In this way, categories gradually change.
4. This procedure continues through the lower priority characteristics until the slips of paper are on the floor, arranged in rough categories.
5. Group discusses the categories and makes any necessary changes and adjustments. There is usually a 'miscellaneous' category with characteristics which don't seem to fit anywhere. Headings are agreed for each category.
6. Group broken down into pairs and threes, with one or two categories (including the 'misfits' pile) allocated to each.
7. Each pair or three is now responsible for 'finalizing' the characteristics in each category by
   (a) eliminating duplication or overlap   *and*

> (b) after careful consideration, passing certain slips to other sub-groups for inclusion in their categories.
>
> The sub-group in charge of 'misfits' should try to find a home for each slip in the pile, or should create new categories, as necessary.
>
> 8. A consolidated list is produced, including the agreed headings, with all the remaining characteristics listed under each heading.

This procedure led to an extremely lively, sometimes heated, discussion, as they explored each other's thinking and defended their beliefs. Some of the excitement and sense of progress which was felt during and after this session is captured in the following summary, produced by one of the participants on behalf of the group as a whole:

Session 4 Summary
THE 'GREAT LEAP' TOWARDS THE PRODUCTION OF AN OBSERVATION INSTRUMENT

i) Having discussed the assessment requirements of our trainee teachers in the teaching practice component, we noted the following aspects:

   a) students are observed by many different tutors
   b) students are observed in many different lessons, all of which are graded for certification purposes
   c) there is a need to have a common observation instrument (one common 'observer language')
   d) for purposes of developing 'self-evaluation' in our students, we need to have a self-evaluation instruments (for the student).

ii) Rod, realising the urgent requirements of the 'patients' administered his double dosage through the long and penetrating syringe[1] called:
   "WHAT ARE THE CHARACTERISTICS OF A GOOD LESSON?"
   Through individual, group and class dynamics the following 'good lesson' characteristics were noted, thus making <u>a great leap forward</u> in the production of an <u>observation instrument</u>. (These are yet to be refined, of course):

---

[1] We were very struck by the perpetuation of the 'clinic' metaphor in this participant's notes!

1) STATEMENT OF OBJECTIVES
   - had clearly defined objectives
   - clear lesson objectives
   - clear objectives should determine the number of activities in a lesson
2) AIDS
   - uses teaching and learning aids
   - should show the learning/teaching apparatus the teacher or pupils are going to use
   - list of material to be used (nicely tabulated)
   (Note: these last two characteristics plainly refer to the lesson plan rather than the lesson as an observed event.)
3) TASKS AND ACTIVITIES
   - variety of activities
   - what type?
   - how?
4) INTERACTION
   - pupils work individually, in pairs, in groups and as a class
   - pupil-to-pupil interaction
   - teacher-to-pupil interaction
   - pupil-to-teacher interaction
5. SUBJECT KNOWLEDGE
   - language awareness
6. PERSONAL CONSIDERATIONS
   - teacher resourcefulness
   - accepting criticism
   - teacher flexibility
   - teacher's interest
   - audible voice
7. PLANNING
   - integration of skills
   - integrated language skills: listening, speaking, reading and writing
   - should spell out the roles of the teacher in that lesson
   - well planned lesson
   - good organisation of the materials and groups
   - should show the activities pupils will do at the end of the lesson
   - organisation of class

Inside a Training Course

Plan should show:

EXECUTION	ORGANISATION
Classroom management	Column for teacher self
Timing	evaluation
Good presentation	Systematic
Progressive	Easy to follow
Moves at a steady pace	Shows sequence of lesson –
Progression – clear	stages
sequence of tasks	Space for
Clear instructions	Feedback
Varied teaching modes	Presentation
Introduction	Accuracy
Conclusion	Fluency
Logical lesson progression	Spells out pupil roles in a lesson

8) <u>ACHIEVEMENT OF OBJECTIVES</u>
   - good teaching/learning outcomes
   - should have a central learning point
   - objectives achieved
   - one which achieves the objectives at the end

9) <u>LEARNER FOCUS</u>
   - link experiential knowledge with new knowledge
   (n.b. this was an early sign that the participants were coming to terms with some of our terminology and working principles)
   - in a language lesson, learners should be involved in communicative activities: near-real-life situations.

Reflection and Forward Planning 4

As facilitator to the group, I had decided to take no part in the discussion which led to the production of this list of categories. I functioned solely as a timekeeper and 'pusher', ensuring that the overall deadline was met. The reader will note, as I did, a number of features of this interim summary.

- *the underlying preoccupation with the 'lesson plan' as part of the process of lesson observation*
- *the overlap and lack of clear distinction between certain of the categories and (especially) within the large and subdivided category entitled 'Planning'*

- *the 'unevenness' of both the categories and the characteristics: some of them are general almost to the point of vagueness while others are much more sharply focused*
- *a fairly clear emphasis on the more formal (and easily observable?) characteristics.*

Reflecting afterwards on the session, and on its tangible product, I felt that a lot had been achieved and that I had learned a great deal in my 'outsider' facilitator role:
- *the group had really begun the process of exploration of each other's thinking*
- *the group had worked very effectively under time pressure*
- *the working atmosphere was positive and supportive, though there were plenty of challenges and disagreements*
- *I had become much more aware of participants' beliefs and values*
- *the group accepted my facilitating role and were content to work, for the time being, within their own conceptual and experiential framework without demanding 'expert' input*
- *I realized how important the **product** orientation (towards an observation instrument) was to the group: they wanted to return to Zambia with something tangible and usable*

In thinking about the way forward, I decided to prompt the group with some questions aimed at getting them to tidy up their categories, and to offer them a range of existing observation instruments to consider and, maybe, learn from before they proceeded to designing their own. This latter decision was based on my conclusion that participants were robust enough, and confident enough in their own thinking ability, to resist the temptation to go for 'external' solutions.

Commentary 4: Developing The Agenda

The sequence of activity followed in Session 4 demonstrates how in a training course the trainer can effect a transition between 'thinking/discussing' and 'doing/discussing' modes. The 'Good Lesson' activity enabled the participants to begin to identify the parameters of the observation and feedback instruments which they wished to develop for use at home. They were thus in a position to use their new and clarified ideas in a design task. Starting with their concerns and developing a series of discussions had enabled the trainer to stimulate thinking both on initial and new ideas about classroom observation.

The role of the trainer in prompting this process is acknowledged in the participant notes - following a brief discussion of assessment requirements for trainees in the Zambian context, the activity is introduced. The group makes the connection between the activity and the construction of the instrument. A series of criteria and classroom features emerge from the activity. These, as the note-taker points out, are to be developed in subsequent sessions. The trainer's questions on the categories are a means of assisting the participants in refining their thinking and conceptualisation of the issues involved in observation of classroom activity.

Summary
The first four sessions proceeded by working from participants' initial concerns, through their existing ideas on observation to a definition of a practical product to take from the programme. These are summarised in Figure 1.1. This was achieved by activating the following working principles:
- Start with participants' existing concerns when appropriate - in this case it was essential as the trainer had only a limited knowledge of the participants' context
- Work from existing to new knowledge and constructs; build on what is already known, sorting out misconceptions and ideas 'blocking' thinking
- Provide ample opportunity for group discussion as a means of articulating ideas and subjecting them to inquiry - this also assists group formation and development as a common language emerges, and participants get to know each other's points of view
- Allow for group involvement in decision-making about course direction and process (including note-making and summary by participants)
- Trainer's inputs and contributions are designed to provide structure and direction, as well as 'expert' input when required

The overall aim of the initial sessions was to activate thinking on classroom observation and to facilitate the identification of a product with which all group members felt that they could identify and contribute to.

Subsequent sessions - Exploring Concerns
Having described the first four sessions in considerable detail, I shall now go on to give a résumé of subsequent sessions and some of the processes and products involved. It may be helpful for the reader to know that the group was accommodated on campus, and that much of the good work on their course as a whole, and on this component in particular, was carried out in whole-group or small-cell mode in kitchens, study bedrooms and common-rooms. It may

Inside A Training Course

also be helpful to point out that participants spent a proportion of the course on school attachment in and around Plymouth, which permitted them to hone their own observation skills and to experience different teaching styles.

Session	Group activity	Trainer Activity During Session	Trainer Activity After Session
1. Establishing Concerns	Group Discussion	Initiates discussion, listens, notes	Decides on organisation of course
2. Opening up Participants' Existing Knowledge and Ideas	Discussion of questions set by trainer (individual/group/plenary)	Sets up discussion; structures discussion stages	Works on summary – adds thinking questions
3. Exploring Terms	Discussion of thinking question on summary; plenary discussion of terms; setting objectives	Structuring discussion; board summary; set follow-up reading	Sets writing task; reads accounts; writes summary + questions
4. Further Exploration of Existing Ideas; Developing An Agenda for Action	Discussion of assessment criteria for students; 'good lesson' activity	Time-keeping, 'pushing'; facilitating discussion	Writing questions to assist pps. in refining categories developed in 'good lesson' activity

Figure 1.1 Summary of training sessions 1-4

My class sessions were usually spent reviewing progress, engaging in seminar discussions, and (especially towards the end) working furiously in product-oriented task groups. My role defined itself as these processes unfolded. I felt myself to be most useful as:
- *a facilitator of discussion and collector of feedback*
- *a summarizer (usually 5 minutes at the end of a session, often prompting the group's thinking with questions and possible ways forward)*
- *a provider of back-up reading (some examples are given below) and of other resources (e.g. sample observation instruments)*

Inside a Training Course

- a consultant during group work and (sometimes) a scribe and recorder, though the examples above show how well individual group members took to this task, too
- a brake on the headlong rush towards products (often asking the group to consider alternatives, to try another angle etc.)

In all of this, I gave occasional short inputs, but, above all, "thinking questions" (either written, on handouts and summary sheets, or oral, during feedback).

After the fourth session, three sub-groups worked both in class time and in free time on the design of their trial observation instruments. Three were produced, and these are reproduced, along with guidelines for supervisors, subsequently trialled in Zambia, and a standardized, final version agreed on at a later project seminar.

The group also went on to design a self-evaluation checklist for post-lesson use by trainees after considering some possible models, notably those proposed by Gibbs and Habeshaw (1989). They felt that trainees needed to take more responsibility for the development of their own teaching during school practice, and believed that an instrument of this sort would help them to do this. The trial version of this checklist was the result of a group brainstorming activity, feedback from me and from each other on the first draft and, ultimately, concentrated work by an elected sub-group.

One problem the group particularly wanted to tackle was the poor lecturer/trainee ratio, which created an impossible workload for lecturers, and adversely influenced the quality of supervision they were able to offer. During school visits in and around Plymouth, they became interested in the Partnership in Practice scheme operated by our College, whereby experienced teachers support trainees during school practice by acting, in liaison with college lecturers as mentors, I offered them articles by Malderez and Bodoczky (1992) (describing a successful initiative in Hungary), by Williams (1989) and by Sheal (1989). Discussion of the latter two articles took place after the group had been divided into two for reading purposes, with each sub-group preparing questions for the other group on one of the two articles. (They enjoyed this kind of task focus for reading assignments and resolved to try it out with their trainees at home.) The outcome of all of this thinking and discussion was an outline scheme for "surrogate observers" to be implemented on their return. It was important that the Ministry representative was keen on this scheme, and he promised to lend his weight to it in Zambia.

A further preoccupation, the reader will recall, was the inadequacy of the link between college-based methodology courses and school practice. On the basis of a series of "thinking questions" which I provided, they went on to draw up some guidelines on "Preparation for School Practice" to be discussed with, and used by, colleagues in each of the colleges in Zambia.

Finally there was the whole issue of supervisory skills, particularly the giving of feedback. They all felt that they were too directive when giving feedback, and wanted to consider alternatives. Time was very short for work in this area, so I provided a brief input summarizing Freeman's (1982) three approaches to supervision and asked the group to read King's (1985) much shorter article on Counselling for Teachers. They also considered Cogan's (1973) eight-phase cycle of supervision as a possible working framework. This was followed by shared viewing of a video lesson, and a role play in which they practised giving and receiving feedback in a less directive way. We would all have liked more time to work on this area but the group also felt they had learned a lot about supportive, non-directive feedback from all the tutors on their course.

A Final Reflection
During the course, the group felt that their existing experience had been respected and built on and, significantly, that they had been empowered to develop some new approaches within this problem area, which would be helpful and relevant back home. I felt that my initially tentative and exploratory approach had been vindicated, and that both the initial work plan and the decision I took to keep a low profile and to resist the temptation to provide 'expert' input as a starting point had borne rich fruit in terms of the outcomes and products of the course.

The structure and sequence of the course emerged from the process more or less as it was originally conceptualised by the trainer after the first session (see 'Reflections and Forward Planning 1). A similar menu of activities as had been used in the first four sessions was employed for each of the main topics as the group dealt with them. The overall process of the course reflected the miniature version followed in Sessions 1 to 4, working from participants' initial experience, ideas and knowledge to new understandings and products, via a process of thinking and discussion, facilitated and structured by the trainer. The overall aim of participants returning to the context with new ideas and practices was based on the principle of working from existing experience through a process of reflection and new learning to a series of action-planning tasks.

Figure 1.2 on page 20 summarises the whole course process.

In Chapter 2 we outline the conceptual framework which underpins the procedures used on the Zambians' course. This conceptual framework informs all of our work at session level and we also use it to organise longer sequences of work on courses.

Inside a Training Course

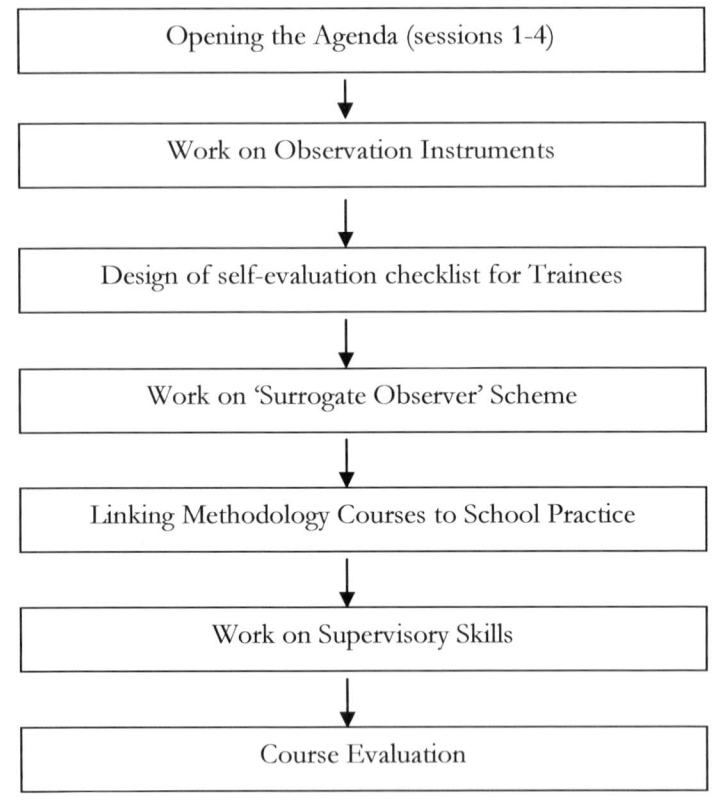

```
┌─────────────────────────────────────────────────┐
│       Opening the Agenda (sessions 1-4)         │
└─────────────────────────────────────────────────┘
                        ↓
┌─────────────────────────────────────────────────┐
│          Work on Observation Instruments        │
└─────────────────────────────────────────────────┘
                        ↓
┌─────────────────────────────────────────────────┐
│   Design of self-evaluation checklist for Trainees │
└─────────────────────────────────────────────────┘
                        ↓
┌─────────────────────────────────────────────────┐
│       Work on 'Surrogate Observer' Scheme       │
└─────────────────────────────────────────────────┘
                        ↓
┌─────────────────────────────────────────────────┐
│    Linking Methodology Courses to School Practice │
└─────────────────────────────────────────────────┘
                        ↓
┌─────────────────────────────────────────────────┐
│            Work on Supervisory Skills           │
└─────────────────────────────────────────────────┘
                        ↓
┌─────────────────────────────────────────────────┐
│                Course Evaluation                │
└─────────────────────────────────────────────────┘
```

Figure 1.2 Main stages of the Zambian teacher trainers' course

References

Freeman, D. (1982) Observing teachers: Three approaches to in-service training and development. TESOL Quarterly, 16/1.

King, D. (1983) Counselling for teachers. ELT Journal, 37/4.

Cogan, M. (1973) Clinical Supervision. New York: Houghton Mifflin.

Gibbs, G. and T. Habeshaw (1989) Preparing to Teach. Bristol: TES.

Malderez, A. and C. Bodoczky (1992) Co-trainer training. Talk: IATEFL Conference, Lille.

Williams, M.D. (1989) A developmental approach of classroom observation. ELT Journal, 43/2.

Sheal, P. (1989) Classroom observation: Training the observers. ELT Journal, 43/2.

Wallace, M. (1991) Training Foreign Language Teachers: A reflective approach. Cambridge: Cambridge University Press.

CHAPTER 2
A FRAMEWORK FOR TRAINING

The previous chapter presented an extended sequence of training activities, typical of the way we choose to work with groups of trainers in the training room. We also took the opportunity to comment on the sequence of activities as a way of introducing readers to the principles informing our practices as trainers. The purpose of this chapter is therefore to outline the thinking framework which underlies our working practice as trainers. We shall present what we see as the essence of our training approach, and illustrate the discussion with reference both to the activities already described in Chapter 1 and other sequences of activity we use in training.

We naturally choose to use sequences of activity with training groups as a way of initiating new learning. For us, training is not a series of 'one-off' events with the onus on the participants to make the connections. We believe that trainers should actively structure and sequence training activity over periods of time as well as in single sessions. We see our own work running in cycles, in many ways similar to the learning cycle described by Kolb (1984). However, for us the learning cycle is a starting point; we are indebted to the original conception, but find in practice that working in this cyclical way is richer and more complex than the idealised progression implied by the diagram. It can also lead to unexpected discoveries, side tracks and difficulties which we acknowledge in this chapter and discuss in more depth in other parts of the book. In this chapter we shall discuss an extended conceptualisation of Kolb's learning cycle with reference to our own training practice.

The Learning Cycle

Before discussing our own work, we shall briefly examine Kolb's learning cycle (Figure 2.1), as it is the jumping-off point for the discussion.

Kolb sees a cycle of learning activity beginning with 'doing' - activity of some type by participants. Activity is followed by 'reflection' on the activity. From the reflective stage, participants move into a stage of 'abstract conceptualisation', or 'learning'. We prefer to think of this stage as one of 'making meaning' - we find the notion of 'abstract' not in keeping with our view that we also learn to articulate emotions at every stage, and that they can become a vital part of a teacher or trainer's vocabulary of experience. The process is not all entirely 'cognitive'. Having moved to this type of thinking, the trainer is then in a position to 'plan' for further experience, actively integrating the new learning into their practice.

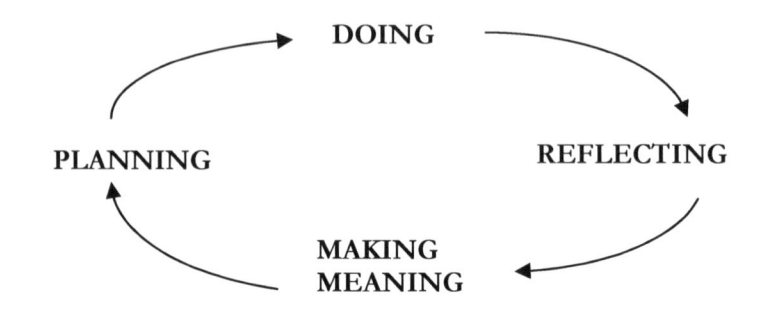

```
                    ──▶ DOING ──
                   ╱              ╲
                  ╱                ╲
                 ╱                  ▼
         PLANNING                  REFLECTING
                 ▲                  ╱
                  ╲                ╱
                   ╲              ╱
                    ── MAKING ◀──
                       MEANING
```

Figure 2.1 The Learning Cycle (after Kolb 1984)

The basic logic of Kolb's model is that in order to learn from experience, a learner must move into a 'thinking' mode before embarking on new activity. We find this logic entirely consistent with the processes of professional learning inherent in teacher education. Teachers and trainers are, on a day-to-day basis, practical, active 'doers'. They also think and learn and develop, although not always in obvious ways, and rarely do they articulate the processes of their learning and development. We have found that the learning cycle affords opportunities for participants in training to think about professional issues and articulate their thoughts, free in the main from the burdens on everyday work. It has proved for us to be a helpful means of conceptualising the training process. In the ensuing discussion, we shall use Kolb's four main stages as broad headings under which to discuss our training framework, before providing readers with an overview of the whole cycle as we have experienced it over our years of practice.

1. Doing
The basis of our work as trainers is experience, both our participants' and our own. In training, we work on experience in two main ways: **previous** experience and **shared** experience on a training course. There is, as we shall see, no clear-cut boundary between the two types of experience. However, when we consider training activities, we can distinguish between those sequences of activity which begin with a definite focus on

previous experience, and those which are intended to involve the participants in some form of new experience. Before looking at these in more detail, we examine the role of experience in training.

The Role of Experience in Training

What is the role of experience in training? It might be helpful to picture our life's experience as a lake, an organic body of thoughts, images, memories, feelings, knowledge, in circulation, the water constantly in motion, although the depths remain fairly static. Attitudes, values and beliefs are partly in the depths, and also in the general circulation of water. New experiences feed into the lake in a variety of ways - through rainfall, the wind on the surface of the water, the lives of creatures like fish in the water, of birds which might float on the surface, of craft moving over the surface, from the streams and rivers which feed into the lake, and which originate in the lake and go elsewhere. In training sessions, through the activities, we might decide to dive below the surface, or to go 'fishing', in search of past experience. Or we might choose to create a breeze on the surface, or launch a boat and go for a ride on the water, the point at which new experiences are first perceived.

Experience thus has two distinct but linked faces. The boat trip or the sudden rainstorm will be experienced immediately at the surface of the water, as they happen. Of course these experiences will also subtly alter the lake's circulation and composition. A dive to the bottom of the lake will enter the past; it will be quite risky, as it is dark in the depths, and our knowledge of what is there is limited. We need special tools to help us in the depths in addition to our ability to sense what is around us.

How then does the process of working with experience happen? Experience is Janus-like, the surface of the lake that marks the boundary of the past and faces outwards into the uncertain world. It is the nature of the surface itself that we are interested in, and how it receives and accommodates new sensations, its colour and texture too. When we work with experience, we use activities which explore the surface and also which take us below the surface. The training activity is what we do at the surface, whether we alter the surface or whether we go through into the depths. Whatever we do has the potential to change permanently the lake - rainfall is absorbed into the body of the lake; waves change the shoreline and thus the shape of the lake in small but significant ways. Our dives may also disturb the depths, and bring to the surface material which might otherwise remain hidden.

Working with Previous Experience
At its most fundamental level, we draw from our own **previous** experience in the training room as trainers and participants, in the classroom as teachers and observers, and in other teacher education settings such as school practice. In addressing professional issues as they affect us either as trainers or teachers we aim to **make sense** of this experience. Because we find it quite difficult to separate personal and professional aspects of our experience (to us they seem to be inextricably interwoven, an issue we examine later in the book) we see experience as having a strong affective dimension, as well as more cognitive and 'instrumental' dimensions in terms of skills or knowledge. By inviting participants to make sense of their experiences as trainers, teachers, trainees, students, and of life as a whole in a number of different ways, we believe we can make available a range of possibilities for personal and professional learning of different types among our participants.

In the course for Zambian trainers described in Chapter 1, the early activities all worked on the participants' previous experience, what they had brought with them to the course in terms of professional concerns, knowledge, ideas, beliefs and attitudes about observation as part of teacher training. By setting up a series of activities in the training room, the trainer was, from several different angles, able to provide an opportunity for participants to examine their experiences as working professionals and the beliefs and ideas which informed their experience. Two types of 'doing' are involved in these activities:
1. Previous professional activity (perhaps over 20 years, or more recent, but PRIOR to a course) - what participants have done
2. The active exploration of this experience and knowledge - through activities such as metaphor (the classroom); recall (the incident) and so on.

These activities are not confined to **doing** alone, as we shall see in the next section. Active exploration of previous experience leads quite naturally to - some may say *is* - reflection.

New Experiences in the Training Room
As well as reaching into the past through training activities - both recent and more distant - we also believe in providing participants with the opportunity for **new** experiences in the training room. These take place in the immediate or 'current' training situation, and are the jumping-off point for new learning, such as the acquisition of new teaching ideas or knowledge about teaching. Let us look at an example.

At the outset of a training sequence, participants are asked to take part in a series of say, 5 or 6, activities which illustrate a particular theme, for example, communicative language teaching. Each activity will illustrate a different aspect of the theme. By taking part in the activities and recording their responses, we aim to involve participants in a shared experience of communicative language teaching as the first stage in learning about the area. The basis of this stage of the sequence is the **shared** training room activity. Naturally, participants' current states of knowledge, previous learning experience or teaching experience, attitudes, beliefs and values are engaged by the activities, but in a quite different way from those activities which explicitly focus on past experience.

The first type of 'doing' activity naturally leads to reflection on experience. The second does not, and here we have to be more deliberate in our efforts to encourage participants to reflect on the experience. If a group of trainees merely experiences the communicative learning activities designed ultimately for classroom use, they could be forgiven for saying 'so what'. A key working principle to which we adhere is that activity in a training session should always incorporate or be followed by reflection.

2. Reflecting

Training activities which concentrate only on the description of past or current experience, individual or shared are, in themselves, of little real use in helping participants develop a deeper understanding of the events which occurred during the experiences. In order for meaning to be derived from any activity, structured and, if necessary, guided reflection need to take place. This section will explore different types of reflection and the process of awareness-raising.

What Is Reflection?

Following, in particular, the work of Schön (1983, 1987), 'reflection' has become a key term in teacher and trainer education, rather in the same way that 'communicative' has become synonymous in some circles with contemporary approaches to language teaching. At this juncture we would like to say that we cannot imagine successful training experiences which do not, at some time, feature an element of reflection, but we would also like to say that reflection on experience is only a **part** of the learning cycle in training. This is, in common trainer parlance, often referred to as 'the reflective cycle' or 'a reflective model'. This could be misleading because reflection is a vital part of the training experience, but only a part. It is also worth remembering that reflecting is a thinking style which comes more naturally to some people than to others; activists and pragmatists may initially find it hard to 'get into' reflecting.

What happens when we reflect in the training room?
Participants experience training activities as individuals. By asking them to reflect, we are asking them to step back from the experience and to share their perceptions of the experience. The stepping back process involves a shift from activity that is principally '**doing**' in nature to one of **thinking**. It can also involve them in beginning to share their perceptions of their experience with colleagues in the training group. This is a major reason for structuring activities so that participants first have time to respond as individuals and then to share their responses with others in the group.

Stages In Reflection
We see reflection in terms of at least two main stages - attending to feelings and analysis. We believe that in the initial stages of reflection, participants need to 'unload' their feelings about an experience before proceeding to describing or reconstructing it. At this stage the role of the trainer is to allow participants the time and space to do this and to support them as they try to express clearly what might be coloured by strong emotions. Unexpressed feelings can block understanding of the purposes of an activity, and can dilute the quality of thinking and talk about the experience in question. The emotional dimensions of experience are also so important to an understanding of an activity like teaching that rehearsal of talk about them can pave the way for a deeper understanding – at an affective level. Once feelings and descriptions have been dealt with, participants are able to proceed with analysis - often analysis will accompany description - but only when the affective dimension has been addressed.

Reflection thus means looking back at past experiences (e.g. through story-telling as in the Zambian group's course - session 3), **reconstructing** them and beginning to ask questions about these experiences and **deconstructing** them. Reflection on immediate experiences involves both **reconstructing** and **deconstructing** them, and beginning to make sense of their purposes. When working with previous experiences, we might also invite reflections on the *activity of recalling the past - how it felt, what the stages of the activity were* and so on. Thus two levels of reflection can be involved in these types of activity - reflection on the past and reflection on the new. We see these two types of reflection as being fundamentally different in aim and outcome. If we pursue our earlier analogy of the lake of experience, the reflective process is akin to lingering on a boat ride across the lake, or paying attention to the breeze's effect on the surface, or staying still long enough under water to catch sight of something. If experience is found on and beneath the surface, then reflecting is finding out about the nature of what is above or below and its relationship with the surface.

Awareness Raising

We have mentioned the **shift** as a central aspect of sequences of training activity which progress from doing to reflective modes. Our experience is that it is during this shift, not always experienced in the same way by all participants in a group, that awareness is raised. It is at this stage in a sequence that participants are likely to make jumps in awareness, to *notice* things in past and present experience. It is for this reason that we see all activities inviting reflection on past or present experience as **awareness-raising** activities. The shift in mode of operation from activity to introspection, combined with a shift from individual experience to collective talk about the experience, appears to contribute to raised awareness about a wide range of phenomena, from feelings to ideas.

We would like to note at this point that the transition from recalling experience through reflection to exploring its meaning is not a linear sequence of events. This is far from the reality of our experience. The Zambian experience reported in the last chapter bears this out, as the trainer had to change plans to accommodate the participants' changing thinking. It is at the reflective stages of a training sequence that we become most aware that the process is out of our hands. We are no longer in control. We are dependent on what participants do, what they say, what they feel. We may find ourselves processing experience by running back and forth between reflection and the experience. Indeed, sometimes we deliberately keep a group in the experience/reflection mode for a series of activities so that there is time for the issues they are working on to become as clearly focused as possible, or for the principles behind a training approach that we are working on to become as transparent as possible. It is not worth moving on until participants have properly processed an experience. The main processes of working from experience to reflection are summarised in Figures 2.2 and 2.3 below:

A Framework for Training

```
┌─────────────────┐
│ PREVIOUS        │      RECALL EVENTS, FEELINGS
│ EXPERIENCE      │─────▶ *AWARENESS RAISING*
│ (Individual)    │
└─────────────────┘             │
                                ▼
                        ┌─────────────────┐
                        │ REVIEW and      │
                        │ REFLECTION      │
                        │ (Individual and │
                        │ shared)         │
                        └─────────────────┘
```

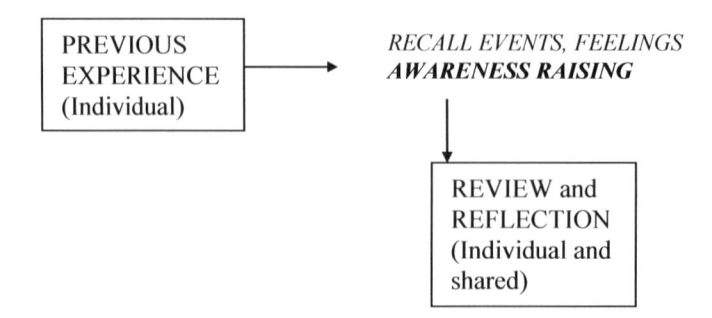

Figure 2.2 Activity structure for reflecting on past experience

In Figure 2.3 the experience and reflecting elements are bracketed in order to show that the reflection element is the means by which previous experience is reached. In a trainer training session, we would do such an activity as an illustration of a training activity, and then move to a reflective stage, thus following the full sequence in Figure 2.5.

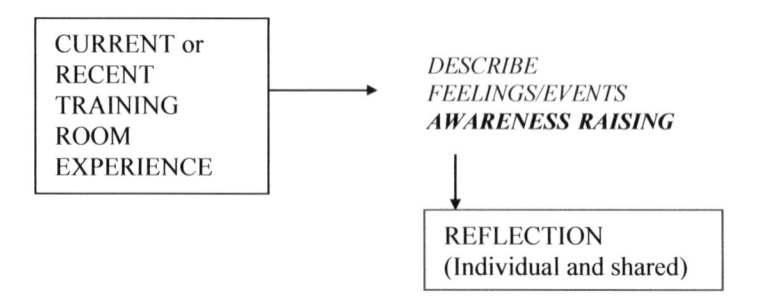

```
┌─────────────────┐
│ CURRENT or      │      DESCRIBE
│ RECENT          │      FEELINGS/EVENTS
│ TRAINING        │─────▶ *AWARENESS RAISING*
│ ROOM            │
│ EXPERIENCE      │
└─────────────────┘             │
                                ▼
                        ┌─────────────────────────┐
                        │ REFLECTION              │
                        │ (Individual and shared) │
                        └─────────────────────────┘
```

Figure 2.3 Activity structure for reflecting on 'present' training experience

This completes, in outline, the second phase of the learning cycle. It is often an energetic, exciting and risky time in the training process. It is a time of unlocking experiences, opening up possibilities, raising questions. Trainees can be assisted in moving forwards towards understanding of what their experiences, past and current, might mean, and examining the personal and methodological bases of their practices as teachers or trainers. As this understanding becomes clearer, participants come closer to creating meaning for themselves, and this is the next major stage in the process of professional learning.

3. Creating Meaning

Once participants in training sessions begin to analyse their reflections on experience, they open up to opportunities for the exploration of ideas. At the reflective stage, talk may be fairly rudimentary, anecdotal, still to some extent anchored in the experience it describes. The next phase of a training sequence is aimed to lead participants making sense of an experience and beginning to think in more abstract ways about it. They can do this by (a) articulating a set of principles which may underpin a teaching or training activity or (b) drawing out themes from an experience retrospectively. The latter may well precede the former in a sequence of training activity. In the Zambian course sequence described in Chapter 1, the material that was summarised in sessions 2 and 4 is a good example of material still to be processed further.

Processing Experience

During this type of work in the training room, the participants are involved in thinking at successively more abstract levels through various tasks and questions that we provide to structure and guide the process, such as 'thinking questions'. At this stage, as thinking becomes more refined, it is less and less open to our direct influence as trainers. Paradoxically, this is when the trainer might need to 'insert' ideas and material to help move the group forward, as happened in session 3 of the Zambian course, when the group decided to focus on terminology.

The essence of this process from a cognitive point of view is the analysis of the experience and the consideration by participants of various alternative ideas about the meaning and significance of the experience, first to them as individuals and then in more general professional terms. In order to create meaning from an experience participants have to distance themselves from it, and to objectify it as far as possible. It never becomes completely abstract, however. The most productive concepts usually seem to be grounded in experience and are recoverable with reference to experience. Here lies the importance of the affective thread within experience. We have found that completely abstract ideas on training and training processes mean little to participants without the concrete reference point of personal history or shared experience in the training room.

How do we explore ideas?

In order for this part of the training process to succeed, group perceptions are essential, shared and refined by focusing on a 'product' of some kind (for example in sessions 2-4 of the Zambian course). The 'raw' data of experience needs to be explored in order for it to make sense and for further insights into its nature to emerge. We might call this 'deep reflection'. It is also The articulation of ideas in a small working group, offering and receiving constructive feedback on each others' ideas, and the use of questions which explore and subsequently focus participants' thinking are all parts of the process of making sense or creating meaning. It is at this stage that opportunities for new learning and deeper understanding of experience are created. To return to our lake analogy, it is rather like flying above the lake and observing the wave patterns or drawing a map or a diagram of the depths of the lake.

The Trainer's Role
It is at this stage in the cycle that we, as tutors, think it is relevant to begin to offer our own perceptions and ideas, to complement and to help clarify what participants have come up with. We become, effectively, members of the learning group as co-participants. Opportunities for us to engage as co-participants are presented in whole group discussions (or plenary sessions). Our aim is not to provide 'the answer', but hopefully to enrich the process from our own experience and background knowledge. Our role is to help to structure the talk and contribute to the process of discovering meaning. At this stage we could be seen as experienced explorers of a country which may be new to participants, offering our representation of whatever part of it that we or the participants have chosen to focus upon, and providing some routes through the landscape. Part of this can be to provide the participants with pointers to appropriate reading material to further explore the concepts.

From Making Meaning to New Experience (Transfer from Abstract to Concrete)

What do participants take with them from a training session in terms of new knowledge, skills or awareness?' One way of expressing this is to talk of 'concretizing' - the process of bringing an idea about training into clear focus and to identify what has been learnt that can be integrated into a teacher or trainer's thinking and practice. For example, a training participant may say 'I now understand some principles for teaching reading' or 'I have learnt that it is important to listen actively to a colleague' or 'I realise that I could be more sensitive to a range of different values held by participants in a group'.

Every individual participant hopefully takes something tangible away with them from a training experience, and develops a sense of 'owning' any new idea, concept or skill. The process of exploration, of making sense, opens up to participants the possibility of **discovering for themselves** principles or ideas, or coming to understand, or provide a new interpretation of an event abstracted from the lake of experience through firstly reflection and then refinement.

Processes such as concretising are activated during the journey from one main stage of the training cycle to the next and are mediated by passing through a **filter** of talk and action by training group participants (including the tutor). As participants begin to concretise their thoughts, so they pass from group perceptions back to individual ideas. It is at this stage that they can become open to the possibility of owning any new idea. As individuals they are also ready to return to the world of action in one way or another, ready to begin the process of actively exploring their ideas in practice in the training room. We call this stage of the process **linking**. It marks a transition from the deep thinking at the meaning making stage to decisions about future action.

The process we have described is summarised in figure 2.4:

```
┌──────────────┐                    ┌──────────────┐
│ REVIEW and   │ ─────────────────▶ │ MAKING SENSE │
│ REFLECTION   │    Exploring       │              │
└──────────────┘     Ideas          └──────────────┘
                                          │
                                          │ Linking
                                          │ and
                                          │ Concretizing
                                          ▼
                                    ┌──────────────┐
                                    │ PLANNING FOR │
                                    │ ACTION       │
                                    └──────────────┘
```

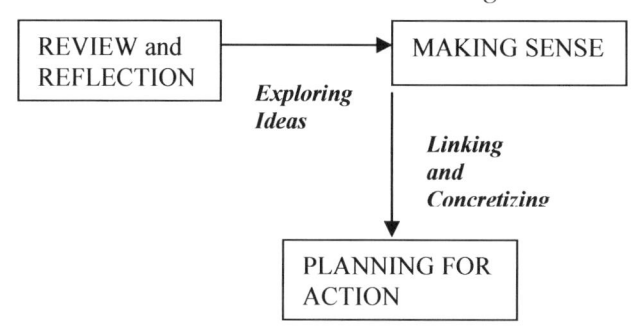

Figure 2.4 From Reflection to Planning

4. Planning for Action

When participants have a sense of gaining something new from a training session - for example, when they can articulate a set of principles or a heightened awareness of a teaching/training practice, they can now begin to think how they can integrate this into their own practice. This can mean either testing out the new idea in practice, or be entering another training activity designed to further refine thinking. (See, for example Session 4 in the Zambian training sequence) Although this is a stage at which individuals often work alone, we do not preclude collaborative planning, as well as the need for participants to elicit feedback on their plans. Our experience has revealed that the potentially more developmental or 'do-able' plans usually evolve from a combination of making plans concrete plus good feedback or 'pre-testing'.

It is at the action planning stage of the cycle that we invite participants to project themselves into the future and to achieve some form of closure on current training activity. We invite participants to decide what action they do wish to take on the basis of the training experiences up to this point in the cycle. Plans could include the following, for example:

- writing a lesson plan
- preparing some teaching or training materials

Whatever the nature of the plan, we anticipate participants facing the difficult prospect of testing any change in their thinking or practice. It is our responsibility at this stage to provide support and assistance for participants in achieving this.

By now, we have completed the cycle, working from experience through reflection to making sense and finally planning for action. We have moved through the filters of group and individual talk on this journey and engaged in different processes at each stage, awareness-raising, exploring, making concrete and linking and finally preparing.

The Completed Cycle

So we return to experience. However, it is likely that our perceptions of experience - past, present or new - will have in some small way been **transformed** by working through the cycle. As well as transforming past or present experience through reflection, making sense and then planning, it is possible that in subtle and possibly in ways unknown to participants at the time, perceptions have changed - outlooks have been transformed.

The training cycle provides us with a flexible and developmental means of structuring training activities and at the same time supporting participants in their learning about training or teaching. The cycle itself is a way of 'making sense' about the training process. Our expanded version of the cycle as presented here is the representation of our current state of knowledge and thinking about training. A final point is that although the diagrammatic representation and the way in which we have written about the cycle gives a very linear and neat picture, the reality in the training room is much more organic, unpredictable and less open to objective description than we might have portrayed it, and we hope that the case study in Chapter 1 realises this. Figure 2.5 draws together the elements discussed in this chapter into a full portrayal of the process.

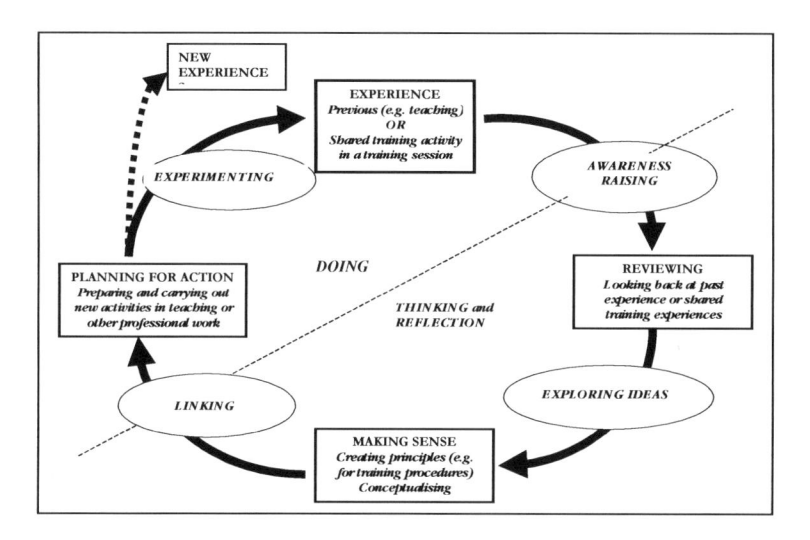

Figure 2.5 The Learning Cycle in Training (after Kolb 1984)

The next few chapters will examine in more depth what we do at each stage of training by way of different training activities. We also explore the social and psychological processes, and issues that are raised by working around the learning cycle.

References

Kolb, D.A. (1984) Experiential Learning as the Science of Learning and Development. Englewood Cliffs, NJ: Prentice Hall. 3rd edition.

Schön, D.A. (1983) The Reflective Practitioner. San Francisco, CA: Jossey-Bass.

Schön, D.A. (1987) Educating The Reflective Practitioner. San Francisco, CA: Jossey-Bass.

CHAPTER 3
WORKING WITH GROUPS IN TRAINING

The training programme described in Chapter 1 was a group experience. Many of the strategies used at the outset of the Zambian course were designed to aid group formation and development. We believe that the bedrock of a training course is the group of people who experience the course, both participants and trainers. For the duration of the course a learning community, a social group with a life of its own, is formed; the quality of the eventual outcome of the course will to a considerable extent be forged in the interactions between the members of the learning group. A positive 'social climate' in a learning group is essential for the release of the potential of the learning cycle we described in Chapter 2.

Chapter 3 focuses on working with groups in training. We begin by describing typical activities which we use for group formation, management and maintenance. We then explore problems arising during courses such as conflict in groups. We complete the chapter by exploring personal and interpersonal issues for trainers, such as 'distance' and power relationships.

3.1 Activities for Group Formation

A teacher embarking on a training course is leaving behind for a while the autonomy and isolation of classroom work and joining a group with the aim of learning something new. The Zambian group described in Chapter 1 had not worked together before their course, and the Masters group, which we describe in Chapter 9, was like many groups of professionals we work with, heterogeneous (multi-cultural, multi-ethnic, multilingual). It always takes some time, and considerable care on the part of trainers, to enable groups like this to 'form' and to reach a stage where they are personally secure, and trusting of each other and the trainer, enough to start learning. Course participants have reported anxieties to us at the start of a course which include the following:

> * *I'm 43. I'm not sure I can cope with being a full-time student again.*
> * *I don't think my English will be good enough.*
> * *I have never written long assignments.*
> * *I'm afraid of appearing ignorant - I've hardly read anything.*
> * *I'm so much less experienced than the others.*
> * *The others in the group all sound so confident!*
> * *I'm missing my family a lot.*
> * *I can't read quickly enough.*

Working With Groups in Training

All these are, in different ways, signs of insecurity, self-doubt, or temporary dislocation. They are often there to a lesser extent even in more homogeneous groups such as the Zambian college lecturers described in Chapter 1. Groups of initial trainees, new to higher education, may have different worries, dominated perhaps by the seeming immensity of the career decision they have just taken. Of course, there are usually other emotions at play, too. There is often a genuine sense of excitement and anticipation about being part of a group on a new course, and it is just as much as part of our job as trainers to release and build on the positive energy which individual group members bring to these early encounters as it is to dispel doubts. The activities which we describe below are all aimed at different aspects of the group-forming process. It is our experience that lack of attention to this type of activity, even on the shortest of courses, is likely to diminish the effectiveness of the course as a whole.

3.1.1 Icebreakers and Warmers

The sooner that everyone in the group realises that everyone else is 'only human', the more quickly each individual will begin to feel secure and able to start contributing to the group. This means hearing everyone's voice, learning everyone's name and making 'eyeball to eyeball' contact with every other group member. We look for icebreakers which will facilitate this process, drawing on a range of published sources (see booklist at the end of this section) as well as on ideas of our own and those of colleagues. We also, at this early stage, tend to use 'low disclosure' activities, which allow participants to reveal 'safe' information (e.g. about likes and dislikes in food, music, sport etc) rather than activities which probe more deeply into personal matters, values or beliefs. One activity which fulfils these criteria is an adaptation of one proposed by Moskowitz's (1978) – 'Clock Line Up' - which we offer as an illustration on page 37.

We have been made aware by a number of course participants and groups of the value of starting each training day with a 'warmer' such as this one. Even if the group is already well formed, each new meeting requires attention to re-forming: re-entering the public world of the group from the more private world of family or workplace. These warmers are often contributed by group members in turn, a practice which shares the responsibility and gives everyone a chance to learn from peers. As the course progresses, such activities may draw on previous shared experience and may serve to remind everyone of the value of the group to each individual participant.

3.1.2 Trust-building Activities

No group can function well in the absence of trust. When participants from different cultural backgrounds come together, and even in mono-cultural groups with little experience of openness or co-operation, we have found that mutual trust cannot be taken for granted. There may be prejudices in one participant's view of another, suspicions about motivation, or caution about disclosing anything to comparative strangers. As trainers, we are part of this. Participants need to learn to trust us, and we need to trust them. We are aware that the process of trust-building is often a long one, and that it is fragile: there have been times when our own actions and behaviour, or those of individual participants in groups we have worked with, have undermined or even sabotaged the hard work that has gone into trust-building, and we know that trust, once lost, is very hard to regain. In long-term groups, much of the trust building goes on in all sorts of ways which we, as trainers working largely in training room sessions, only partly perceive. On shorter, more intensive courses, we often make conscious use of trust-building activities, many of them derived from drama or group therapy handbooks. Activity 2 (Lighthouse) is one we particularly value, borrowed and adapted from Brandes & Phillips (1977).

A number of things have struck us about 'Lighthouse'.

- the feeling that everyone in the room is willing the captain and the lighthouse keeper to succeed. There is often an almost tangible tension;
- the spontaneous applause from the 'lifeless' rocks when the ship eventually arrives safely;
- comments from the keeper about the sense of responsibility he/she feels and from the captain about the absolute faith he/she has to place in the keeper;
- the way the keeper tries to use his/her voice to reassure the captain.

As trainers, we have found it useful to stand outside the activity, near the lighthouse-keeper, offering support through our presence, during the first run-through; subsequently, however, we can also safely participate by becoming rocks. This brings us back to the point about participants' trust of us, as trainers. To win that trust, we have to be open about our objectives, and be ready to participate in activities on an equal basis whenever it is possible or makes sense for us to do so.

ACTIVITY 1 **Favourite Time of Day**
Time required: 10 - 15 minutes
Materials;   None
Space: A good expanse of open floor

Instructions to participants:

Stage 1: Stand in a big circle. Imagine that your circle is a clock face. Here are some points of reference (Trainer locates 12, 3, 6 and 9 o'clock on the floor using chalk or other markers, such as A4 sheets with large numbers drawn on them.) Now think back to your regular routine at home. What is your favourite time in the day? Without speaking, please go and stand as close as possible to that time.

Stage 2: Trainer arranges participants randomly, as they stand, in an inward-facing and an outward-facing circle, and in pairs, thus:

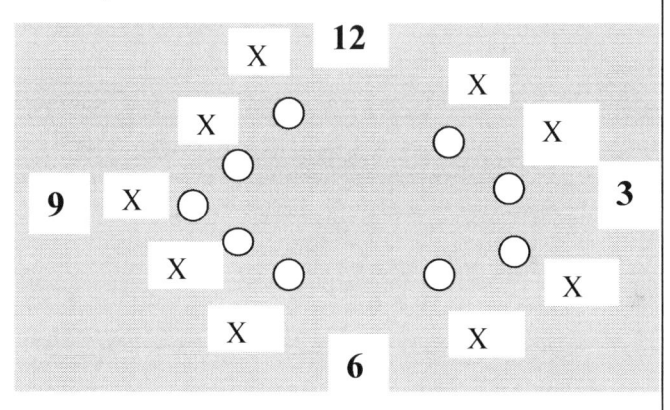

(The spread around the clock is likely to be uneven, but each pair should be as close as possible to their chosen time.)

Each pair has 1 minute to exchange names and explain their reasons for choosing that time.

Stage 3: Outer circle remains stationary, inner circle moves clockwise to the next partner. Once again, one minute is allowed for the same conversational exchange. (A variation here is to pass on what your last partner told you rather than your own information). There should be three or four more clockwise movements of this sort.

Stage 4: Everyone moves into an inward-facing circle and trainer mentions each participant by name, inviting anyone else in the group to reveal this participant's favourite time

and the reasons for it. (e.g. 'Martha likes 11 o'clock in the evening because she finally gets time for herself')
Alternative Extra Stage When every group member has talked about themselves and each other, ask the group to split into 2 sub-groups - 'morning people' (or 'larks'), and 'night people' (or 'owls'). Ask the group if anyone wants to comment.
Note : **Trainer's role** This activity requires careful timing and management, and the trainer will probably need to be responsible for this, rather than take part. It is a lively and often noisy activity!
(After Moscowitz, G. (1978:63))

ACTIVITY 2   **Lighthouse**

    Time required: 10 minutes approx.
    Materials: A scarf or other means of blindfold; a steady chair
    Space: A good expanse of open floor

Procedure
1. Ask for two volunteers, one to be a lighthouse-keeper and the other to be a ship's captain.
2. The two stand at opposite ends of the room, facing each other. The lighthouse-keeper stands on a chair and the captain is blindfolded.
3. Ask all other group members to be rocks. They should distribute themselves randomly in the space between the lighthouse-keeper and the captain, but facing the lighthouse-keeper. Remind them that rocks cannot move (even a centimetre!) or speak.
4. Explain that the light in the lighthouse has broken down, and that it is night-time. The lighthouse-keeper can see the lights of the ship as it approaches the harbour. Using a loud-hailer (cupped hands!) the lighthouse-keeper has to guide the captain through the rocks safely to the harbour below the lighthouse.
5. Once the ship is safely in port, remove the blindfold, and ask the keeper, the captain and the rocks how they felt during the activity. Repeat with further volunteers if time allows.

3.1.3 'Baggage'
On short in-service courses, participants frequently arrive with preoccupations relating to their work, their families etc or

preconceptions about the course itself. We find that these preoccupations can prevent them from being fully 'present', particularly in the early sessions of the course. They can even lead to physical withdrawal on occasion. It is often these 'preoccupied' participants who gain least from in-service courses and who are most critical in end-of-course evaluations. So it is in everyone's interests to spend a little time removing this potential block to learning. We have used the next activity – Activity 3 - with groups on residential courses overseas as well as at home:

ACTIVITY 3 **Laying Down Your Burden**

Time required: 10-15 minutes
Materials: Pen and paper
Space: Chairs in circles of 5-6

Procedure
1. Ask participants to form group of 5-6, and to take a pen and paper.
2. Ask them to jot down, silently and privately, something which is on their mind from the 'world outside', and which they don't mind talking about (this is important).
3. Invite them, if they wish, to give this 'problem' a pictorial image (n.b. It's not always bad news: one participant in Austria drew a picture of a church because her sister was to be married the following weekend and she was very excited about it!).
4. In each circle, participants take it in turn to 'lay down their burden' (the piece of paper) on the floor in the centre circle, and to talk about it to the others in the group.
5. In plenary, take some feedback from groups, asking how they felt about sharing their 'burdens'.

This activity has often enhanced the 'social climate' of training courses. It allows people to 'share' and helps them to avoid the trap of believing that they are the only ones with a problem. It also explains why participant X rushes off to his room every evening (to correct a pile of examinations, maybe) instead of joining the others socially. But above all, it helps to 'unblock' many participants who, having had an inner need acknowledged and having had a brief opportunity to talk about it, seem much more receptive and ready to participate more fully in the rest of the course. As trainers, we should also feel free to take part in this kind of activity; it can help us, too.

3.1.4 Setting the Agenda for the Course

Even when sponsors lay down objectives for a training course in advance, we find it important to involve participants in setting as much of the course agenda as possible. A totally imposed syllabus and framework often alienates participants, particularly on post-experience courses, when they already have a well-defined position in the profession. We are also aware that participants come to courses with set agendas, and that the quality of the group experience is enhanced by collective work on learning agendas.

ACTIVITY 4 Agenda Setting

Time:	Up to 30 minutes
Materials:	Overhead transparency, pens, paper
Space:	A normal training room with flexible seating

Procedure (for a group of 16):

1. Ask participants to write down, individually and privately, their **three** main learning priorities on the course. Ask them to be realistic in accommodating known constraints (e.g. time, sponsor's objectives etc).
2. Ask participants to work with a partner and to draw up **three** priorities for both of them. (There may be overlap, but individual priorities may have to be sacrificed).
3. Now ask each pair to join another, to form a group of four and to agree on **three** priorities.
4. In the meantime, cut an A4 transparency into four equal sections across its width, and divide each strip into 3 numbered 'boxes':

1st	2nd	3rd

5. Give a strip and a pen to each group and ask them to write in their priorities.
6. Display the four strips simultaneously on the transparency, and allow time for contemplation, questions and clarification. As trainer, ensure that you fully understand all the expectations and point out anything you feel is contradictory or unrealistic.

We use a number of different procedures in order to arrive at our common agenda, but one of the most democratic is the 'pyramid' discussion. It allows every voice to be heard, and points out graphically the need for a compromise between individual (and sometimes idiosyncratic!) priorities and the realities of working together in a group within a given time-scale. The example activity – Activity 4 - which follows is based on the 'pyramid' principle.

This activity can be carried out where the agenda is relatively open, but also where a syllabus or 'menu' is offered for participants from which to choose. We find that pair and group discussion helps participants to clarify their ideas, strike compromises, and become more realistic about what can be achieved on a course. This can, and often does, have a positive effect on individuals and the group, and plays a valuable part in group formation as well as establishing course priorities. Above all, it gives a sense of shared responsibility for what is to come: participants become, in a real sense, stakeholders in the course.

A sample agenda, set by participants in the opening session (on a Friday evening) of a Weekend Mentoring Course in Hungary in early 1996 appears below.

The display of these priorities was followed by a lively plenary discussion of important areas of common concern, and the two facilitators also used it as a basis for planning the programme for Saturday and Sunday.

Priority	1st	2nd	3rd
GROUP A	How much help to give trainees?	To what extent can we be flexible with trainees' lesson plans?	How can we persuade trainees to give grades for oral work?
GROUP B	Marking	How do you talk trainees into your views about grades?	Time allocated to Teaching Practice [T.P.] (observation & effective teaching)
GROUP C	How to assess the improvement of less-gifted	What counts more in assessing T.P. - preparation or implementation?	How to teach trainees to assess their work after T.P.?

	trainees who put a lot of effort in T.P.?		
GROUP D	How to give feedback on poor/negative performance?	Checklist or guidelines for evaluation	Get overall picture of T.P. in the country
GROUP E	How to be a bastard in feedback?	How much space shall we give to self-evaluation?	Grade criteria

Fig 3.1 Sample agenda set by participants

On the basis of an agenda like this, a trainer can negotiate with the group issues such as time allocation, resources, modes of working, assignments, and action plans. It **is** important for the trainer to draw on his/her own experience at this stage to ensure that no promises are made which cannot be kept. It may be useful to keep the agreed agenda on display for the duration of the course, and to refer to it whenever necessary during the course and at the end when evaluation is under way.

3.1.5 Establishing Ground Rules

Anyone who has been involved in a course, as a trainer, teacher or participant will know how irritating it is when the flow of the session is interrupted by late arrivals or early leavers, how difficult for everyone it is when one or two participants hog the talking time or use the force of their personality to impose their agenda, or when someone uses sarcasm or a dismissive remark to 'put down' someone else or to devalue a contribution. This is where ground rules come in. We have found it valuable to devote time, especially on longer courses, to discussing ways in which everyone can help to ensure that group learning opportunities are maximised and that the training room remains a 'democratic' forum. These rules are of little use if imposed by the institution or the trainer. They seem to work better if they are devised and 'owned' by all participants. On this basis, they can make an invaluable contribution to the health of the group (c.f. Brandes & Ginnis 1996). The process of discussing and arriving at them is often a healthy way of opening up beliefs in the group about the nature of the process of professional learning. As trainers, we may start this discussion in the following way:

Now that we have worked together for a few days, you may like to establish some ground rules for the group. You may want to consider turn-taking, punctuality, assignments, and so on. How do you feel about spending 15-20 minutes on establishing some rules?

If the answer is positive, and in our experience it almost always is, it may then be helpful to divide the participants up into four working groups, and to have each group display its chosen rules on a poster or overhead transparency. A final list can then be drawn up in plenary, for display on the training room wall on a poster which can serve as a reminder whenever anyone feels a need to refer to it. Here is an example of a set of rules drawn up for Classroom Investigation by a Masters group.

GROUP GROUND RULES

1. Active participation
- Everyone should contribute (equally)
- Don't rely on other group members
- Work schedules should be equally distributed

2. Regular communication between group members
- Commitment
- Responsibility
- Everyone should agree on topic for investigation

3. Keep appointments when made
- Keep to scheduled meetings

4. Work out a schedule

5. Meet deadlines

6. Set up objectives
- Do what you say you'll do

7. Be focused but open-minded

8. Enjoy!

Subsequently, a nod or a gesture from the trainer or one of the participants in the direction of the 'ground rules' poster is usually enough to remind participants of their commitment. The rules may need to be revised or elaborated as the course progresses.

Ground rules can also be formulated later in a course, or for a specific part of a course in which activity will be slightly different

Working With Groups in Training

from what has already been experienced. We very often set ground-rules at the outset of a course. Sometimes we don't, however, and have to do repair work later on, as we shall describe in 3.2.

3.1.6 Multi-purpose Group-forming Activities

On short, intensive courses, it is often important to save time by combining some of the elements described in a) to (e) above into a single activity. 'Suitcases', described below (Activity 5), is one such activity. It serves the purposes of ice-breaking (requiring close discussion between group members), 'baggage deposit' and agenda-setting, and may also contribute to trust-building and the establishment of ground rules, depending on the 'compartments' that you choose to put in the suitcase.

ACTIVITY 5 **Suitcases**
  Time required: 15-20 minutes
  Materials: Paper and pen, blu-tac
  Space: Normal classroom with wall-space for display

Instructions to Participants
1. Take a sheet of A4 paper and draw a suitcase on it. It should almost fill the paper.
   Draw this on the board as an example.

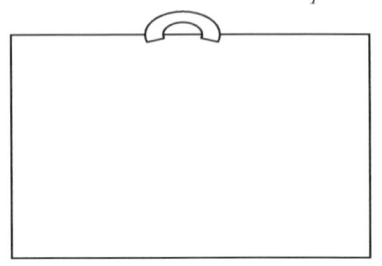

   [suitcase drawing]

2. In the top left corner, note down any expectations you have of the course.
3. In the top right corner, write down any problems or worries you have brought with you and which are still on your mind.
4. In the bottom left corner, note down any ideas or resources you have brought with you to share with others.
5. In the bottom right corner, show anything you have brought with you to occupy you in your free time during the seminar.

Working With Groups in Training

> 6. Now 'tie' a luggage label to the handle and write your name on it.
> 7. When you have finished, stick your suitcase to the wall with tape or Blutac.
> 8. Stroll around and look at the contents of all the suitcases. If you see anything that interests you, find the owner of the case and talk to her/him about it.

As an example, on the next page we reproduce the suitcase of a Hungarian participant on a one-week Mentor-Training course which we co-tutored in Plymouth. (We have changed her name)

JUDIT

<u>Experience</u>
- 3 years of teaching
- 2 years as a mentor

<u>Expectations</u>
- Getting to know the SW of England
- Some stimulating ideas

<u>Resources</u>
- an umbrella
- cigarettes
- a good book
- chewing gum
- some ideas

<u>Problems/concerns</u>
- Everyone expects me to take a present home
- first time I've left my daughter
- tests to mark

We have found that the activity has the following benefits:
- It creates an easy and relaxed atmosphere. Because it is based on a strong image, this seems to help. At the beginning of a course, we do not want to overload participants with complex abstract thinking tasks, and find that 'light' thinking activities such as this one have a positive effect in preparing participants for deeper thinking later in the course.
- It makes participants consider and respect the background and expectations of others (thus preparing them to make the compromises which are necessary on every course).
- It helps participants to identify shared problems and interests.
- It allows the trainer to assess the 'human resources' in the training room at the start of the course.

- It combines the personal with the professional, and the cognitive with the affective.
- It is 'democratic' in that it gives all participants (and trainers!) an equal voice.
- It enables participants to put their problems into the 'public domain' if they wish - participants only reveal what they choose.
- It is a good starting point for reflection.

It is also versatile. We also invite participants to form groups and pool the material in each 'compartment' of the suitcase to create a composite picture of the group's experience, resources etc. This is very useful for setting an agenda for a course. Another variation we like is for participants to include a couple of items of advice to the trainer on conducting the workshop or course.

The same image is useful as a basis for evaluation at the end of a short course. In the closing session, participants can be asked to re-examine the contents of their arrival suitcases and then, on the back of the same sheet, to redraw it and to show what they are taking home after the course, (resources, ideas, solved and unsolved problems, etc).

3.2 Working with Groups - Issues and Processes

In our experience, time spent on group forming is seldom wasted, and it is most often the key to a successful and productive training experience for everyone involved. When we have given insufficient attention to activities such as those described above, we have almost always regretted it later. As trainers, we see it as our responsibility to ensure that these steps are not neglected, and to make their importance clear to the groups we work with.

The purpose of this section is to examine various issues which can arise during the course of working with groups in training. Through our discussion we shall examine some of the group processes we have experienced through our work, and how we draw from this experience in managing groups.

3.2.1 At The Beginning

A central aim of the ice-breaking and 'warmer' activities in 3.1 is to enable the training group members to get to know each other. This section elaborates on these activities and discusses the importance of disclosure in training, with reference to the Johari Window (Luft 1974).

Here, and throughout the rest of the book, we introduce our participants' voices into the discussion to provide another perspective on training issues.

- **NAMES - 'GETTING TO KNOW YOU'**

> *'The whole week of activity has built up the friendship between the teachers and the students and the students ourselves. We feel more at home and are more confident that we can be successful.' (Haiyan)*
>
> *'Feels like I've known everyone for longer than 5 days.' (Graeme)*

Knowing participants' names at an early stage is important. It helps establish an informal and friendly working relationship. We find that this contributes towards breaking down barriers to learning and enhances a strong flow of information in a group.

Knowing names sends a message to individual participants that they are valued, with their own unique identities. It is not easy to learn everyone's name in a training group, and the 'warmers' and 'ice-breakers' in 3.1 are ways of getting to know people's names. The repetition of names in an activity can help all group members to remember them. If you are the trainer, it will not take long for participants to learn your name. The onus is on the trainer to learn names. On the other hand, the group members may already know one another from their working contexts, so how can a trainer remember all the names in a group, and help group members remember each others' names?

- Rote learning a list after the introductory session is very helpful, especially if each individual on the list has divulged a personal detail or two in an activity which can be 'hooked' to the name.
- Finding an opportunity to write names down during an ice-breaker can reinforce memory.
- Saying a person's name every time we talk to them in the initial stages of a course is also very helpful as a 'cementing' device.
- Above all, we seek opportunities to talk with group members during activities in sessions and at breaks, informally.
- We encourage groups in sessions to put their names on products from group activity, such as posters or summaries - it enables them to take 'ownership' of the products and, of course, it is another opportunity to read names and refer to individuals by name in feedback sessions.

- **SHARING BACKGROUND AND PERSONAL DETAILS**

> *'In the first week we were introduced to each other as part of the process of learning. It enables us to know each other personally and professionally. The latter reflected our differences.' (Habteab)*

Icebreaking, 'warming' and other group forming activities which encourage the exchange of personal details, can assist in creating openness of exchange in a group, and in laying the foundation for the often risky and challenging work we do in subsequent training sessions, as Habteab points out in his diary entry.

Group formation is also enhanced by our remembering specific contributions that participants have made. The thoughts and information individuals choose to reveal in training sessions also become part of the identity that we build for each individual. The more we know, the closer we are able to get. The feeling of closeness adds to **security**, and when participants are secure, they are more likely to reveal details of their lives, work and ideas. Professionally, this is essential, because secure participants will feel able to open up with their peers, making ideas available for public scrutiny, and thus creating opportunities for learning from each other. We also find that if we share some of our own personal details with groups that we are more able to quickly establish a good working relationship with the members of the group.

'Safe' activities which share personal details like family backgrounds, likes and dislikes and personal biographies are also a very helpful way of establishing a common language in a group because common points of reference are established. A group's collective memory begins with these events. We are often amazed at how much a group invest in an activity like 'Favourite Time of Day'. We have encountered groups who, when searching for common ground, return to this activity and remember who the 'owls' and 'larks' in the group are. We, too, try to remember these important small details. This shared personal knowledge is, we believe, part of the internal dynamics and cohesion of a group.

Problems
Despite our best efforts at creating a 'sharing' atmosphere in a group, problems can occur, sometimes outside our immediate influence.

- Latecomers to courses, who have missed all the opening activities, often struggle to relate to peers who have already begun to establish common points of reference. These participants have to be inducted into the group's insider talk, or they can quickly feel excluded.
- Another issue that this type of work raises is the question of whether or not participants wish to reveal personal details. We might hold back from using 'high disclosure activities, concerned that the group will not

like them, for 'cultural' reasons, or personal reasons. We have found, however, that groups all over the world respond positively to the socialising process. Knowing about each other seems to be a universal human need, and participants themselves know what can and cannot be disclosed.

- We have also had difficult experiences with training groups when we have not spent time sharing personal backgrounds and details. In these circumstances, we find we have carelessly overlooked the importance of enabling participants to share something, or holding back our own details. Trainees, already isolated from each other at the outset of a programme for all sorts of reasons, have this feeling of isolation amplified in such circumstances. This can create undesirable tensions in the group.
- Personal isolation can also be the root of unnecessary competitiveness among group members. It seems easier to compete against people you with whom share nothing, or feel you have nothing in common with.
- If we don't reveal anything of our 'real selves', participants might also think that the trainers are aloof or uninterested in them. Again, communication is blocked.

When things have gone wrong in a training group, and we wish to diagnose the problem, we find that this is a good place to start - to ask whether or not we have done enough facilitation of the 'getting to know you' process. While we can attempt repair, we have often, to our cost, found that it is difficult ever to achieve this fully. The learning experience suffers as a consequence.

- ***DEALING WITH EXPECTATIONS***

'I was a student now, but different from the sort of student I'd imagined to be. The feeling was reinforced by the other tutors (apart from the course leader). They were willing to listen to us whenever we had discussions, and seminars in class. Strangely we didn't have the sort of lectures I'd expected, in which we have to take a lot of notes with definitions of obscure academic terms followed by long lists of characteristics of certain principles, or quotations from certain gurus. Instead what we'd got was all from ourselves, from our own contributions.' (Yijie)

'Towards the end of the term , those with more experience or knowledge in the profession expected more input from the tutors e.g. their answers, solutions to the tasks given, opinions decisions etc' (Mul)

I was a little disappointed at first, as I was expecting the usual lectures, note-taking and mugging up routine. (Hamid)

> *'I didn't expect lecture-type sessions and I certainly expected group work.'*
> *(Mirela)*

These comments from participants are very common in our experience. We ignore them at our peril. Participants arrive on courses or at workshops with a vast range of expectations about the work they are going to do, what they hope to achieve, relationships with other participants, with trainers and so on. It is one of a trainer's main responsibilities at the early stages of a training programme to help participants 'air' their expectations, and to make them public. False or unrealistic expectations can block an individual's capacity for learning and development if they remain submerged. Or they can emerge some time later in the course. Whenever we have failed to examine participants' expectations, we have suffered the consequences with damaged relationships which we cannot completely repair.

The following examples will illustrate the expectations issue:
- An individual may arrive at a course with a ghost to lay and expect the course to do the job for them.
- Another might turn up with a totally open mind, ready for anything, and be disappointed when the agenda is fairly tightly controlled.
- Another might come to a course simply for a 'piece of paper' and expect the course to provide her with the simplest means of getting that piece of paper.
- Perhaps the most sensitive area concerns expectations of trainers' roles - participants have often expected us to be lecturing from Day 1 of a course - 'giving input', not 'playing games'. In these cases we find it best to respond with clear statements about our roles and the methods we are using. When we haven't done this, we have paid the price. All participants will, at one time or another, want to seek confirmation of their own and the trainers' roles. It is our responsibility to see that this happens.

Trainers are the most influential people in the training room. The ways we choose to work may disappoint some expectations. We need to explain ourselves, and not to act defensively. We have beliefs about training which it is only fair that our participants should feel able to discuss and question. Our own openness, although hard to achieve, is central to effective practice in this domain.

It helps to have some inkling of participants' expectations early on in a course, and to help them articulate these expectations. The following are ways we have used:

1. Group formation activities and activities which invite participants to explore their past are very helpful indirect ways of enabling participants to voice their expectations, as in 3.1.
2. A needs analysis questionnaire (pre-course) can sometimes help an intending participant to express their wants and expectations. But often in our experience, the real want or expectation is unexpressed (perhaps the participant thinks that this information might prejudice their chances of acceptance on a course? or their chances of success?), or it may have changed by the time the participant arrives for the course.
3. One-to-one tutorials are extremely helpful in sorting out confusions and misunderstandings, as these students note:

> *'I find the tutorials very helpful especially in clarifying matters which I find confusing in class.' (Pat)*
>
> *"Had my tutorial with T. I put my questions which he's very good at bouncing back at me and making me do the thinking...' (Doug)*

We find that they work best if the individual (like Doug) is invited to come along to the tutorial with some ideas on what they'd like to achieve on the course, as a prelude to setting goals, which can be reviewed from time to time in subsequent tutorials. This has the advantage of not pushing the participant into statements without previous consideration, and for the participant to set the agenda for the tutorial. This can be followed up with an extra section in a written professional biography in which the individual writes about what they expect from the course, and what they will contribute to the course.

Another way of making our trainer perspective explicit is to give a short talk near the beginning of a programme about the overall principles upon which a course has been designed. For longer programmes (up to a year), this also has the useful function of being a point of reference for every individual throughout the course (it can also help participants see goals which they might otherwise not have seen) and is a way for us to articulate our own training agenda. We, too, have strong principles and ideas about training. These principles can become the subject of dialogue between participants and trainers when looking at, for example, training methodologies on a trainers' course.

Here is an example of a set of guidelines for professional development that have evolved on our Masters programmes. It is presented as a short talk, with thinking tasks following exposition of each principle.

> **Professional Development**
> **Some Guidelines**
> 1. **Experience - past and present - is the basis of professional development.**
> 2. **Relationships between theory and practice need to be explored.**
> 3. **Autonomy is a professional goal - self-development.**
> 4. **We can learn from and with our peers and colleagues, given good working conditions - collaboration.**
> 5. **There are different types of learning, all of which are valuable.**
> 6. **Change - personal, professional, institutional - is a basic process, and can be worked on and with.**

Some responses to an invitation to share experience after the first guideline on the list had been discussed appear on the next page – 'Types of Experience in the Group'.

Another brief task set after group discussion about the principle referring to learning is for the participants to list as many ways as they know in which people learn. The trainer can then take the opportunity to say that training can take place in some or any of the modes specified, with concrete examples. Individuals are then free to raise doubts and questions at this stage, and later in the course. A commonly expressed doubt is that participants don't know enough to contribute to group sessions. This has to be taken seriously and addressed through activities which appeal directly to participants' present knowledge and experience, with enough time for reflection on the learning modes employed. An example appears overleaf.

A final point on expectations: very often, as a course proceeds, participants' hidden expectations emerge, or their original expectations change, as Gertrude (below) realises.

> *"'A paradox of education is change." This statement also has a great impact on my view of the teaching and learning process. I do believe that change should take place. But who should change? And to what extent should one change?' (Gertrude)*

Participants' expectations can and do change as a course unfolds. We need to remain in touch with participants to follow these changes, and to respond to them wherever possible - usually by publicly noting changes and initiating discussion in the first place. A training experience will produce new expectations as well - participants may become very accustomed to a particular exploratory type of activity with a particular trainer. The trainer then opts to give a lecture - participants wonder what's happening. It sometimes seems that trainers can never win! They can't, of course, unless they let course participants know what's going on.

Working With Groups in Training

> **Types of experience in the group**
> - *working in a research team*
> - *writing teaching and training materials*
> - *experience with having struggled with something and succeeded*
> - *experience with changing one's approach to teaching and being involved in the change*
> - *experience of taking on responsibility*
> - *experience with different levels of work (classroom teaching to undergraduate level, to serving teachers and initial trainees)*
> - *experience of teaching in problematic situations and difficult circumstances (large classes, difficult politics etc.)*
>
> (Masters Group)

3.2.2. Group Problems

Groups come in all shapes and sizes but they can all face difficulties, even when the greatest of care has been taken in forming and establishing a group. This section discusses some of the main problems that we have experienced in our work with groups, and how we have tried to deal with the issues raised.

- ***DOMINANCE and RETICENCE***

> *'There are undoubtedly frustrations of peer group work as well. Sometimes there is a danger of the dominance of the most assertive being reinforced; sometimes there seem to be personality clashes.'* (Julia)

All groups have their extroverts and their introverts, their dominant personalities and the silent ones. In groups, we all tend to behave in certain ways, even if outside the group situation we behave differently. Many participants come to training with us having for many years been trainers themselves, leaders of groups. They can find it difficult to adjust. We have been with groups, who, during their 'forming' stage, seem to have only one spokesperson, who answers any direct questions or our open invitations to the group members to speak. The voice and the personality dominate. As they move into the 'storming' stage, new voices emerge to challenge the dominant voice. Tolerance of those who 'hog' turns diminishes. The group begins to 'spark'. (For a valuable account of this process, see Jacques (1991).)

We notice too that in small group work, there is often a dominant character, or that two dominant characters tangle. But in plenary, whole group mode, the dominant voices do the reporting back, and take the lead in expressing points of view, often (uninvited) on behalf of the rest of the group.

Dealing with the Problems

Throughout these often 'difficult' periods, we need to be particularly alert to the signals from the less dominant, but still valuable, group members. When do they want to speak? How do we recognise their need to speak?

Perhaps the simplest way is to 'test the water' by inviting the quieter members of a group to speak during a group discussion, but not insisting that they speak. It seems to form a useful bridge between silence and self-selection as a speaker. Sometimes eye contact is made, or a hand shyly rises. We need to keep our eyes and ears open for these signals - we do not always succeed, but a way of increasing our chances of success is to insist on seating arrangements in which all participants can see each other, such as circles and horse shoes. We find that this enhances communication in a group.

We also have to overcome the apparent aversion to silence in learning groups, or silent participants. Some may not be 'ready' to talk; we cannot force them. We try to recognise the individuals who are 'quiet', who need time, to talk with them in one-to-one tutorials about the issue. Our experience is that the 'silent' ones do end up talking in plenary, and make increasingly strong contributions to small group work as a course proceeds, as long as we don't push them, or if we invite them to contribute on terms agreed with them in private.

- **CONFLICTS and COMPROMISE**

> *'Group work was not always positive. Negative things came along with the process as it went deeper. I had different problems working with different people. They might think I was difficult too. I remember how I felt uncomfortable, how I compromised all the time, how I got upset and became passively resistant. (...) More conflicts happened when people got closer. Dealing with conflicts is a knowledge which can only be acquired through real experience. For a time I felt weak and powerless confronting conflicts which I couldn't avoid. This feeling twisted and upset me. Then I locked myself in my thinking world. I took time to review and rearrange my feelings. This became a source of power for my next action.' (Qiyan)*

We don't agree all the time, as Qiyan notices. Training groups often consume large amounts of energy in disputes. Unless this is transformed into creative energy, it can undermine a group, and prevent it from making constructive progress. Most disputes occur early in a group's existence, or when they cannot find a way of reaching a compromise, they regress to an earlier 'storming' stage.

Again, we can turn the spotlight on these problems and use the group's resources to unpick the issue of conflict, to ask why a conflict breaks out - case studies of conflict situations, created by the trainer, are particularly effective, as they are neutral in terms of personality. Activity 6 on page 53 is an example

By inviting small groups to focus on this type of problem as a part of their training, and then sharing responses in plenary, we find there is ample opportunity to air attitudes to conflict, and to discuss it openly. The level of openness will be to some extent dependent on the length of time the group has been together, and the self-awareness of the group. We would regard sessions which explored these issues as central to a training programme in any case - if the discussion is informed by participants' immediate experience, so much the better.

ACTIVITY 6   Problem Buster (suitable for trainers' and teachers' groups)

Step 1. Explain to the group that they are going to spend some time examining a situation in which a team cannot agree. The aim is to come up with as effective a solution as possible in the circumstances:

Step 2. Give out the following description, and tell group members to respond individually to the questions after reading it through:

> *A team of 5 teachers have been discussing students' discipline problems at a departmental meeting. 2 members of the team are adamant that a greater degree of control, with strong sanctions such as unlimited after-school detention, is required. They are convinced that discipline will only be restored if there is a stricter regime. They are vigorously opposed by 2 members who believe the problems are related to self-esteem, and that the low level of discipline is due to students not having enough say in the setting of standards and 'rules'. The lack of input on their part has meant a refusal to accept responsibility, and consequently refusal to conform, or even sabotage of efforts to improve things. The fifth member of the group can see both sides and believes that the first stage is to open dialogue with the students before making any decisions. She believes that the problem will only be addressed through dialogue. The temperature in the room has reached boiling point.*

a. What is the source of this group problem? Are there any 'hidden' factors contributing to the problem which you think may be important, but are not mentioned?

b. What means would you suggest to this group for solving their dispute? And how would you go about implementing your ideas?

Step 3. After 5/8 minutes, form pairs to share ideas and agree common measures (10 mins.).

Step 4. Now form small groups (either 2 or 3 pairs, or splitting pairs), again to agree a strategy for helping the group. (15 mins.)

> *Step 5.* Plenary to share all groups' ideas. Trainer collects ideas on board or flip-chart, but does not interfere except where a speaker needs to keep the floor.
>
> *Step 6.* When all contributions have been made, pose the following questions to the group:
>
> a. How do you feel at the end of this activity? Are there any lingering emotions from your own discussions? What are they? Why do you think there might be 'left-over' emotions?
>
> b. Did you have any difficulties in agreeing during the discussion? If so, what do you think were their origins? Did you solve any difficulties? If so, how?
>
> *Step 7.* Allow time for either group discussion, or open plenary, or set these as overnight 'thinking questions' for further work the next day.

Sometimes a conflict may rumble on and even spill outside the training room. We have to stay neutral, no matter what our private feelings about an issue might be. In extreme cases we may have to provide the conditions which will result in the solution of the problem, such as privacy in which individuals can talk through their dispute. We have, on occasion, sat in with participants as they attempt to resolve a problem. It demands immense patience and we find ourselves having to resist the temptation to offer solutions. Sometimes, participants are able to find their own ways through problems, as June indicates in her comments below.

> *'Small group work has been full of pleasures and frustrations. The composition of a group is crucial to the amount of satisfaction I get out of a task. (...) Even when a group task has been full of frustrations, I've come away feeling that at least I've further developed some more interactional and interpersonal skills, even if I've made no progress on the content of a task.'* (June)

A group generally finds a way of accommodating a conflict, either by ignoring it or absorbing it. But the group suffers in the long run if the conflict is unresolved. Our own attitudes towards conflict, and our ways of dealing with conflict are factors in these cases. Occasionally, our own personal failure to face up to conflict has led to a worsening of the situation.

Trainers In Conflict With Groups or Individuals

How do we avoid becoming enmeshed in the personality clashes in the group? How do we resist challenges from dominant group members who are perhaps unaccustomed to being anything less than group leaders, or address conflict between group members or with us? We do not always succeed. A particular individual might get under our skin to such an extent that we end up in open conflict with them. This is close to a worst-case scenario - such conflict can, and does, deeply damage group relations and strains everyone's tolerance. We all have 'hooks' - things which people do or which happen and which get under our skin. Examples are when a dominant participant hijacks the agenda in a session, or when a person exaggerates to make a point.

We are irritated by these small things, and we are thus less able to deal with the business of enabling the group to work together for mutual benefit. As well as being aware of group behaviour, we thus need to remain aware of our own behaviour when working with a group, and to work on those aspects which inhibit group development. Dealing with conflict is, without doubt, the most difficult of these areas.

3.2.4 Outside the Sessions

Group health is essential for an active learning community, in which participants feel that they are able to learn from their peers as well as their trainers, and in which trainers can also learn from the participants. We know that a great deal of important work is done outside the training room. There are two ways in which we feel we can assist a group in this regard - by setting tasks for discussion outside the training room, and by providing opportunities for the group to 'get away from it all'.

'I like the fact that we are given tasks which involve working with others outside the classroom.' (Margit)

Group life continues after the training room sessions are over. In fact, training room sessions may only be a catalyst to the more intense, yet more informal work that participants undertake out of hours. We know that this out of hours work is an important part of the process of training. Residential courses can often create the conditions for the continued training work outside the training room. This work is a vital part of the processing of course content and experience, and is probably just as likely to lead to long-term learning and change as the work in sessions. Simply put, new ideas take time to process. Talk aids this process - it may be easier to talk over a cup of coffee than to talk in a room full of peers, deeply involved in a training activity. There are certainly fewer time constraints, and it is not unusual for impromptu sessions to lead to late nights and bleary eyes the following day. And yet participants seem to have just as much, if not more, energy than if they had all stayed in their own accommodation and said nothing to anyone about their thoughts and perceptions of the previous day's events.

> *'Gratifying that our tutors can think of the stress and fatigue we go through during the course - we really needed the break. It was indeed refreshing to go out on the trip.' (Winnie)*

Group life outside the training sessions also involves purely social activity, as Winnie acknowledges in her diary. This may mean running trips away from the learning institution to foster group spirit and for a 'breath of fresh air' to clear away mental cobwebs. Participants also find it easier to approach us if we are away from 'base', and this, too, can act as an important part of the social process of a programme. In short, any device which lowers social barriers and opens up channels of communication is going to be of value to a learning community. Social talk is not idle talk if it leads to more effective and more trusting working relationships. The 'class sessions' need to be complemented by 'out-of-class sessions', both arranged and spontaneous. Walks, outings, late-night debates: all aid a group's learning processes.

3.3 Participants and Trainers - establishing and maintaining relationships

> *'It is nice to have a warm teacher/learner relationship' (Meher)*
>
> *'What struck me positively is the open-mindedness of our tutors, ready to accept any criticism, opinion or suggestion from us.' (Dolou)*
>
> *'The tutors regard us learners as their colleagues, so that it is easy for them to explore our experiences and the share them with others. At first I didn't really understand what they were actually doing' (Idris)*

Even on a one-day workshop, we believe that its success will to some extent be dependent upon the quality of relationships we establish with the participants, both as a group and with individuals. Obviously, on a short course with a large number of participants, we are unlikely to be able to make individual contact with every member of the group. However, it should not prevent us from trying. This raises the question of how we can reduce distance between trainer and participants.

3.3.1 Closeness and Distance

> *'The most valuable contribution of our tutors for me is the establishment of trust between them and ourselves' (Uwe)*

Uwe's comment about trust raises issues about how we were able to establish that trust. Imagine being at a training session as a participant. You spend some 8 hours in the company of 20 other professionals away from your workplace. By the end of the day, you feel that you 'know' your trainer, and that she 'knows' you. You are on first name terms and have been since the opening hour of the session. You feel as if you have been able to participate as an individual, and yet you have only actually exchanged words with the trainer on two occasions, once over coffee, and once when you asked a question during a session. Why do you feel so 'close' to the trainer and the other participants?

Let's try an alternative scenario: The same length of time in the same place. You have worn your name badge all day but the trainer - Ms Strong (you have read her name badge) has not addressed you by name. The trainer is apparently aloof, and does not socialise. She even insists on being called 'Ms. Strong' in sessions. You feel you know nothing about the trainer by the end of the day, except that she is very 'professional' and 'efficient'. The sessions are immaculately presented and timed to the nearest minute. The learning load was just right, you have a file full of useful handouts and yet you feel as though you've not really had a worthwhile experience. It has been 'cold' - you feel distant from both the trainer and the other participants.

These may be two extremes, but they are nonetheless real training experiences for many participants. We believe that forging good relationships with participants on training courses is essential if we are to work effectively as a group and to maximise the learning potential of the group. This works at the individual level too.

- **WHAT IS 'CLOSE'?**

There are days when I was very sensitive and exhausted resulting in interpersonal and intrapersonal conflicts, not to mention conflicts with the tutors' (Anonymous Student)

This student's diary entry and its candour is perhaps a reflection of how comfortable its writer was with the tutors who read it. How close can relationships between participants in training be? Teaching is often referred to as a 'passionate encounter', and that the quality of learning can be profoundly influenced by the involvement of individuals in the educational encounter. Sharing in the learning experience of an individual is bound to create a bond between the individuals concerned if the learning has been significant and meaningful. We all remember our favourite teachers with some affection - exploring the root of the affection we feel even many years later is often related to significant, shared learning experiences. Or we might hear someone say something like 'My history teacher really cared for us.' This is an acknowledgement of a natural process at work. When teaching or training experiences are memorable, we feel a part of a shared experience. We have 'been through' an experience together, invested in it. Such shared experience brings people closer. Very often, this is unacknowledged by individuals - somehow, to acknowledge it strips away the excitement of the closeness that we feel. And yet, if we do find ways of giving voice to the awareness of closeness - psychological and emotional - we often find that it opens up new possibilities for learning about teaching and training.

- **DANGER SIGNS**

> *'Power is in the tutors' hands, even though on the surface we learners feel we are in control' (Jamilah)*

Jamilah's comment is very apt: trainers are always in control of the learning experience, no matter how much work groups do on their own, and negotiate their programme. Trainers have power over course content and direction. A danger is that we direct covertly without making our intentions plain - we need to open up issues related to trainers' roles from the very beginning of course in order to keep alert to the dangers that lack of awareness of this issue can produce.

Another danger is of a group - possibly including the trainer - becoming too group-focused. Seen from the outside, a 'cosy' working relationship between a trainer and the individuals in a training group can seem too close, in danger of being manipulated or subverted by individuals who may feel less valued by the other individuals in the group, or by the trainer. There are other dangers too, threats of different types from both inside and outside a group and threats from outside a group. Jealousy, anger, exclusion, mistrust: learning groups are as open to normal human emotions as any other groups of individuals.

We try to guard against this by acknowledging our responses to groups and individuals in diaries, by talking about our feelings with colleagues who may or may not be teaching a particular group. We are also aware that the 'waves' of energy created by a powerful group learning experience in an institution can have the effect of making colleagues not immediately involved feel insecure and excluded. Our own absorption with a group can blind us to other commitments to our colleagues and institutions.

- **THE TIME FACTOR**

> *I feel in a position to crystallise and personalise what I have learnt so far. There seems to be so much that I have learnt about myself and working with others that has emerged from working together. (Rose)*

Time is an important factor in the group process. Over a year, one gets to know an individual very well if one is in daily contact, particularly on training courses which involve constant interaction. Relationships are inevitably going to be closer the more that is revealed of a personal and professional nature by participants. Our role as facilitators is to allow these processes to develop in their own time, with 'gentle' help when necessary, in the form of activities or thinking questions, to push a group forward.

Teaching and training are very personal activities - teachers and trainers have it in their own hands how close they wish to get to their students or participants. Our experience is that a helpful form of closeness on training courses is one which emanates from a sharing of experiences and gradual disclosure over time. Trust and mutual respect are the basis of this closeness, as is openness about intentions and roles.

It is the trainer's responsibility to get to know individuals, to see what makes them tick, to find out how they are experiencing the course and so on. As a trainer, you can't support an individual's development if you don't know that individual well or if that individual doesn't trust you. The same applies if you don't know yourself or trust yourself.

3.3.2 Likes and Dislikes

Some groups we like a great deal. Some groups we get along okay with. A few groups we do not get on with. One or two groups have been, for us, the proverbial 'groups from hell'. We know why we like groups - they are 'open for business', full of energy, playfulness; they challenge us, listen to each other, accept each other's differences and work towards understanding them. They look for compromises, absorb potentially 'difficult' colleagues, want to be autonomous, and can even tell us to keep clear of their work. Any group which exhibits the opposites of these behaviours can 'turn us off' unless we remember that they have the right to be as they are.

We can try to influence groups in their development towards our ideals, but in reality our influence is fairly minimal. If we find ourselves in conflict with a group or an individual it is painful, both to us and the persons involved. Some of our worst experiences have occurred when we have been unable to resolve conflicts or face up to them. What is important is that the group's learning may be adversely affected. It is therefore up to us to seek to solve the problems, to face them and to face our own shortcomings. Not easy, but made easier when working with a supportive team, who might be having similar problems themselves.

We all carry our likes and dislikes about with us - our psychological baggage. We also signal these to a group or to individuals in that group. We have overcome difficulties with groups and individuals we don't get on with by acknowledging our dislikes. It is often painful to learn about oneself in this way, but a valuable learning lesson nonetheless. The emotional side of being a trainer is one that poses us some of the greatest challenges in our own development and learning. The risks of working closely with a group, and which are most graphically illustrated in disputes, are not to be underestimated.

3.3.3 The Trainer As Participant - Dealing With Demands

We have presented a picture of the trainer as a participant in the group process. No matter how participant-centred training might be, the trainer is still a key player in the process, and is *expected*, more often than not, to provide leadership - social, emotional and psychological as well as professional and intellectual. The demands are intense if we accept these multiple roles. Stress is an inevitable part of the work. We recognise that we broadcast how we're feeling to trainees and colleagues in a multitude of ways - whether or not we're nervous, under stress, happy or angry. We can't deny stress, but we can manage it, and learn better how to manage it.

Participants on courses sometimes appear to want to eat up all our time, finding all sorts of ways of engaging us in conversation as a way of laying their own doubts to rest, to think out loud, or sometimes, fortunately rarely, to destabilise us in order to protect themselves from unpleasant decisions. Handling disputes, uncertainty, change and development are very demanding. Somehow we have to absorb negativity and doubt with a smile when we're actually feeling quite impatient and anxious to move on to the next learning experience. We are not always the best time managers, and we may succumb to the temptation of passing time talking to participants in order to avoid unpleasant duties of our own, or we may enjoy the social contact in its own right.

Burnout is a constant threat if we are not aware of how our time is eroded, and if we are unable for one reason or another to cope with the emotional demands of running training programmes with a strong process agenda. All this serves to remind us of the stresses and strains people are under when they are involved in intense intellectual and emotional activity on training courses. For example, expectations about the role of the trainer may not be met - a stress point for many participants. How do we, as leaders of the process, first acknowledge that people do not appreciate what we are doing, may oppose us, may withdraw from the learning process, and then take appropriate action to deal with it? In short, how do we creatively protect ourselves from ourselves?

The following extracts from our own diaries illustrate the problems, if not the solutions:

> *'My problem will be to work on the plateau of mid-term expectations, and to work towards a productive second part of the course (when the disruption of assessment begins). It'll soon be time to feed in some reading and to set up classroom visits.'*

> '... trying to balance all these demands, pressures and influences, and to keep focused on the teaching which I feel is suffering at the moment.'
> 'The whole day yesterday was frantic. I couldn't devote full attention to the Course meeting. TOO MUCH GOING ON!'

Summary

'Why don't you just tell us the answer and put us out of our misery?' This is a common question from a participant frustrated by apparently endless group discussion, wanting closure, wanting to move on. We could easily make the decision to spoon-feed participants, and avoid this question being raised. That would, however, be too simplistic a response to the problem. Once we take the decision to involve training participants in open discussion of training issues, to interact as a learning community, to acknowledge the resources for learning available in a group, and to set out deliberately to understand and work with the social and emotional world of trainees, we create a challenging agenda for all concerned. In this chapter we have outlined the types of activity we find valuable when managing groups. We have discussed the issues and the processes that are raised by the social lives of groups, and illustrated them with extracts from our own and participants' reflections on the process, and illustrations from our training experience. Central to the process is talk between participants, and this theme will be further developed in subsequent chapters.

References

Luft, J. (1984) Group Processes: An introduction to group dynamics. Palo Alto, CA: Mayfield. 3rd edition.

Moscowitz, G. (1978) Caring and Sharing in the Foreign Language Classroom. Rowley, Mass.: Newbury House.

CHAPTER 4
WORKING WITH PARTICIPANTS' EXPERIENCE

In Chapter 3 we discussed at length the social aspects of training courses, through the lens of a group's common experience and the issues raised by working closely with a group. In this chapter we turn our attention to the process of opening up participants' previous experience as a starting point for new learning in training courses. In Chapter 2, we identified this as one of two main ways of beginning work on a learning cycle. We shall outline examples of the types of activity we find helpful in this work and follow this with a discussion of the process issues that this type of work entails, both psychological and social.

4.1 Activities for Opening Up Experience

As we have seen in previous chapters, one of the basic assumptions in our training work is that the previous experience which participants bring into a course is of central significance to the ensuing learning process - thus, for example, the statement of experience in the 'Suitcase' activity in Chapter 3. The time spent on opening up this experience is worthwhile for a number of reasons:

- as a means of signalling strongly to the whole group that their experience is valued
- as a way of giving each individual a voice.
- as a way of 'advertising' the experience to all group members - it thus becomes a resource which can be drawn on in both formal sessions and informal exchanges outside the training room
- as a way of identifying starting points in the training process which are relevant to the needs and aspirations of the participants
- as a point of departure for exploration of participants' beliefs and attitudes

In trainer training there are at least three areas of professional experience to draw on: training experience, teaching experience and experience of learning. In teacher training, usually the latter two are of importance, although initial trainees generally have only learning experience to draw upon. We would also add that life experience is of great value in the training process. All types of experience are relevant in different ways. In this section we present some of the activities we have found useful in opening up existing experience.

ACTIVITY 1 **Centuries of Experience**

Time Required: 3-5 minutes (depending on size of group)
Materials: Poster paper (and a pocket calculator, maybe!)
Space: Normal room layout

Procedure

Ask each participant in turn to call out the number of years teaching and/or training experience she/he has had. Give one of them the task of totting up the total number of years. (The group leader's experience should be counted into the total). Then make a large poster like the one following and put it somewhere prominently in the room.

> **THERE ARE OVER THREE CENTURIES OF PROFESSIONAL EXPERIENCE IN THIS ROOM!**

Adaptations

1. Trainers working on pre-service courses can use the same activity but referring to years of ***learning*** experience.
2. Add an 'experience' compartment to the 'suitcase' activity

---

Participants often find this process cathartic; most find it refreshing and pleasurable to have their experience acknowledged in a public forum. However, we have been told by some less experienced participants that they find it threatening to be confronted by so many seasoned professionals.

While the activity may contribute to an initial feeling of well-being in the group, its product is in itself nothing more than a rough statistic. It reveals nothing about the quality, variety or depth of the years of experience which have been counted. The activities which we now go on to describe go a little further in exploring the experiences that individuals bring; many are strongly autobiographical in nature.

ACTIVITY 2 **Career Pathways**

This is an activity which we use regularly with in-service teachers' groups and trainers' groups. We find it is worth devoting a lot of time to sharing and discussion of common features of experience, as part of the disclosure we discussed in Chapter 3.

Time Required: 15 - 20 minutes

Materials: A4 paper, pen or pencil, 'Blutac' or tape
Space: A normal room layout; plenty of wall space for display

Instructions to Participants

1. Take a piece of paper and a pen or pencil.
2. Think back over your career to date and imagine it as a kind of pathway. Think of the turning points, people and events that have influenced you, courses you've been on, books you have read, etc. Close your eyes if you need to, and try to visualise the pathway in three dimensions. Work quietly by yourself at this stage.
3. Now draw the pathway as you see it, using whatever images you like for the key events and encounters. Your pathway should lead right up to today.
4. When you've finished, write your name on the corner of the paper, and hang it up on the wall. (An alternative here is to discuss the pathways in pairs or small groups **before** they are displayed, thus giving participants a chance to talk to peers about their careers which is often a pleasant experience: everyone enjoys talking about themselves, particularly when it is legitimised in this way!)
5. Now walk around, look at all the pathways, and talk to anyone whose career interests you in any way.

Individual pathways range, in their design, from the simple and schematic, to the highly ornate and elaborate. A sample, produced by a participant on one of our training programmes appears in Appendix I. The viewing stage usually gives rise to animated talk, as participants discover common ground or even mutual acquaintances, and ask questions about each other's experience.

The activity seems to have the following benefits:
- Participants become more aware of the collective experience in the room
- Everyone contributes on an equal basis (trainers can take part too!)
- The pathway metaphor seems to be powerful, yet simple and clear
- Participants have time to think back over their professional development and to take an evaluative stance
- The activity highlights differences as well as similarities, enabling participants to see both opportunities for learning from each other and the need for compromise over personal objectives on a training course

- Individual experiences are valued and talked about
- Participants disclose only what they choose to
- The activity helps to promote a sharing and open group climate
- Trainers can gain speedy access to important background data about each individual participant, which is often valuable as a training resource during the course. If trainers find it valuable to have a more detailed account of participants' careers, which may be the case on a longer course, they can ask participants to write a 'professional autobiography', based on the pathway, as a follow-up assignment. This has proved particularly helpful to us as trainers when we encounter participants whose home context is unfamiliar to us.

Taking the image further, a course in itself can be seen as a brief interlude during which a number of pathways become entwined, only to separate and go their different ways once the course ends. (See figure 4.1) Seen this way, a course offers a rare opportunity to work intensively in a group within a career which is more often characterized by professional isolation.

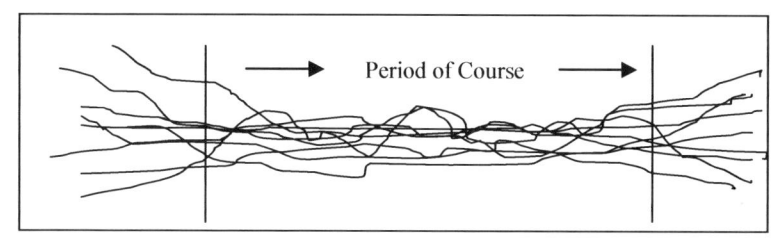

Figure 4.1 Course pathways

The kind of **narrative account** which participants run through in their minds in the *Career Pathways* activity, and which may be articulated in spoken or written form, is useful on a smaller scale, too. **Accounts of lessons** (such as the one solicited from the Zambian trainers, see Chapter 1) or of other professional episodes and events, can provide valuable data for the group and the trainers to work on. It is common practice, during and after school practice, for initial trainees to record in some form the 'story' of their teaching experience, and to recount incidents from it in seminar discussions. We find this useful for trainers, too, who may wish to highlight incidents from their own experience in order to compare notes with peers and, possibly, to make sense of them in retrospect. The following is another example of the type

Working With Participants' Experience

of story-telling activity we use, based loosely on critical incident analysis (Tripp 1993).

The activity 'Success Stories' illustrates how personal theories can be explored. 'Stories' offered may range from informal anecdotes to more formalised reports, but nearly all of them help us, as trainers, to gain insights into our participants' backgrounds and, importantly, their beliefs about training, teaching and learning, an issue we discuss in greater depth in 4.2. We may respond to these accounts with questions or with comments, but we would never attempt to pass judgement on them, or on the professional attitudes which they seem to reveal. Our feedback is aimed at affirming the value of the experience ("This was a fascinating account which really made me think about ....") and at nudging participants into a more reflective mode ("What do you think the students in your group spoke about *after* the lesson you described?")

ACTIVITY 3: Success Stories	
STEP	**COMMENTS**
1. Participants are asked to recall a time or event when they felt they had been particularly successful (e.g. as teachers or as students) and get ready to tell a colleague about it.	*Recall of past experience opens up personal theory.*
2. Pairs exchange stories. They are asked to speculate actively on the ingredients of success in each case and to note these.	*Articulation activates personal theory. 'Ingredients' capture aspects of personal theory.*
3. Participants are asked to write a title for their story on a slip of paper, fold it up and to put it into the centre of the room in a suitable container. When all titles are in, each participant draws one (if it's their own they put it back in and take another) and reads it out and is asked to speculate on its theme regarding success. Trainer records this on the board or flip chart (spider diagram is helpful). At the end, all participants identify their story and comment on the accuracy of the speculation.	*Giving stories a title encourages focus.* *Sharing of 'ingredients' can raise awareness of diversity and commonality of personal experience and conceptualisation.*

Working With Participants' Experience

4. Participants, in small groups, are now asked to look for themes in the stories regarding success. These are then elicited and listed on the board. Participants are asked to decide privately which themes best describe them and which don't apply They also consider how they might cultivate ingredients they don't currently have. These are shared in pairs or small groups (experience shows that participants want to share with as many people as possible - this type of activity draws participants together).	*Themes move participants towards an understanding of the ways in which they conceptualise their experience, and open up possibilities for expanding awareness of different emotional states.*
	Theorising is encouraged, as well as introspection on personal theories.
5. Participants are invited, in plenary, to share what they feel they have learned or become aware of in themselves and others as a result of the session. This can be followed up with diary writing or a similar activity.	

Judgmental or evaluative comments on such personal accounts have, in our experience, resulted in a lessening of trust and a decrease in self-confidence in participants. In future activities they would take care not to disclose so much and might even 'clam up' altogether. Section 4 2 has further discussion of these issues and includes other story-telling activities. Chapter 10 also features a narrative-based activity to review a recent training experience.

We often start our longer (1 month or more) programmes with individual **case study** presentations of their most recent working contexts and jobs. Here are the instructions we give to participants.

ACTIVITY 4: Case Studies - Your Professional Backgrounds
You all come from a wide variety of backgrounds, and in the early stages of the programme we aim to enable you to get to know more about each other and your work.

Specifically, during Week 1 we would like each of you to prepare and present a 10 minute case study of the teaching or training situation you have most recently come from. The points you may

wish to cover will vary according to context, but you may find the following checklist useful as a guide (choose the areas that you feel are relevant):
- your institution (size, organisation etc.)
- the English department (role, size etc.)
- the role of English in your country/institution
- the state of teacher training in your country/institution
- your colleagues (background and training etc)
- courses and syllabuses in use or about to be in use
- teaching or training materials in current use
- problems and constraints
- your own particular interests and work

We shall ask you to prepare a poster and/or overhead transparency to illustrate and provide a record of your presentation. Through the case studies, you will begin to know about each other professionally - they will also give you some early experience in oral presentation. We shall have to work to a tight schedule, so please do not exceed 10 minutes - remember to include a little time for questions and comments. Please don't go into too much detail; remember that most people in your audience will not be familiar with your context and will need a 'gentle' introduction to your professional concerns. These case studies will not be formally assessed, but we shall carry out an evaluation as a group and we will give you feedback on your individual presentations. This feedback will be the first part of a process to be continued throughout the course.

These presentations, given semi-formally in front of the group, have a number of valuable functions.
- They allow each participant in turn an opportunity to talk in some detail about their most recent working context (in most cases they left it behind them only days or weeks before the start of the course, and so the preoccupations and problems related to it are still fresh in their minds).
- They give everyone in the group an opportunity to get to know each of the others better from a professional point of view, and to identify similarities and differences in their respective working contexts.
- Each participant also takes a turn to chair a presentation, and to write up another presentation, thus contributing to the profile of two other participants within the group.

- The course leader may invite other course tutors to attend the presentations, so that initial knowledge about the individual participants is passed on to the course team at first hand and can be used for diagnostic purposes in planning the rest of the course.
- The course leader can make an initial assessment of the presentation skills of each participant (this is particularly valuable, since almost every trainer has to make a professional presentation sooner or later).
- Finally, the write-ups of each participant are kept on file as background data which can be referred to as the course progresses, e.g. when a tutor prepares for a tutorial, or when participants write assignments relating to their working context.

Subsequently, individuals and the whole group evaluate the whole experience of case-study presentation. This allows feelings and cognitive responses to be expressed openly. This process of 'debriefing' is also valuable: it helps to objectify the experience and to deal with any negative emotions and anxieties which it may have given rise to.

Here again, it is vital for us as trainers to avoid judgmental comment and to affirm each contribution: Many participants, still adjusting to the demands of life and study in a new and unfamiliar environment, are unsure of the value and relevance of their experience, and they need to feel accepted by both the tutors and the rest of the group. However, many feel proud to be on a course, and proud of what they have achieved so far in their professional roles back home. Thus, a well-handled set of case study presentations can help to make the temporary transition from full-time professional involvement to full-time study among fellow-professionals relatively smooth and painless.

ACTIVITY 5 Metaphors

Most of the activities discussed in this section so far have involved fairly direct accounts of previous experience. All of them allow participants themselves to decide what to disclose and what to keep 'under wraps'. This can, and sometimes does, prove problematical, since there are many cultures in which openness, for one reason or another, may be risky, as we discussed in Chapter 3.2. Some of our participants may not even be fully aware that they are 'censoring' their own contributions, since the avoidance of self-disclosure or public self-doubt may be so ingrained in their ways of behaving. Other participants may never have had the opportunity to 'dig' beneath the surface of their

Working With Participants' Experience

experience, and their accounts may come across as superficial or as event-bound rather than issue-related. However, we have to take responsibility for encouraging our participants to re-examine some of the beliefs, assumptions and attitudes which they bring with them to the course. In order to achieve this, we need to be sure that we are gaining access to this (sometimes subconscious) area in our participants' minds. This is one reason why we find **metaphor - based activities** useful in training.

All of us make use of similes and metaphors frequently, both in personal and in professional life:

'The session just took off!'
'That classroom is a minefield'
'She's a closed book'
'I think we can open up this issue'
'Let's nudge this idea forward a bit!'

Often, such figures of speech allow us to express ourselves with far more conviction and feeling than literal language ever could. Sometimes, too, a metaphor can say in one or two words what might otherwise take many. So why should we not use them in training and teaching? They can be a powerful tool (sic!), but they do need to be handled sensitively.

One example of a metaphor-based activity was the one used with the Zambian trainers in which they were asked to offer metaphors for the classroom. (Chapter 1) The images they came up with were both colourful and productive. They provided the group with much food for thought and a basis for reflection and further work. When we teach Course Design as a component of one of our courses for trainers, we often start by examining perceptions of a course through images or metaphors. The following activity outlines the procedure.

ACTIVITY 6:   **A Course Is ....**
Time Required: 30 - 40 minutes
Materials: Paper, pen, posters, markers, glue, scissors
Space: Flexible seating, open floor space, wall space for display

Instructions to participants

1. Individually, think back to a course that you have experienced either as a tutor or participant.
2. Find a way of expressing the essence of that course, either through a metaphor, or a simile, or a visual image. Write this down or depict it on a piece of paper.
(Note: if any participant is 'blocked' at this stage we encourage them to resort to a more literal definition.)

Working With Participants' Experience

> 3. Now form groups of 8-10, and arrange your chairs in a circle, with an open space on the floor in the middle.
> (Trainer places a poster, glue, scissors and a marker on the floor within each group.)
> 4. Taking turns around the group, call out or show what is on your piece of paper and place it on the poster paper. If your view if a course resembles that shown on another paper which is already down, place yours correspondingly near to it.
> 5. When everyone's paper is down, discuss the connections and distinctions between your views. Adjust the positions of the papers to reflect anything which is revealed by this discussion.
> 6. Once all positions in the group have been clarified, use the paper, the marker and the glue to create a poster for your group, reflecting what has been discussed.
> 7. Display the posters. One member of each group should stand by the poster, ready to answer questions. Everyone else should walk around the other posters and ask questions, make comments etc.

Posters produced in this session may vary both in quality and in clarity, depending not only on graphic ability, but also on affective factors such as the degree of cohesion and the quality of relationships which have developed within the group, and on cognitive factors such as the degree of consensus which the group has been able to reach. An example poster produced by a group in a session we co-facilitated at a Trainers' Seminar appears in McGrath 1997:36.

An alternative, and rather shorter, version of this exercise involves the trainer in collecting contributions from the whole group, and with their help, building up a collage in front of them either on the board or on a ready-mounted blank poster or flipchart. However, this deprives the participants of the opportunity to explore each others' ideas in the security of smaller groups, and may inhibit contributions from less confident group members.

A possible follow-up activity would focus on roles, leading on from a participant's metaphor with a question: "If a course is a jungle trek (this really came from a Malaysian participant), who is the course leader, and who are the participants?" To which the participant replied "The guide – course leader - is an experienced local who knows the territory, and the trekkers, who are often city people, unused to the jungle, are the participants".

This kind of activity has a number of features which are worth pointing out here:
- It is a 'right-brain' (or image-rich) entry point to 'left-brain' (or logical/rational) issues: it is a starting point for in-depth work on topics such as Course Design, Classroom Management or Classroom Observation on trainers' courses
- It often reveals fresh dimensions of participants' thinking and attitudes
- It provides a way of looking for patterns and connections in participants' thinking
- It is culturally rich, allowing trainers and participants to explore images which are familiar to their peers in other contexts
- Everyone contributes to the thinking and the end-product
- It can promote teamwork in the whole group or in sub-groups
- It appeals to participants' sense of fun

These points are explored in more depth in 4.2.

ACTIVITY 7 Personal Constructs

A further way of opening up our thinking is to explore our personal constructs (after Kelly 1955 and Bannister and Fransella 1986) in a fairly systematic manner, using an adaptation of Kelly's procedure for eliciting constructs and peer interviewing. Knowledge of the underlying bases for our responses to professional and personal issues in training is an invaluable tool for development and problem-solving. An example of the type of activity which encourages this type of work is to elicit constructs about teaching as the prelude for a discussion and exploration of bias in observation and how we invariably find ourselves judging what we see when observing teachers at work, despite protestations of innocence.

The activity is structured as follows:

Exploring Our Personal Constructs

Time required: 40-45 minutes
Materials: Blank 'repgrid' sheets (An example follows on page 71)
Space: Flexible, open seating for pairs

Instructions to participants

1. Ask the group individually to recall 6 teachers, past and present who have left some sort of impression on them - good or not so good. They can give them pseudonyms or initials or leave them

with their real names, and number them 1-6. They write these in the 'slots' on the vertical axis of the repgrid.
EXAMPLE: 1 – P; 2 – LT; 3 – WS; 4 – OT; 5 – RD; 6 – GS
2. With a partner, in turn, develop a series of constructs (words or phrases) using Kelly's 'triadic sorting technique'. Put simply this involves taking 3 of the teachers at random and asking your informant or partner what makes two of them similar, with one odd one out. Write down the phrase or word your partner used.

EXAMPLE (A and B are partners)
A: 2-5-6
B: Uuum – I can see a strong similarity between 2 and 6. Both were quite systematic and organised, whereas 5 was a bit chaotic and improvised.
A: Shall we say 'systematic' is what they have in common?
B: Yes.

The process continues until, say, 6 or more constructs (either positive or negative) are written down. 8 is more than enough to work with.

	1- PL	2- LT	3- WS	4- OT	5- RD	6- SG
Systematic		x		x	x	
Good listener						
Impatient						
Lively talker						
Loves subject						
Gives us time						
Indifferent						

Repgrid – Completed Example. Constructs are on the left.

3. Ask your informant to prioritise the list of constructs without any further reference to the original list of teachers. The paired participants can then explore reasons for the listing, starting with the most preferred construct. (Another technique is to explore one of the most favoured constructs and to elicit anecdotes from the informant to illustrate the construct.)

> 4. The group can share the effects that the experience has had on them, or collect group construct lists, or begin to explore the implications for practice in either teaching or observation.

Personal construct work has the benefit of making available in a relatively 'safe' form, the basis of an individual's value or belief system. From this stage, a connection can be made to professional practice, and to an understanding of how much it is influenced by personal constructs. It is a 'private' activity, too, in which participants do not need to reveal their constructs to any other group member apart from their partner. For many, the experience of exploring personal constructs is a gateway into understanding themselves better, and of understanding others, too.

Through these activities we have re-stated, with examples from our practice, our belief in 'starting where participants are'. If a course is a journey we, as trainers, have to locate the starting point, join our participants there and travel with them. We can't expect them to start where we are.

4.2 Opening up Experience: Issues and Processes

In this section we shall explore some of the issues which working with participants' previous experience raises. The activities we have outlined in 4.1 are usually well received by participants, who invest a great deal in them. However, there are also 'negatives' which we think it important to discuss.

4.2.1 What Participants Bring - The Starting Point

> *'I liked the way in which everyone's experience and knowledge was tapped, thus making all of us feel important.' (Uwe)*

Uwe's comment is one echoed by many participants, despite vast differences in their backgrounds. What is it about exploring previous experience that is so valuable?

In training, we are working with adults and young adults who share basic *categories* of characteristics despite differences between them.

- All have personalities, previous life experience and probably professional experience, and skills, knowledge and awareness acquired in previous activity and experience.
- They also have well-developed value systems, attitudes and belief systems, (we can call these VABs for convenience) built up over many years' life experience. They may or may not be aware of the content and nature of their VABs.
- They have stores of memories, pleasant and unpleasant.

- All come to programmes with varying levels of self-esteem, varying degrees of sharpness of self-image, differing capacities for expressing thoughts and feelings.
- Participants also have misconceptions (some of them pretty well-entrenched), ideas currently being digested, and expectations of themselves, their trainers and their co-participants.

A participant exhibits far more in person than an application form could ever capture, or even the most thorough of needs analyses (although the latter can help if well-focused on the types of categories already referred to). All of these personal traits have to be accommodated and encouraged by a training programme because the training programme will undoubtedly provide a forum for self-discovery as well as the acquisition of knowledge from 'out there'

- ### *WHY EXPLORE EXPERIENCE?*

We explore experience to establish its influence on our current practice. We want to see both what the experience consists of and what it might mean to us as individuals and as training groups. The exploration of previous experience can have the following benefits:

1. Increased awareness of one's own personal VABs and their influence in teaching and training. Deeper self-knowledge is of inestimable value to teachers and trainers, and all activities designed to probe previous experience lead inevitably to a confrontation with VABs once the events of experience have been revealed. What lies behind these events is the key.

> 'Perhaps one of the most tangible features of the last few weeks has been the 'making explicit' of what I'd previously thought or felt.' (Jane)

The exploration of personal theory can have the following benefits:

- Increased awareness of one's own personal VABs in teaching and training.
- Knowledge of others' VABs and experiences can lead to further introspection and examination of one's own personal theories. Deeper self-knowledge is of inestimable value to teachers and trainers.
- Increased awareness of the influence of personal theories on practices in teaching and training.
- Informing trainers of participants' VABs as a foundation to the work that can be attempted on the course - a form of 'needs analysis'.

- Articulation of VABs and the exploration of practice provides opportunities for change. Change is unlikely unless we make our principles public.

2. Knowledge of others' VABs and experiences and comparisons with our own can lead to further introspection and re-examination of one's own personal theories. By encouraging participants to share their previous experience and VABs in pairs and groups, we are contributing further to group formation, and enabling the group to develop an open attitude to the sharing of ideas. We believe that this incidental training has real and tangible outcomes in increased openness in group discussion, and the enhancement of teamwork, both valuable learning outcomes for working professionals, with an influence long after they have finished a course.

3. Increased awareness of the influence of personal theories on practices in teaching and training. We do not normally have time to stop and think about why we do what we do. This is a luxury for the vast majority of teachers and trainers in our experience. The activities enable teachers to see the importance and influence of their 'personal theories' (or Theory I, as we shall call it) in their practices. This is the theory of practice that we build up, often unconsciously in practice (it is often available to others in the form of 'tips'). Participants often come to a course without an awareness of Theory I, and expect 'new ideas' (Theory II - from the books or the lecturers) - they are often disappointed to find a course beginning with an examination of their own experience. Our experience is that the activities enable participants to 'reconnect' with their experience and to begin to do some deep reflection on their professional action. Training that explicitly draws upon participants' personal theories and the capacity to theorise is likely to be perceived as more 'relevant' by participants. Sadek's diary comment is quite a common one:

> *'Many a time and during group work, we reflect on our own experiences, trying to devise new criteria, principles etc. (...) These things strengthen my belief that practice precedes theory' (Sadek)*

This type of work also facilitates agenda setting, as participants, through reflection and analysis of experience, become more aware of the questions that they want to address. It is a form of 'needs analysis, and of much more use to a trainer than the answers to questions on a form.

It helps participants to have an insight into our VABs too, and by participating in the activities, we have the opportunity to reveal them. This we find helpful as a way of signalling our personal value systems and acknowledging their influence on proceedings. For example, in metaphor activity, we usually share our own images with the group, but are careful, in doing so, not to devalue any of the contributions made by participants. One way of doing this is to participate in the activity from the beginning, rather than revealing ours at the end, after the participants. Once again, it is important to accept *every* contribution without judgmental comment of any kind.

4. Articulation of VABs and the public exploration of practice provide opportunities for learning and change. New learning builds on the foundation of existing knowledge and practice. By encouraging participants to make explicit what they tacitly know and believe, we contribute to the creation of learning opportunities. Inconsistencies in beliefs might be revealed - we must treat these sensitively, and again not judge. The individual needs to accept the dilemmas and inconsistencies before they can contemplate change.

The extract from Basseng's diary sums up the importance of this activity at the outset of a course

> *'The story (of the course) so far is like entering the Palace of Hasanul Bolkiah, the Sultan of Brunei, I knew that the palace has got an enormous number of big rooms, and I was sure that all of them were elegantly furnished. I could not wait to absorb the enjoyment of walking around these rooms.'*
> *(Basseng)*

4.2.2 Time and Space to Talk

Participants need time and space to explore their personal theories. In this way they can prepare themselves for new learning, learning which is integrated into current states. (Remembering the potential destabilising effects of such a strategy - Section 1.4) Activities such as personal story-telling, explorations of personal metaphors, exploring career pathways, and so on all require time and space. What may have been planned for 15 minutes very often ends up taking an hour, so absorbed and so vocal do participants become. There is a need for time to talk things through, to explore each other's experiences, values and so on. This deep reflective work does not follow logical pathways, and does not have 'right answers'. Such work may, in fact, open up more possible directions for learning. It also enables participants to see that education is value-laden, hence the passion with which practitioners pursue it. These processes are not encouraged by quick fire, 'zappy' activities. We have found that the time spent is time well spent, because of the **depth** which participants are able to reach through the activities. Contemplative work may not suit all participants, and it may not suit all trainers who see questionnaires as 'light relief' from the serious business of learning principles and 'new things'. We dispute this - new knowledge is built on old.

- **METAPHOR ACTIVITY - *Exploring Laterally***

'In the core studies we used a lot of metaphors. The following is one of my comments on metaphors in my diary:
Unlike brainstorming, my thinking comes from my deep deep mind. I can explore myself, what I am thinking about a topic, and I think it is fun to go into the deep thoughts and to discover the little things I usually miss (...), I can clarify my thinking - concentrating the picture would make me think more and more deeply.' (Ritsuko)

'These metaphors are a great way of raising issues and getting to the heart of how people see classrooms.' (Doug)

Ritsuko and Doug attest to the value of metaphor work. Training participants need a varied diet of thinking activities. Apart from the obvious canon of variety in training, it is also useful to enable participants to draw upon their 'creative' resources, and to think their way around issues in unusual ways with the aim of developing new insights.

- Creative thinking encourages visualisation and therefore enables better prediction and planning in future professional activity
- Creative thinking enables participants to understand that what we see is not always what is actually there, and to see below the surface
- Creative thinking can 'loosen' old, redundant concepts enabling new ideas to take root
- Creative thinking is a necessary precursor to systematic thinking, as it enables the generation of ideas, images and even ways of organising them.

Work which involves response to music, visual display and design, metaphor and imagery (*haiku* can be particularly effective), modelling with real materials, brainstorming and thinking about the day-to-day in unusual ways can be both liberating and generative, and can lead to striking developments in ways of seeing things.

The image which appears in Appendix I were produced by a group of Advisory Teachers when considering the ingredients of a successful training course, in the form of a 'stew'. The variety of ways in which the groups portrayed their material provided the opportunity to discuss different ways of seeing things and also to look for common ground among the group members.

4.2.3 Difficulties

> *'Since I am the kind of person who needs time to turn things over in my mind, I don't always feel at my best during brainstorming or other related activities like metaphors'* (Mike)
>
> *'Some of the strategies are not to my liking, e.g. metaphor work. I don't like it because it switches my way of thinking from analytical to figurative. It is double work:- to convert logical thinking into employing images to reveal these images' broader themes'* (Iryna)

The comments from Mike and Iryna are a reminder to us that not everyone likes metaphor activity. We have learned not to use metaphor-based activities too frequently, as they don't suit everyone's learning style. Both of us have experienced 'groan' reactions from participants who have been over-exposed to this kind of activity. We accept that not all participants like visualising or thinking non-logically, and we respect these differences. However, we think it is important that participants see that there are different ways of thinking and that individuals have differing preferences, and the relevance of this for their own teaching. It is also possible to become more comfortable with less rational modes of thinking and the richness of these modes. We find that if we open up discussion of the techniques, it can assist participants in becoming more analytical and understanding of the contribution to the learning process that their own experiences and mental images can have.

- **'I DON'T LIKE THESE ACTIVITIES'**

Participants often express misgivings about 'dredging up the past' or taking part in self-awareness activities. We understand their difficulties and their doubts. It is never easy to introspect, especially if one is working in the company of strangers. However, with care and a gentle introduction, combined with ample opportunities to discuss the aims and goals of the activities, as well as the difficulties and doubts participants express, these activities can become a central part of the training process, and a rich source of knowledge and awareness about learning and teaching.

Summary

In this section we have re-stated, with examples from our practice, our belief in 'starting where participants are'. If a course is a journey we, as trainers, have to locate the starting point, join our participants there and travel with them. We can't expect them to start where we are. This, of necessity, takes time, but we have come to believe that it is time well spent. We have often heard the argument, from both teachers and trainers, that the kinds of procedure we have described here are time-consuming, and may prevent us from getting down to the 'real' content of the course. For us, this **is** the beginning of the real content of the course. To begin by telling them what we know, or what various experts in our field have written about, may only serve to emphasise the gap between our participants' thinking and our own. It is only natural that such a gap should exist, but it is **our** business, as trainers, to recognize it and to try to bridge it, not theirs as participants.

References

Bannister, D. and F. Fransella (1986) Inquiring Man: The psychology of personal constructs. London: Croom-Helm. 3rd edition.

Kelly, G. (1955) The Psychology of Personal Constructs. New York: Norton.

McGrath, I. (1997) (ed) Learning to Train: Perspectives on the training of language teacher trainers. Hemel Hempstead: Prentice Hall.

Tripp, D. (1993) Critical Incidents in Teaching. London: Routledge

CHAPTER 5
NEW and SHARED EXPERIENCES in TRAINING

In Chapter 2, when discussing the Kolb learning cycle, we identified two kinds of experience which are valuable as a training resource - "past" and "present". In Chapter 4, we outlined activities to enable participants on training courses to explore their past experience as a 'jumping-off' point for new learning. We also discussed issues which arose from using this type of activity in training. In addition to the opening up of past experience, another valuable source of training data can be created through activities and procedures which are shared by all group members in the training room. These can be used as a basis for awareness raising, reflection and further learning. There are many ways of creating such shared experience. In the first section of this chapter we briefly describe some shared training activities which may be used for different purposes. In the next section, we shall examine the processes initiated by use of these activities, and also some of the problems and difficulties we have experienced when using such an approach.

5.1 Experiential Activities
There are a number of alternative means of providing a shared learning experience for training participants. In this section, we shall outline two procedures we often use.

5.1.1. 'Shared Classroom Experiences - Being Learners'
It is common practice on teachers' courses and seminars for the trainer to expose participants to *classroom activities* as a means of ensuring immediate practical relevance and to enable the participants to *experience* them before exploring principles which inform them.

When we decide, for example, in a Methodology or a Language Awareness course, to expose participants to teaching or training activities, we usually follow this sort of procedure. The example procedures below are from a Language Awareness course for Austrian teachers on an in-service programme, and the rationale and trainer action are included for each step.

During the session, we would manage the activities, thus freeing up participants to involve themselves fully and then to give us the opportunity to pay full attention to their responses. After the activities themselves, we allow time for participants to compare notes in groups. To save time, we usually allocate one activity to each discussion group with a 'secretary' appointed to give a summary of the group's main findings. Thus, for the Language Awareness sequence, there were five discussion groups.

PROCEDURES	RATIONALE/ACTION
1. Decide which activities will be appropriate to the learning needs and objectives of participants.	*Participants have asked for a fresh look at some key grammar areas, and so a number of activities are prepared and selected to enable them to see how grammar works in authentic contexts. The first topic is article use. Trainer feels it is important to raise some questions about 'received wisdom' in this area.*
2. Make sure that the first activity in the sequence is not too demanding and encourages participants to draw on their existing experience.	*A metaphor-based activity on 'The Definite Article' is chosen as a starter: "If the Definite Article were an animal which would it be? Why?" (Wright 1994)*
3. Sequence the activities in such a way as to ensure variety, relevance and opportunities for learning and follow-up.	*Four more activities are chosen: one which encourages participants to evaluate published learning material on article use, one which asks them to examine real text in order to see how articles are used, a third which takes them through some of the common difficulties faced by German speakers with the article in English and one which asks them to question some of the common rules about article use found in reference grammars. The activities are varied both in terms of their data sources and in the tasks participants are asked to carry out.*
4. Prepare an Activity Record Sheet (a 'grid'). There are, of course, other ways of recording experience, but we find this one to be relatively quick and convenient, for participants to record their responses to each activity after it has been completed.	*The grid used for this sequence is reproduced in Figure 5.1 (after Bolitho and Wright 1993)*

5. Plan the timing of the activities in such a way as to allow participants to make their notes between activities, and to discuss their findings in groups and report back at the end of the sequence. (We nearly always find it difficult to plan the timing of a session like this accurately because the final discussion is usually unpredictable. .	*The Language Awareness sequence was planned for completion within a two-hour session.*

The groups then report back in turn (we call this whole process, rather unattractively, 'de-gridding' (!) because it is based on the information and impressions they have recorded in their grids) and we build up a collective, mind-map of the findings on the board or a poster. At this stage we may prompt with questions, or ask for clarification, but refrain from intervening in any other way: we see our role as to accept and record each group's conclusion without evaluative comment. We then work from the 'mind-map' between sessions to produce either a summary or questions, or a combination of both, which we then give participants as a handout in the next session.

These were among the feelings and responses of the Austrian group:

- We felt rather upset by these activities as we have been used to teaching the article in a certain way.

- The study of the coursebook exercises worried us because we realise that they only deal with a small sample of problems with the article

- Looking at the newspaper texts made us realise how articles are part of a wider system of reference in real language use - perhaps we should look at some real texts with our learners

- We'd need to prepare simpler activities for our own learners

- Can we do language awareness activities with our learners, too?

Activity number	Name of Activity	Purpose of Activity	Your feelings about the Activity	Notes on Trainer's Role	Other comments

Figure 5.1 Participants' grid (NB Grids are normally presented in A3 or A4 size, or participants can arrange their own grids.)

The 'thinking questions' and follow-up task for this activity were given on the following handout. These activities are typical of those we use when trying to move a training group out of the experiential mode and into a more analytical mode (See Chapter 2, Section 2)

LANGUAGE AWARENESS - THE ARTICLE

1. What have you learned about the article system in English through the activities and the follow-up discussion?
2. To what extent do you think your course books (note: these were largely UK publications) cater for your learners' needs and difficulties?
3. Which key points would you wish to focus on when teaching the article to your learners at intermediate level?

TASK *Prepare a piece of teaching material on the article for use with a typical group of learners in your institution. Work in groups of 3/4 and share your ideas*

Thus the shared experience of a sequence of activities becomes the basis for awareness-raising, reflection, making sense (in the example) of a key language area, and planning for further action. This follows every stage of the learning cycle, as outlined in Chapter 2. A similar procedure can be followed when introducing participants to new classroom activities (for example, reading comprehension, or writing) or training activities. In 5.2, we shall discuss the value of these types of activity in enabling participants to understand the principles behind the practice, especially valuable in initial teacher training, or in-service work, where new teaching ideas are being introduced.

5.1.2. Shared Observations

All teacher training courses refer ultimately to the classroom, yet it is often difficult to recreate the immediacy of classroom situations in the training room. With small groups, it is sometimes possible to share the observation of a real class, and to discuss it together afterwards. More frequently, however, we have to resort to the less satisfactory, two-dimensional medium of video. This allows a training group to share an observation experience for any one of a number of purposes:

- (for teachers) to see certain teaching techniques and procedures in action
- (for teachers) to observe aspects of teacher and learner behaviour
- (for trainers) to discuss criteria for lesson evaluation
- (for trainers) to provide the basis for a role-played post-observation feedback session

It is this last purpose which we shall use here as an illustration. We have employed the following procedure with a number of groups.

ACTIVITY   *Video Lesson*

1. Trainer introduces video-clip with some information about the context, the teacher's background, the learning group, etc.
2. Trainer distributes lesson plan (if available).
3. Participants from groups of 3 for viewing 'in role'. **A** will role-play the teacher, **B** the observer/supervisor, and **C** will view the lesson from a neutral perspective. Each is asked to make notes on this basis during the lesson.
4. Viewing of lesson.
5. Participants are then asked to role-play the post-lesson feedback session, with the 'teacher' (A) responding to the 'supervisor' (B) under observation from the third party (C). [The 'supervisor' may use this opportunity to experiment with a more or less directive feedback style].
6. After the feedback session is concluded, the neutral observer (C) gives the 'teacher' and the 'supervisor' comments and feedback on it.
7. Debriefing on the role play with the group as a whole.

This kind of procedure is popular with many trainees, partly because it enables them to see other professionals at work, partly because the lesson data is 'neutral' (in contrast to the more threatening scenario of micro-teaching/training), and partly because of the very real opportunity it affords for them to work on feedback styles and interpersonal skills. Indeed, the role plays often become very intensive as participants identify with their role enthusiastically and sometimes even fiercely! The debriefing stage, usually in plenary, is vital if the whole experience is to be properly evaluated and understood in the light of course objectives.

Good quality classroom videos which can be used for training purposes are, unfortunately, still comparatively scarce, although the Cambridge University Press package *Looking at Language Classrooms* is a notable exception. However, a few have been published recently, and these are mentioned in the resource list below. All classroom videos suffer inevitably through the absence of the third dimension, but as camera technique and sound reproduction improve, they are likely to be a necessary part of a trainer's 'arsenal' for some time to come.

5.2 Issues and Processes

The types of activity we have outlined in Section 5.1 have proved very valuable training tools in our experience, but they are not without their problems. This section examines some of the more common difficulties and issues we have encountered when using them. We also identify some of the main processes that these activities appear to set in motion.

5.2.1 Problems with activities
ACTIVITIES - AN END IN THEMSELVES
This kind of approach **is** valuable as long as there is time and opportunity to reflect on, make sense of and evaluate the experience. We have both participated in courses where the activities seemed to be an end in themselves, with the trainer taking no real responsibility for any kind of follow-up. Such an approach seems to reduce training to recipe-giving, and denies participants the opportunity for real professional learning. Reactions from participants often remain superficial ("I liked that activity. I'll use it with my class next week" or "I felt uncomfortable during that activity") and are voiced in the coffee break, usually out of earshot of the trainer. The excitement of taking part in the activity and the feeling of being involved could also become an end in itself, at the expense of any real

consideration of underlying principles and rationale. We feel that professional learning has to do with deeper understanding of what makes an activity work, or of why it may work with one group and not another, and that teachers and trainers need to know not only how to shape, adapt or extend a particular activity to meet the needs of their own students, but also how to use the underlying principles in order to generate further activities of their own. (Didn't Confucius say something about "teaching a hungry man to fish"?)

TIME and EXPECTATIONS

The range of activities offered to us in 3 days was extremely diverse, challenging beneficial. Step-by-step, activity after activity (...) we synthesised a perfectly balanced , (...) multi-level structure which will serve as a mapping for my future teaching career. (Lena)

I expected (a) product-oriented content which will lead our team to creating a training syllabus. That is why some initial activities such as 'warming up' or 'what makes a good teacher' at first seemed trivial. Almost 2 days passed before it began to dawn on me that we are not going to collect techniques, but rather reflect on why we use them. (Natalia)

We have often run up against individuals and groups who have questioned the activity-based approach. 'Why waste our time playing games? Why not just tell us about the principles and get on with it.' These reactions are in stark contrast to the almost euphoric responses of many groups and individuals to activities. In these cases we are compelled to spell out the reasons for our approach and to take time out to explain what we are trying to do. Experience has also taught us to explain BEFORE we begin a sequence of activities precisely what we are aiming to do and why. It seems to go wrong when we don't invest the time in preparation.

The creation of shared experience, and the follow-up work which is needed to capitalise on it, are both time-consuming. We have been told (Chadwick 1994), for example, that 'gridding' and 'degridding' are simply too time-consuming in real training situations. We beg to differ. Our experience is that professional learning cannot be hurried if it is to be valuable and that time spent on follow-up procedures like these is an investment in depth and quality of learning.

Participants may also say that going straight to the principles is more 'efficient' as a learning route. We disagree. It is a question of breadth and depth in training. We believe the time spent in really getting to the bottom of activities and their rationale is time well spent. Better to explore activities in depth and to gain insights that are generative than to attempt to cover too much and spread ourselves too thinly. Again, we meet trainees who expect to be given the principles first - their previous learning experiences in training have been just that. We have to respect these participants' backgrounds, but we also have to ask permission to try something different. Careful setting up and orientation can avoid participants feeling as if they have been cast adrift on a sea of activity without aim or purpose. This can only add to the inevitable insecurity of encountering new ways of doing things. We explore this particular issue in more depth in the next chapter.

As long as the full sequence of training activities is followed, from experience and awareness-raising through to principle formation and transfer into action, principles can be developed, and there are also ample opportunities for participants to voice their concerns, doubts and objections and to have these addressed in the training room rather than letting them fester and return later in potentially more threatening forms. By introducing training groups to new training ideas by inviting them to experience for themselves what an activity is like we invite challenges and discussion - we believe the difficulties, if and when they arise, are part of the learning experience.

5.2.2 Structuring Reflection

We have said in the previous section that it is necessary to go beyond the activities themselves and to 'excavate' them to uncover the principles which lie behind them. We believe that this process needs to be structured, hence the 'grid'. The grid is in itself a tool for post-activity reflection. It is a way in which a training group can be introduced to reflection and reflective processes. Its categories can also be varied and adapted for different purposes, and we have often invited groups to come up with their own categories when they are familiar with the genre. Here are some example 'grid' categories created by a group of Hungarian mentors for use in their training sessions:

Name of activity/description/ELT use/mentoring use/how did it work + feel

Name of activity/aims/purpose/description/skills involved/CLT

> Name of activity/description/aim/student-teacher-mentor role/place in teaching process
>
> What?/how?/why is it useful?/what is it for?
>
> Name of activity/procedure/function/aim/mentor/trainee/feelings
>
> Name of activity/procedure/CLT/mentor
>
> Name of activity/description/aim/CLT/relevance to mentoring/relevance to COT training/comments

The grid enables an individual to go beyond the activity, with the security that such a framework offers, and in the knowledge that there are not going to be direct and perhaps embarrassing questions about, for example, what the learning principles behind an activity are. The principles need to develop at a group's pace, and we see no point in hurrying them. The grid provides the raw material for the development of ideas. Categories such as 'feelings' enable the participants to 'unload' their emotional reactions to an activity before engaging in more analytical work - which can be disturbed by negative or positive emotions left unexpressed. The 'purpose' category enables participants to gain access to principles in non-technical language.

Like any training activity, the grid too can outlive its usefulness. 'Oh no! Not another grid.' is not a reaction we would want to hear too often, though we have both experienced it. The grid has a specialised use, we feel, as an adjunct to the sort of 'experiential' activity we outlined in 5.1. It is a way of making meaning from activity. There are other ways of reflecting on experience which do not need to be structured, particularly if the group has had a lot of experience in reflective activity. Sometimes, all that is required is a sequence of questions- for example, after an observation:

- How did you feel during the observation?
- How do you feel now?
- What, for you, were the outstanding moments in the observation?
- What might you do differently next time?

Here we are interested in what a participant has learned from the observation rather than its **purpose.** The purpose should be apparent or spelled out. We are concerned with letting the experience speak for itself rather than inviting the 'discovery' of principles,

LEVELS
One problem we encounter particularly frequently occurs with teachers' groups when some participants find it difficult to revert to a teacher role when considering shared course experience *as learners* (for example when they try out classroom material), and with trainers' groups when some struggle to distance themselves from the *trainee* role they adopt during shared experiences such as lesson observation in order to reflect on the *training* implications of an activity. Once again, this usually happens with individuals within a group rather than with the group as a whole, but when it does happen, it can block the thinking of others within the group and thus decrease the momentum as we move towards further exploration and the opening up of opportunities for professional learning. We often find that time spent on 'sorting out levels' (as we have come to term the problem) is very worth while, and removes what might otherwise be a block to moving on and developing new concepts.

5.2.3 Supporting Participants' Performance
Asking training participants to 'perform' in the training room (e.g. through micro-teaching, micro-training or presentations) raises many issues. Security and 'safety' are the first which any trainee would consider. Training or teaching one's peers can be a most difficult experience, and yet, often without the luxury of 'live' participants to try things out with, it is often the only way. We have to provide support for the 'performers' in order for them to maximise the benefit of the experience. Practical ways of doing this include creating ground rules (see 3.1), briefing participants individually before their sessions, and providing the post-session discussions with structure and support. A full account of how we might go about this appears in Chapter 10.

5.2.4. Other Experiences
If a training course takes place only in the training room, without contact with the outside, either institutionally, or with real trainees and learners, inevitably lacks an important dimension. We try therefore to build in a range of experiences to courses which enable participants to 'escape' the inevitable narrowness of the training room. This we feel is especially important on long courses, but no less vital on shorter courses. The types of experience include:
- school visits and attachments
- research projects with teachers, trainers and students

- attachment at 'sister' institutions
- observing live feedback sessions

It is, again, imperative to follow up these experiences with structured reflection and sense-making, as well as supporting participants with meaningful tasks while they are in the experience, such as interviewing people, completing observation sheets, writing 'experience' reports, or analyses of lessons observed. It is also important to review such experiences as soon as possible after they have been completed, to establish difficulties, high points and so on. The reflection process is in our view indispensable to these activities.

One activity sequence we have employed successfully follows.

Activity Sequence

1. Group experience 6 communicative activities, grid these, and establish principles.
2. Observe lessons and record instances of similar principles at work, supported with audiotape or video if necessary.
3. Plenary to compare the principles observed in the live classes with those experienced in training.
4. Planning of teaching or training activity by participants (trainers could create a sequence of experiential activity for their context; teachers could produce or adapt 'communicative' activities for their own settings)

The collective experience of such sequences of activity can also contribute towards the bonding of a group by providing a common frame of reference for the discussion of professional issues.

Summary

In this chapter we have looked at ways of providing and building on shared experience for course participants in the training room. We have explained that this is almost always necessary as a means of establishing a common foundation on which to construct new learning, and have given some examples of activities we use for this purpose. In particular, we have highlighted the need for participants to have ways of recording their immediate responses, both cognitive and affective, to shared experiences but we have also pointed out some of the difficulties which have arisen with the procedures we regularly use.

References
Bampfield, A. (1997) Looking at Language Classrooms. (Video Series) Cambridge: Cambridge University Press.
Bolitho, R. and T. Wright (1993) Grids as reflective tools in teacher education. The Teacher Trainer, 7/2.
Chadwick, J. (1994) Grids for recording and reflecting in teacher training sessions. The Teacher Trainer, 8/3.
Wright, T. (1994) Investigating English. London: Edward Arnold.

CHAPTER 6
THE AWARENESS RAISING PROCESS AND ITS CONSEQUENCES

Increased awareness is probably the first step on the way to change in professional behaviour. Before our thinking can develop in productive ways, we need to take stock of where we are, to acquire an understanding of issues and problems which concern us, and to know where we stand in relation to them. Many of the procedures described in the previous two chapters include a strong element of awareness raising, but in this chapter we wish to focus more closely on some ways of raising participants' awareness of issues in teaching and training and, crucially, of their own beliefs, values, attitudes and aptitudes. This, in turn, leads to further exploration of issues which awareness raising triggers, like the impact of new awareness on one's emotional state.

6.1 The Nature of Awareness-Raising
We start from the premise that raising awareness can be interpreted either as *increasing* awareness that is already present in an individual, or as *helping* someone to be aware of something to which they were previously oblivious.
Two models aid our thinking here. The first is the much cited but always valuable Johari Awareness Model (Luft 1974), which is outlined in Fig 6.1.

This model enables us to see how individuals may be aware of certain features of their own beliefs, attitudes and personalities, and unaware of others. The public domain (square A) is relatively straightforward. However, the private domain (square B) is the home of private agendas which often inhibit progress in meetings and change in individuals. We reveal material from this area under conditions of disclosure - but we also have control over what we choose to reveal. Square C ("blind") shows us how we may need the help of others in order to become more aware of ourselves, and we believe that this is an important part of group processes in training. Under conditions of feedback, we can reveal material to others which they may previously have not been aware. The hidden or unknown domain (square D) is there to be explored in all sorts of unpredictable ways for each individual course participant: it is, for example, the key to hidden potential such as may be revealed when a previously quiet participant gives a first-rate presentation, surprising herself as much as other group

The Awareness-Raising Process and its Consequences

members. It is also probably the area where 'forgotten' material rests. Awareness-raising activities have the effect of releasing hidden material into any of the other three areas. As trainers, we need to be ready for this to occur. Such revelations are not "under control" as material in areas B and C are and there are always risks to be assessed.

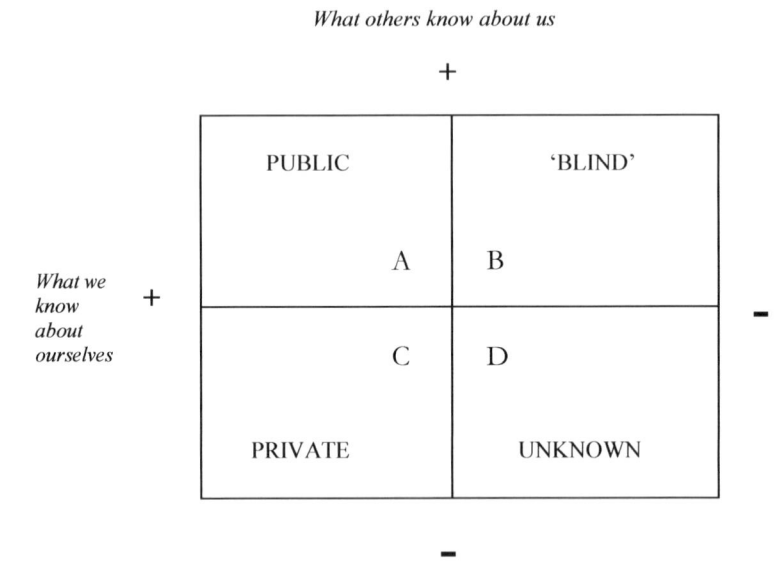

What others know about us

+

PUBLIC A	'BLIND' B
C PRIVATE	D UNKNOWN

What we know about ourselves +

−

−

Fig 6.1 The Johari Awareness Model (Adapted from Luft 1974)

The second useful model for conceptualising the awareness-raising process with teachers and trainers is one we first came across in Handal and Lauvas (1987) and later found in another form in Claxton (1989). It concerns the levels of teachers' thinking and action, and our version of it appears in Figure 6.2.

Classroom Behaviour
Interpersonal factors and received knowledge
Values and beliefs

Figure 6.2 Levels of Teacher's Thinking in Action [adapted from Handal & Lauvas (1987) and Claxton (1989)]

In this model, a teacher's classroom behaviour (the way she teaches, manages a class, interacts with learners, etc.) can be accounted for at one level by what they **know** about teaching and learning (usually in the form of knowledge handed down on their initial training courses) and also by the norms established in a particular institution. Most teachers want to "belong" (Maslow 1976) to a profession, to be accepted by colleagues, and to confirm to some extent to institutional and societal expectations of them in their roles and teachers. As British trainers involved in professional development programmes with teachers and trainers from a wide variety of different cultures and backgrounds, we can only gain second-hand acquaintance with many of these factors, and yet it is important for us to try to understand them and to take them into account when working with our trainees. We become aware of them, for example, when an Indian teacher tells us that she is reluctant to use group work because there are no walls in her school's classrooms and colleagues in neighbouring areas (not to mention the school principal!) would object strongly to the increased noise level caused by forty children in animated discussion.

Deep down, however, this teacher may **believe** in the value of group work in language classes, and it is here that we reach the third level of thinking in the model. A teacher's actions may be governed by values and beliefs which are either clear and articulated or deeply embedded in a complex web of cultural, personal, religious and social traditions. Once again, as trainers, we cannot gain full access to these beliefs and values and to what they might mean for each individual, but we **can** encourage our course participants to be more aware of what they mean for themselves. Often, we see this awareness growing in participants' contributions to open discussions. It is also revealed in written assignments and, most frequently, in dissertations. For example, a Japanese postgraduate student (Maeda 1996) used her Masters dissertation to explore both her own development as a teacher and the reasons why Communicative Language Teaching has made such limited headway in most Japanese institutions. In doing so, she 'visited' all three levels of our model and came up with some stunning and valuable insights into language teaching in Japan, from historical, cultural and social perspectives. In exploring her context so thoroughly she had become much more aware of herself as a professional working within that context.

We attach a great deal of importance to awareness-raising and in-depth exploration of self, values, attitudes and beliefs as steps towards professional development in our work. Finally, the real confrontation on any training course is between each individual participant and herself. The sense participants make of a course is essentially derived from the degree to which they are prepared to explore their own thinking and to relate it to their own context in the light of wider trends and findings. Awareness raising is the crucial first stage in this process. We now go on to mention some of the ways in which we as trainers can encourage awareness raising and exploration, in addition to the ways we have discussed in Chapters 4 and 5.

6.2 Some Activities to Enhance Awareness

The first set of activities is designed to raise awareness quite directly, while the second set is for developing awareness and insights which have arisen because of activities.

6.2.1 Self-awareness and self-discovery exercises

Finding out about one's own attitudes, strengths and potential is always interesting and valuable, and we make use of a number of exercises, questionnaires and inventories on our courses in order to 'open up' some of these areas. Two examples are given here, the first focusing on self-assessment and professional development, and the second on team roles.

ACTIVITY 1   **The Teacher I'd Like To Be**

Time Required: 25 mins. (approx)
Materials: Paper and writing implement

Instructions To Group
1. Take a piece of A4 paper and draw a table like this on it

THE TEACHER I USED TO BE	THE TEACHER I AM NOW	THE TEACHER I'D LIKE TO BE

2. In the first column, write a list of adjectives to describe yourself at the beginning of your teaching career. Make sure you include some positive ones!

3. Now, in the third column, write down an adjective, corresponding to each one in the first column, to describe the teacher you'd like to be.
4. Use the centre column to show, either in words or by using a symbol, what progress you have made towards your aim.
5. Make notes on anything you'd like to work on in each area.

[Adapted from Brandes & Ginnis (1996)]

One participant's completed chart looked like this:

The teacher I used to be	The teacher I am now	The teacher I'd like to be
enthusiastic	*I've lost some enthusiasm*	enthusiastic
very active	———X———	active
noisy	————X—	calm
dominant	——X——	student-centred
nervous	—————X	confident
grammar-oriented	———X—	communicative
idealistic	*I don't want to be cynical*	realistic

We normally let the exercise rest here, without any pressure to share insights with others; it is an activity which is based firmly in the private domain and enforced self-disclosure would not be appropriate. However, many participants have reported that it has given them food for thought and has helped them to set personal development targets.

We also make use of a number of management-derived inventories and questionnaires to raise awareness of self in relation to others. Most of these are derived from the professional literature. Here is one which we devised for looking at individuals' responses to change, based on work of the Kirton (1989).

Managing Change in Education

The aim of this questionnaire is to explore the way you respond to change in education. Please read each statement and decide whether or not it is a statement which describes your behaviour or attitude. Score 1-4 for each statement: 1 for VERY MUCH ME to 4 NOT LIKE ME.

1. I think that the best way to change is to improve what we have, not to try to create something new

2. It is important to work only on projects or schemes which can be completed

3. We must take decisions carefully and be very aware of the consequences of our actions

4. I accept change when it improves or strengthens the status quo

5. I tend to be methodical and prudent

6. I would make sure there was widespread support for changes before proposing them

7. It is very important to maintain high levels of efficiency in a system

8. I'm not really one for "sticking my neck out" against prevailing opinion

9. I don't like changes that challenge the cohesion of my working group

10. I prefer to solve problems rather than to look for them

11. I can work effectively for long periods, doing detailed work

12. I usually agree with criticism from close colleagues

13. I hate to feel rejected or others' hostility

14. I tend to regard innovation as rather threatening or unsafe

Adapted from Postle, D (1990) [See also Kirton, M.J. (1989)]

After participants have completed the questionnaire, we give them a 'key' as a handout. This appears in Appendix II.

The success of our initiatives in teacher education depends to a considerable degree on how individuals respond to change and most teachers and trainers face change at some point in their careers. This exercise often highlights previously unknown strengths and tendencies in individuals, and helps them to decide how best to contribute to work in "change situations". It is frequently followed by an excited buzz of talk among participants as they exchange their findings and consider the implications. We explore some of the change dimensions which training activities can touch in the next section (6.3)

Other topics which we find productive for self awareness work with individuals and groups are as follows:

- Team Roles: how we work in teams; what roles we are strongest in, and most need to develop
- 'Learning Styles': ours and others' preferred ways of learning
- 'Intelligences': drawing on the work of Gardner (1983) on multiple intelligences
- Personality Types: for example Briggs-Myers (1988) indicators
- Leadership Styles: based on key texts in the literature on management

These explorations do not provide us with definitive answers, and it would be very naïve to imagine they did. Frequently participants object to 'personality tests' on the grounds that they are not 'scientific', or are 'reductionist', or just plain misleading. We feel that these criticisms mask a belief held by individuals that there should be an 'answer'. This is not, however, the point of the activities. These instruments and activities are a jumping-off point to self-awareness, which we believe is a lifelong quest. Seeking feedback from close and trusted colleagues on the outcomes of questionnaires is a valuable exercise - do we see ourselves as others see us? Where are the gaps in perception? In a safe and non-threatening atmosphere, these activities can be the beginning of important personal learning.

6.2.3 Following Up On Awareness

Awareness in itself may or may not be valuable. Real learning only begins, in our experience, when awareness and insight is followed up constructively. Here we share a few ideas on this aspect of the training process which we have found of value.

Thinking questions
We formulate thinking questions in response to written or spoken contributions from participants during a course, most frequently following experiential and associated awareness-raising activity. We do not always seek answers to these questions, often preferring to allow participants to mull them over privately or discuss them in groups out of class. Our questions may lead to further questions, or to a line of research or enquiry which participants may follow up in their own time, or through an assignment. Here are some examples of 'thinking questions' in response to a group presentation by Hungarian teachers on Coursebook Evaluation. (For more examples of thinking questions, see Chapters 5 and 10).

> **Thinking Questions**
> *Could Headway be used with secondary classes in your context? Give reasons*
> *You mentioned that many teachers in Hungary would 'like' the approach to grammar. Why do you think this is?*
> *Do you think Hungarian teachers might resent the widespread introduction of mass-market British-produced coursebooks?*
> *What benefits and problems do you think adult learners might find in Headway?*

Each group had drawn up its own evaluation criteria and had selected a book to evaluate against these criteria. With our questions, we wanted to push this group to think about some of the wider issues relating to coursebook use in their context, looking beyond classroom action into the societal dimension and prevailing attitudes and beliefs.

Helping participants to formulate questions
In any educational culture dedicated to answers and solutions, it is difficult to promote a more open-ended approach. Teachers often go to courses to find solutions, and yet professional development seems to us to have more to do with continuing enquiry than with convergence. As our participants become more aware of themselves and of the issues which matter to them, they start wanting to find out more. Their questions are often, in a very real sense, research questions. Our role is to help these questions to 'be born'. In a tutorial or in the training room the encounter may go something like this:

Participant: *I'm having some trouble with the idea of a teacher releasing control in the classroom. I'm not sure it would work.*

Trainer: *Why do you think that is?*
Participant: *In my country, teachers are expected to be in authority. They might lose the respect of their learners and colleagues if they introduced something like project work with a class. It wouldn't seem like real learning, you know, for the exam.*
Trainer: *So you don't think you could do it with one of your groups ....*
Participant: *Well, that's just it! I think it <u>would</u> be useful in promoting active use of English, which is what our learners really need.*
Trainer: *So there's a dilemma for you to resolve there?*
Participant: *Yes, and it will take me some time to understand the best way for me to proceed.*
Trainer: *Maybe there are some compromises you could look at .....*
Participant: *Yes, I think I'd like to see how the ideas we've had on project work could be adapted and tried out in our context ....*

We frequently find ourselves in this role of catalysts to our participants' thinking. In the case above, the trainer has helped the participant, through prompts, to move on from an initial worry to an awareness of a possible line of further enquiry.

There are also more direct ways of providing participants with the opportunity to gain practice in formulating questions:

- to examine the products of colleagues in training sessions, and to ask probing questions. This type of activity usually helps participants see the differences between supportive and challenging questions
- to write their own thinking questions on personal or group reviews of training sessions for other members of the group to work on
- to write questions for authors of articles or books. These can be posed in role-play situations where participants can take the part of an author, having read an article in depth.
- to practise interviewing skills as part of an action research component
- to evaluate and rewrite questions in training and teaching materials
- to practise asking improvised and spontaneous questions during 'micro training' or discussion sessions. Recording these can be a useful source of data to explore as a group when examining the role of questions in training.

One spin-off we find from both the 'thinking questions' and this kind of in-person formulation of questions is that participants working in peer groups become better able to 'ask the right questions' in order to advance the group's thinking in productive directions. As they get to know each other better, they find ways of raising each other's awareness and self-awareness, thus contributing significantly to the developmental process of the course. When participants begin writing their own thinking questions on summaries of sessions, we know that they have made a major breakthrough in their development. Chapter 10 describes how this has taken place with a group.

Giving and receiving feedback

One important way of developing self-awareness is by learning to give and receive feedback. We have learned a great deal about ourselves as trainers over the years by reading and listening to our participants' feedback in formal and informal settings. Many of the procedures we have already outlined involve a feedback stage, and we attempt to ensure that participants have ample opportunity to work on their own feedback skills, both in groups and interpersonally, not as an end in itself (though there is much to be learned about giving and receiving feedback) but as a route to increased awareness of self and others. As a first step, we often set up an 'active listening' exercise along these lines, presented here in the form of instructions to the group:

ACTIVITY 2   **Active Listening**

Instructions To Participants

Please take a little time to think about how the course has been going for you so far. Jot down three things you'd like to mention.

Now, find a partner and follow these steps:

1. A tells B about her/his impressions of the course. B listens without interrupting and without taking any notes (2 minutes).
2. B paraphrases, without interpreting, what she/he has heard from A. A may interrupt only to correct any misperceptions (2 minutes).
3. Reverse roles. B now speaks and A listens as in 1 above (2 minutes)

(Trainer keeps time and signals changeovers)

> Now take a little time in your pairs to reflect on what you have just been through. How did it feel to have your partner's undivided attention? How did you manage to focus on what your partner was telling you?
> (After 2 - 3 minutes)
>
> **Trainer:** *OK, let's sit in a circle and you can tell me about your experience of the exercise. I'd also be glad to have a note from each of you about your impressions of the course so far. Can you give me that at the end of the session?*

Time spent on this kind of procedure helps participants to learn to listen to each other as well as to the trainer. It also helps them to formulate their own feedback contributions carefully and to see how they compare with those of others in the group. There are many variations on the procedure outlined above (see Edge (1992) for some examples) and many other uses to which it can be put, both with teachers and with trainers. For initial trainees, learning how to accept and deal with a trainer's feedback both on teaching practice and on their written work, is an essential step towards becoming a teacher.

6.3 Issues and Processes in Awareness-raising

In this section we shall gather some of the themes raised by a consideration of awareness raising. Awareness raising can have many effects, from the blinding insight - the 'Road to Damascus' experience - to a horrible sense of ignorance or insecurity. We have to be ready as trainers to 'field' these responses, whatever they might be like. It involves us in having our 'emotional antennae' at the ready, as well as drawing on our understanding of the processes that awareness-raising activities can trigger. Awareness-raising activity may involve us in questioning or challenging deeply held assumptions. This may be perceived as a threat to one's integrity - the responses are fairly predictable: fight or flight, but the behaviours and feelings are subtle and complex. This section examines briefly some of the issues.

AN EMOTIONAL BUSINESS

> *'This has been a period of soul-searching, of discovering aspects of ourselves as teachers, trainers and individuals that need to be reviewed and accommodated in that these discoveries are not always palatable. The increasing awareness of the complex world of learning, teaching and training is accompanied by an*

> *increasing awareness of my own development as a teacher and a human being.'*
> *(Reena)*

Reena's comments illustrate for us the emotional investment participants make in the training process, and the potential benefits as well as the potential pain. Training **is** an emotional business. In the first place, being together with others in intensive work and study for long periods, interacting with them, and the process of learning itself involves emotional commitment. When a trainee learns how to teach she makes a huge personal and emotional investment in the process, which is very close to our being or essence. When we teach, we teach ourselves; when we learn deeply and meaningfully, we learn about ourselves.

Training thus has emotional consequences. Emotion can block learning, or it can enhance the depth of the experience. For example, the adrenalin of teaching practice and in other high stress or response states when a trainee is 'up front'. In fact, by staying neutral and aloof from the emotional side of training, participants (including trainers) run the risk of missing the potential learning opportunities presented by emotional issues. Learning is more than just cerebral and intellectual, despite some of the messages about teaching and learning we bring from our previous educational experiences. In fact, working in training, with teachers and trainers, demands an acceptance that the laughter and tears of learning are a necessary part of the process. We would contend that one of the key development areas for us as trainers is in understanding the world of the emotions. Being a student of people is a most valuable stance for a trainer to adopt, and a good proportion of the content of the study of people is their emotional side - how they react to stress, what they laugh at, what makes them sad, what frightens them.

We would prefer to use the term 'emotional', meaning 'feelings' in the broadest sense, as we believe the boundary between 'cognitive' and 'affective' is an artificial one, a way of cutting off the rich emotional world of learning from the more rational type of thinking. The latter is essential, as we shall see in Chapter 8, but has a different role in training from the emotional. We do not have the space to explore all the richness of the emotional aspects of training in this book. However, as an illustration of its importance and significance in the learning process and as a source for learning, we shall discuss the relationship between awareness raising and change.

THE CHANGE DIMENSION

> *'I usually contemplate how change can be introduced in my context and I hope I will be capable to introduce the change bit by bit when I return.' (Endalk)*

Training entails learning. Learning entails change. All branches of education and training are concerned with change - either learning new knowledge and skills or altering current knowledge either in its shape or use. We only have to look at training course aims such as 'to enable participants to acquire supervision skills and observation skills', for example, to see the implicit or explicit change agenda. And yet, even if participants volunteer for courses (as opposed to being 'selected'), they do not, as a rule, come looking for change. Or they might be unaware of the need to change in order to accommodate new knowledge or skills. To further complicate the picture, change in behaviour (for example, to supervise in a non-directive way, compared with prevailing directive practices) may require a parallel change in attitudes or even value systems. By making new possibilities available in training contexts, we unleash the forces of change. How do these manifest themselves in training situations?

UNCERTAINTY

When we become vaguely aware of a new possibility in our practice, or of a lesson learned from previous experience, we question ourselves. Can we really do this? Is that really what happened? Why didn't we see it before? Are we deficient because we can't see ourselves doing this type of activity with our students? We are somehow unable to act, unable to move forward. We somehow become 'infants' again. We seek guidance. The unknown is frightening, possibly overwhelming. 'Tell me what to do' is a common plea.

DESTABILISATION

As well as being uncertain, unable to make decisions, believing contradictory ideas, holding opposing positions, we are also 'fragile'. We want the new awareness to go away. Its consequences scare us. One part of us tells us that we should take up the challenge of the new while another tells us to reject it - it poses a threat to the status quo. In our destabilised state, we are drawn easily into conflict. We 'say things' that we may regret later. Our moods swing rapidly.

Add destabilisation and uncertainty to the group process, where people are struggling to establish identities and relationships, with perhaps undeveloped communication skills, and the training room is an even more stressful environment. Everyone is potentially at risk, psychologically and emotionally.

We have no panacea for these critical moments. Each one is unique - the 'chemistry' subtly differs from group to group, individual to individual. We learn anew with each programme we run. Being committed to the idea that awareness raising is an essential ingredient of training, we have to work with the forces that are released. We do not always get it right. For example, we might offer an individual reassurance and praise for their contributions when what they really want is direction and prescription. We have learned, however, that feelings of uncertainty, doubt, aggression and sadness, as well as joy, must be accepted and allowed full voice. We have learnt that the informal, relaxed atmosphere of supportive pair or small group work is better for releasing emotion than the 'stage' of a plenary. Attempting to remain detached from the group process can help, although there are dangers that we might be spotted not being fully involved in the process. We have learnt that participants demand emotional commitment from trainers. Often they might prefer us to be suffering what they feel they are suffering. We cannot dismiss that lightly, and accept that under conditions of change, we have to carry some of the burden. But to lose our detachment invites difficulty, as we need to be available to support those who are facing crisis or panic. It is a difficult balancing act, made easier if participants are involved in the process as listeners and helpers, and informed by an understanding that all emotional crises are a rich source of learning about educational processes.

RISKS

Awareness-raising activities are designed to help participants in training see the world and themselves in a different light, which may lead to new perspectives and understanding. In the process of 'seeing things differently', a wide range of emotions is possible. For example, by inviting participants in training to go into their past learning or training experiences, we expose them and ourselves to ghosts and buried fears, as well as happy memories of halcyon days. By involving them in activity to experience new ways of teaching and learning, we may invite irritation, anger, fear or silence. Reactions are more often than not defensive, no matter how well intentioned or motivated a group might be.

This is quite understandable - new learning poses a threat to old knowledge, and therefore our self-image, beliefs and self-esteem. Under threat, we are not entirely rational. So participants can say some strong things when they are asked to disclose how they feel about activities:

> *'This is a waste of time - just playing games.'*
> *'What's the point of spending hard-earned money talking about ourselves when YOU (trainer) should be doing the talking.'*
> *'This idea won't work in my context. It's silly.'*
> *'You (trainer) are trying to manipulate my thoughts and ideas.'*

Or there may be defensive or aggressive behaviour - turning away; overt challenges to motives, either verbal or physical; deliberate sabotage of activities by individuals.

We have to try to cope with these comments and behaviours, to accept them and not to be defensive ourselves. Difficult! When someone accuses us of manipulating them, we may find ourselves becoming defensive, too. And the descent into conflict is only a short step away. It is a potentially dangerous situation. A course participant caught the essence beautifully in a diary entry:

> *'Risk-taking is considered to be a way of learning, but usually the risk-taker can end up being a victim. So how can we encourage risk-taking, and at the same time protect risk-takers?'* (Haiyan)

Despite the risks, it is a necessary step in the training and learning process. Working with and from experience *is* highly risky. The outcomes are not immediately apparent or available. The gains are not always what participants might have expected in terms of 'solid facts'. The awareness-raising process may have been probing for emotional awareness, anyway, rather than hard fact. Moments of awareness have their emotional content and we as trainers need to prepare ourselves for what can be contradictory and threatening moments for ALL participants, including ourselves. Developing in this area poses some of the greatest challenges to educators.

Summary

This chapter has highlighted the pivotal role of awareness-raising work in the life of a course and in the professional lives of teachers and trainers. Much of this kind of work involves self-disclosure, and we find it important to share in this process by taking part in many of the activities ourselves. By being open to feedback, we have also become more aware of ourselves as trainers. The emotional aspects of training are also central to our practice. We do not claim to have the answers in this delicate area - it is perhaps one of the greatest challenges we face in our own development to cope with uncertainty, difficulty, challenges and more when participants are affected by awareness raising.

References

Brandes, D. and P. Ginnis (1996) A Guide To Student-Centred Learning. London: Nelson Thornes. 2nd edition.

Briggs-Myers, I. and P. Myers (1988) Gifts Differing. Oxford: Oxford Psychologists Press.

Claxton, G. (1989) Being A Teacher. London: Cassell.

Edge, J.E. (1992) Cooperative Development. Harlow: Longman.

Gardner, H. (1983) Frames of Mind. New York: Basic Books.

Handal, G. and P. Lauvas (1987) Promoting Reflective Teaching: Supervision in action Milton Keynes: Open University Press

Kirton, M. J. (1989) Adaptors and Innovators. London. Routledge.

Luft, J. (1984) Group Processes: An introduction to group dynamics. Palo Alto, CA: Mayfield. 3rd edition.

Maeda, R. (1996) East Meets West in Teacher Development: An approach towards a 'Development and Kaizen' culture. MEd Dissertation: University of Exeter. Unpublished.

Maslow, A. (1976) The Further Reaches of Human Nature. Harmondsworth: Penguin.

Postle, D. (1990) Bringing About Change. Mimeo. London: Wentworth Institute

CHAPTER 7
TALK IN TRAINING COURSES

All the training activities we have discussed so far invite talk between participants, in various modes, in different ways. We believe that talk is the core of training activity, and that talk is a major means of enabling participants to develop their awareness and thinking. This chapter explores the purposes of promoting talk in training, examines briefly some of the main types of talk that we have found useful to encourage and finally discusses issues raised by the encouraging talk in training. t draws on material from the previous chapters and also looks ahead to subsequent chapters. Talk is implicit in everything we have so far discussed - this chapter is to make some of the themes more explicit.

7.1 Purposes of Talk in Training

This section looks at why talk is such a valuable tool in training sessions: how it enhances the group processes we describe in Chapter 3, how in so doing it can help develop a common language and professional vocabulary, enabling participants to find their individual voices and to equip them for moving from the discussion of experience to the articulation of principle.

7.1.1 Talk In Groups

'The group contributions help me see more alternatives than reading. Something I have found fascinating and helpful are the questions which are raised in class.' (Fatima)

'Another thing I like is solidarity among colleagues. Mutual understanding has yielded some significant collaboration within the group so that individuals can learn from each other as well as the group.' (Maliki)

I went through a process of group work, revealing different meanings at different times. From the beginning, pair work and group work made me feel good, because at that time everything was unfamiliar to me and I was not professionally mature enough. I avoided losing face. Group work also opened up a wide range of other people's experience and knowledge. They became part of the material of my professional development. They triggered my thinking and promoted more ideas.'
(Qiyan)

All these diary entries from course members mention the positive effects of working with colleagues - the questions raised;

solidarity and mutual understanding; making others' experience and knowledge available; development of interpersonal skills. All of these involve communicating - talking with colleagues. Talk is to training processes as rain is to river flow. We see the quality of talk among group members as one of the most important elements of the training process. The foundation of a productive learning community is the quality of communication between its members. What are the ingredients?

Trust and honesty are the basis of effective communication in groups, and are built progressively (and not without difficulty) through activities which promote disclosure. (The Johari Window in Chapter 6 is a useful model of this process) Disclosure can help to build mutual respect, and enable members to cope with the inevitable conflicts and disputes that characterise a working group. **Active listening** is the second key element in effective communication - we talk more openly and freely if we are listened to with complete attention. We explore this issue further in Section 7.3.

7.1.2 'Speaking The Same Language'
The quality of group relationships can, in our experience, be enhanced by a willingness on the part of group members to open and develop lines of communication within the group and with the trainers. In this section we shall discuss the process of finding a common language in a training group.

Communication can be a difficult problem in a newly formed training group, particularly one in which there might be a diversity of background, culture, or previous professional experience. The problem may be exacerbated if the course is run through the medium of English which may not be the mother tongue of all the participants, and proficiency among the individuals in the group might vary. Among participants whose mother tongues are different and who have not had the opportunity to listen to speakers of English from other countries, there can be difficulties even at the level of understanding accents. Working with multicultural, multilingual groups presents very specific challenges. However, the ideas we shall share with you here apply to all training groups, including monolingual ones, because miscommunication is possible among any group of professionals. It can block progress in a group's social development and can be a barrier to learning.

PROFESSIONAL VOCABULARY

> '... we participants come from different parts of the world, and our culture and expectation might differ to some extent. But we have one thing in common - English language Teaching. Therefore the participants really have something to contribute for others to share. (...) Through talk and discussion of the processes of foreign language learning and our education systems, we have expanded our sight and know more about English language teaching in different contexts.' (Zhou)

Because we believe so strongly that the collective experience of a group is such a valuable resource in the training process, as it is this experience that any development and learning builds upon, we see it as a major task of the trainer to provide the conditions for the group to explore this experience, to share their diversity and to establish points of commonality. Our professional vocabulary has its roots in experience, both trainers and participants. It is helpful for us to remember that while we, to a very great extent, share a professional vocabulary as trainers, this has developed over a number of years. On a course we have to be careful not to let our vocabulary swamp the participants, and at the same time help them open up communication channels so that they can share their own vocabulary, and develop a common frame of reference.

On a training course which involves a team of trainers working with a group, there are three lines of communication to open and develop and through which to share the language of teaching, learning and training: among the training team (an issue we shall explore in more depth in Sect 7.3), among trainees, and between trainers and trainees. From the trainer's point of view, all three lines are important. However, we have found that when we lead a group, there is a special responsibility to make our own language both accessible and clear to the group. This is an essential step towards enabling the group to find common ground. We often find ourselves asking questions like 'What do I mean by ....(reflective)?' or 'Will the group know what I'm talking about when I refer to .....(awareness)?' **before** training sessions. As trainers, we bear the responsibility of leading a group towards common ground, particularly in areas like language teaching or teacher training, where there is no common vocabulary (just to look at publications from the USA and from Britain, and their clear differences, is very instructive in this matter). We can set the tone extremely effectively by clarifying our own language, especially in the use of terms or professional jargon, which we do have to use from time to time. We need a short hand in training, but the shorthand develops through a long process of illumination and clarification: one term can contain an hour's worth of discussion. Often participants may differ from us in their interpretation of terms: our role is to assist the participants in clarifying and enriching their understanding of their own professional vocabulary, not imposing ours, no matter how tempting this may be.

One device we have found to be particularly useful at the early stages of a course is to establish in a group the use of a 'jargon box' (sometimes it is called the 'dustbin') in which participants are invited to deposit terminology, either from their reading or from training sessions, which they don't understand, or find amusing, or irritating, or mystifying and so on. At an agreed time, the box is unloaded and the items are classified in various ways (a particularly common category is 'saying the same thing differently') and the items discussed. In this way, misunderstandings can be cleared up and new insights brought to bear on professional terminology. If jargon is a persistent problem, and is preventing clarity of expression, we invoke the use of Brandes and Ginnes' (1996:186) 'Jargonometer'. (The 'Jargonometer' is an activity which encourages participants to express mild displeasure when a jargon word is used to explain a simple concept.) The reaction which some jargon receives when this is used is enough to signal that it is time to speak clearly.

When we fail to address the question of developing a common language, we sow the seeds of unnecessary argument in a training group, and leave ourselves open to the possible charge that we are avoiding the issue of 'theory', or that we are trying to prevent the participants from gaining access to what they rightfully see as their professional 'birthright' as teachers and trainers. When we overuse a certain term (we well remember when 'awareness-raising' became a problem term with one particular group) we also run the risk of monotony, and lack of imagination. Currently, for example, the term 'reflective' is much bandied about in teacher training circles. It can be quite irritating to have one's work described as 'reflective' by a participant who might want to be seen as sharing our perception of training, even when what we have done in a training session is far from 'reflective'. It can also be quite flattering - we have to be on the look-out for this as well. We prefer to devote time to doing activities which entail the unwrapping of the term and its meaning in relation to the course we are currently running. The time spent is worthwhile as everyone's awareness tends to be raised a notch, and the elusive common language is brought closer.

7.1.3 Finding Our Voices

A great deal of valuable professional learning occurs when we talk about our professional selves and ideas. In a training session, we are in a position to try to articulate ideas which may have been dormant. Or we may end up creating new ideas of which we were perhaps previously unaware through our talk.

It is often very difficult for inexperienced or reticent individuals to participate in this type of talk, particularly if talk is a 'set piece' activity, for example, in seminars. We believe that working in small groups and pairs is an essential part of individuals finding their voices. We have known participants on a year long course who have said little or nothing in plenary sessions, but who contribute actively in the more private and intimate circumstances of small group work. This type of talk helps participants to

- process ideas from reading or which have emerged from an awareness-raising activity and to find ways of paraphrasing or articulating them
- try out their own formulations of ideas or principles

Both these activities enable individuals to take ownership of ideas. The outcome is often rewarding for the individuals who begin to participate in whole group sessions with more relish, or whose professional writing develops for the better.

We have found that group talk centred on a series of thinking questions is a productive means of enabling participants to find their professional voices, and to articulate more complex thoughts. In Chapter 10, we briefly examine professional writing as a way of bringing together theory and practice. We see the foundation of this type of writing being laid in the talk between peers in training sessions. We must also be careful to remind ourselves that, while these talk-rich activities are of immense long-term value (it is also our experience that the change process involves hours of patient talk between people involved, and that the experience of handling talk-rich activity on training courses is an essential part of professional skills learning) participants need to feel a sense of achievement. When we have failed to stipulate a 'product' or outcome, we have often experienced quite understandable expressions of irritation and frustration from participants:

> *'This is just a talking shop'*
> *'We just go round and round getting nowhere'*
> *'We could just as easily be reading about these issues and learning more'*

The 'product' can be as simply stated that we expect the groups to report back with a specific number of points at a certain time. This helps participants manage the process for themselves. The product can also be a more sophisticated contribution such as a diagram or set of principles. This type of guidance is very much a part of assisting participants in finding their voices.

7.2 Types of Talk in Training

It is not easy to classify talk into 'types' - there appear to be very porous boundaries between any categories that we could create, and, in reality, we tend to slip from one type to another without always knowing how when or why. However, when we set up training activities that are designed to get participants talking, we usually have a particular type of talk in mind. In Chapter 6 we discussed supportive talk such as the giving and receiving of feedback. This section explores two further types of talk we have found particularly helpful in training situations - advocatory and exploratory.

7.2.1 Advocatory Talk

In many educational settings, the dominant talk type is advocatory - normally a 'teacher' advocating a point of view or body of knowledge to their 'students'. In other words, doing what has come to be known as 'lecturing'. We see a relatively limited role for lectures in training courses (See 7.3 below, where we discuss 'Trainer Talk') but see an important role for the trainee in developing skills to put over a point of view in settings such as a formal presentation. Many of the professionals we work with are required by their jobs to make cases for change and reform, and to deny them the opportunity to develop this capacity would be wrong. Professionals are expected in certain aspects of their work to demonstrate mastery of a 'brief', and to present new educational ideas to audiences whose agendas may be significantly different from theirs. We therefore encourage the development of the necessary skills, but not in isolation from other types of talk.

The type of task we set to develop this type of talk works as follows:

Talk In Training Courses

> **ACTIVITY 1   Making A Presentation**
>
> *Instructions To Group*
> 1. Small group discussion to decide on a set of criteria for evaluating an effective presentation of, say, a course design, or training materials. These criteria are shared among the groups in plenary and clarified where necessary. They will include criteria which are specific to the task and also the presentation itself. We encourage the discussion to emphasise the latter.
> 2. Individual presenters make up their own check-lists for distribution to the group when they give their presentation. These also form the basis of self-evaluation. Tutors can assist with hints on such criteria as brevity, clarity and use of visual support.
> 3. Presentations are made, usually to a strict time limit.
> 4. There is room for discussion between presentations, or the presentations can be continuous, as the group decides. There are opportunities for self-evaluation, and group discussion of the qualities of effective presentation.
> 5. Peer and tutor feedback and discussion either individually or collectively.
> 6. Plenary to summarise key aspects of learning. Each individual can be invited to make a short statement about what they have found to be of most value in the process.

This type of activity can be used to develop evaluation criteria for a range of training tasks. It is a form of experiential learning, too, if the process is followed through in every stage (see Ch 5). On a long course, skills can be developed by conducting this sequence of activities on several separate occasions, culminating in a final (or summative) presentation activity.

The skills of advocacy are not acquired without an awareness of what is involved, the uses of this mode of talk and activity for its development. The key is to enable training participants to develop their skills rather than to talk about it as a trainer, despite trainees' expectations or desires.

7.2.2 Exploratory Talk

Talk between peers and with tutors is an excellent tool for exploring received ideas or each other's thinking. It can help move a group's thinking forward as well as enhancing individuals' own conceptual understanding of new ideas. Exploratory talk can be unstructured and 'ruminative', allowing free rein to individual's contributions, or it can be structured around specific tasks which may involve clarifying material developed in an experiential activity, or emerging from the 'unpacking' of a grid. At its most basic, exploratory talk is characterised by brainstorming - a 'classic' training activity in which participants are invited to contribute ideas on a particular issue or problem without interference or judgement from either peers or (especially) tutors. We have found that participants often need some sensitization to the 'rules' of exploratory talk, and brainstorming is a useful 'way-in', its value lying in its non-judgemental nature.

The creation of ground rules for certain types of talk - such as not to interrupt or oppose ideas expressed by colleagues - by participants can also contribute to the training process for exploratory talk, as can a 'mixed diet' of structured tasks to generate ideas, or responses to ideas, or questions. One thing we have learnt from this type of activity is that judgement on new ideas and courses of action is often better delayed until a conceptual framework has been articulated - by generating ideas and clarifying ideas, we are actually moving closer to establishing such frameworks. We must endeavour not to allow ourselves to close down options too early - the patience required for effective exploratory talk ensures that our pace is conducive to the development of richer principles.

Our natural tendency as teachers seems to be to either advocate (fine in its appropriate context) or to dispute points in group discussion. This cuts off access to others' thinking, from which we can learn a great deal - either to become aware of others' worldviews, different from our own, or to learn something new from. All teachers and trainers need to remember that others do not necessarily share one's worldview or beliefs, or have had the same experiences. It is a salutatory lesson for us to participate in exploratory talk sessions, and to see just how much diversity and richness of perspective there is in a small group of people. We may disagree, and it is a real discipline not to express that disagreement; we gain from both listening and being listened to, and can always benefit from having our ideas clarified. In 7.3, we discuss the differences between discussion, debate and dialogue in training, and how the distinctions can assist us in solving conflicts in training.

7.3 Talk In Training - Some Issues

We have hinted in the preceding sections that the achievement of effective talk in training is not a straightforward matter. In this section, we explore some of the difficulties and issues involved, such as the need for active listening, the distinctions between dialogue, discussion and debate, trainer talk and the issue of espoused and true beliefs.

7.3.1 Listening

> *From the very beginning, the tutors showed respect and empathy for all the views expressed, often incorporating them into the course of the session. As the group recognised the value of this attitude towards others, we began to make it our own. Knowing that we would be listened to and not judged meant that we became less defensive of our own viewpoints and better able to listen to that of others. (We were freed of wasting energy on defensive emotions!) (Grace and Jane)*

Jane and Grace here allude to the value of learning to listen, and how tutors on courses can help to promote the listening habit through modelling and incorporation of participants' ideas into sessions. We believe that the basis of good communication in a group is the conscious development of active listening skills. The literature and practice of counselling and the other helping professions is full of material on listening. And yet teaching and training in practice seem remarkably bereft of such messages. The traditional model and culture of teaching, reinforced by the traditional model of teacher training - 'I tell you' - is not a listening model. It is an advocatory model. We try to move towards a version of teacher education which values the art of listening actively, and we therefore have to challenge the traditional model.

We begin this process by trying consciously to practise active listening ourselves. A commitment to listening attentively to a participant as they make a contribution is not easy. We seem to have so much of importance we need (or think we need) to tell our participants. It is very easy, in fact beguilingly easy, to talk to course participants. But they do not necessarily **learn** anything from what we say. And they do not develop as learners themselves, or as independent and autonomous teachers or trainers, capable of taking responsibility for their own teaching or training situations if they only ever listen to tutors declaiming.

We believe that for a healthy group atmosphere to develop and thrive, all participants must listen to each other. All the activities we propose for group formation (Ch. 3) and for enabling participants to share professional views and experiences work best when participants listen carefully to each other (Chs. 4-6 inclusive). Some do and some don't. Some prefer the sound of their own voices, even if they are not aware that they do. We find we have to actively promote good listening, either by commenting on the quality of listening in the group, or to create activities in

Talk In Training Courses

which participants have to listen to each other. The latter strategy is followed in the initial stages, or when we notice that the group is not listening well - as a repair device.

In order to see what might be seen as 'good listening' let's try a scenario: trainer elicits an idea on, say, group work, from a participant. The exchange goes something like this:

>**Trainer**: *What do you think is the main purpose of group work?*
>
>**Participant:** *To create the conditions in which participants have a measure of privacy while they discuss a problem.*
>
>**Trainer:** *Yes. Group work is an excellent way of problem solving.*

A close look at the trainer's second contribution shows that the participant's contribution has not been directly listened to. Perhaps a different trainer contribution more on the lines of the following might give better dividends.

>**Trainer:** *Yes. The small group seems to afford a measure of privacy in which to discuss a problem.*

This acknowledges the participant's contribution through agreement and paraphrase.

Listening shows that we value what the participant says. We may not necessarily agree, and we may choose to challenge what is said, but not until we have we have heard what has been said. We cannot do this if our heads are full of our own thoughts, all desperate to break out. For us, it is one of the greatest challenges of training to develop the quality of our listening. It demands our fullest attention.

Once good listening has been established as a group goal and practice, we can try to move towards the more difficult area of enabling participants to give each other feedback on their contributions and their performance. We have discussed this in Chapter 6.

7.3.2 Helping Participants Maximise Use of Talk Time

> *'Sometimes it's frustrating to work with people who are difficult to understand. There is sometimes communication breakdown, especially when people get emotional. Then it becomes difficult to pin down the point being made.'* (Gwen)

Gwen's diary entry highlights just one problem that can crop up in group activity which involves talk. There are others, too. Some participants often use a lot of 'air time' to make points. Their contributions are not effective in taking the group's work forward, continually referring back to points already covered, for example. Other participants struggle for the words to say what they want. Perhaps it is a lack of confidence, perhaps it is a fear that what is said will be ridiculed. Perhaps the participant has never spoken in front of a group of peers before, having been brought up in an educational culture in which the teacher made the only major contributions. We have to help these participants, whatever the origins of their reticence and silence, to contribute effectively, so that they can see what they offer adding to the group's collective point of view.

We can help this happen in a number of ways. Given an atmosphere of tolerance and mutual trust, necessary preconditions for effective contributions to be made, we can spend time usefully addressing the issue with a group when the need arises - when no progress is being made for example. We can turn the process back onto the group for their consideration with the help of some well-chosen questions. In the case of trainer training, we can focus on the topic of trainee contributions and ask participants to contribute to a discussion of effective contributions in training sessions, in which, in a structured way, the topic is addressed. The following procedure is adapted from Easen (1985).

ACTIVITY 2   Effective Contributions
Instructions To Group
1. Ask each individual to note down what characterises effective and ineffective contributions to group discussion, perhaps relating to recent sessions in the group itself.
2. Form groups of 4 to share their perceptions and to create an agreed, shared list. (You can ask a floating group member to monitor the group discussion to note effective and ineffective contributions, and to feed these back at an agreed time in the session, either to the small group, or to the main group)
3. Each group reports back their agreed lists, perhaps with the assistance of an overhead transparency. Timed.
4. Plenary discussion on the points raised. Trainer summarises main points at an appropriate moment and asks participants to recall the various stages and to ask themselves if they felt they contributed effectively.

This activity models many of the features of training practice in which talk is valued:
- individual contributions made without judgement
- active involvement in the process in different ways (participating in talk, monitoring by participants, using their categories etc.)

- presentation
- trainer's contribution limited to setting up the activity and to facilitating the plenary discussion

7.3.3 Trainer Talk

Trainers have to talk - their contributions are both expected and needed. As we have pointed out in this chapter, trainers need to consider when, how often, how long and about what to talk. We have said that we need to move away from a transmission approach to training towards a more participatory one. So when is it appropriate for trainers to talk?

WHEN? We have found that our contributions to the *content* of a session are best left until a group have made some headway towards establishing their own principles or frame of reference. Sometimes this seems to be taking for ever, and it is easy to succumb to the temptation to step in - we shudder to think of the times we have done this! Perhaps we are most useful at the end of a sequence of activities, when we can summarise key themes and trends, having been fortunate enough to see the 'big picture' which participants, engaged in talk, will not have been able to glimpse.

It is at this stage in a group's progress through a learning cycle - formulating new concepts and principles - that we find inputs from us, as trainers, to be most valuable. Now that we have a clear idea about our participants' interests, working contexts and prior experience, we can tune our contribution accordingly. Normally, it takes the form of a short talk or mini-lecture of, say, 15-20 minutes' duration, and it often has more than one purpose e.g. rounding up and injecting some new ideas, or recounting something anecdotally from our experience in order to point out a possible way forward. We find that regular, short inputs of this kind, slotted in judiciously, can be a valuable contribution to a group's learning, at the same time fulfilling participants' expectations.

ABOUT WHAT? Sharing a personal anecdote during group exploration will not divert a group from its goals. Feeding in our own knowledge and thinking about a topic before they are ready will. As trainers we have a range of educational experiences which are potentially richer than those of our participants. We do not want to become avuncular or patronising. We aim to restrict our contributions to summaries of points made by *participants*, adding points which may have been missed and which we think are relevant. We may give a short mini-lecture on the topic under discussion (see Chapter 8 for discussion). Otherwise, we may wish to restrict our contributions to operational ones. A group may request a talk on a topic, and we have had to oblige on occasions - sometimes groups need a rest from intensive talk, and need to be bathed in talk themselves. This may be a valuable opportunity to contribute one or two specific ideas to the group's collective store.

We often find that, in the excitement of an open discussion, so many ideas are reverberating around the training room that no-one can see the wood for the trees. Our responsibility in this case is to pull things together, to pick out and highlight key *themes* from the discussion so that a set of priorities emerges fro the group to focus on. For example, here is some trainer talk following a discussion with a group of trainers about the differences between development and training:

> **Trainer:** *OK. You've talked through an awful lot of issues there. Let me see if I can home in on some of the things we might find it useful to concentrate on ... I was struck by the number of times you mentioned development as* **continuing, ongoing**, *or* **throughout your career**. *That seems worth examining more closely. In contrast many of you seem to view training as* **time**-*and* **place**-*bound. A few people also seem to feel that development necessarily involves* **change** ... *that's something else we could follow up on ...*

As we identify these themes, we may write them up on the board or on a transparency. Once they are gathered together in this kind of way, they can become an agenda for follow-up reading, for a short input by the trainer, or for enquiry by groups or individuals. This kind of thematizing is particularly necessary and useful after a 'degridding' session of the sort described in Chapter 5.

We also 'talk' with our participants through feedback on their projects and assignments, and find that our comments and questions are useful as long as we maintain a strong formative dimension to them. This often means giving them questions to think about, and maybe to discuss in a follow-up tutorial, as well as comments of a more or less evaluative nature. We see this kind of feedback as most useful if it helps our participants to see a way forward as well as to review the work they have done.

We do have a contribution to make - but we try to keep it focused, and derived from a group's explorations and contributions.

7.3.4 Diaries and Dialogue

Diaries and journals sometimes open up another avenue for dialogue with individual course members. We are cautious in this area, however; while we do often encourage them to keep diaries as records of their own progress, thinking, and responses to the experiences they are going through on the course, we believe firmly that these records are personal, and not for consumption by us as trainers or by anyone else, unless we are invited to look at them. An alternative which we do make use of is to ask our participants, periodically, to look back over their own diaries and to extract from them anything they would like to share with us. In this way, we are given access to an edited version of each individual's current thinking, and we may respond to this, in writing, with observations and questions. When we can, we also like to keep our own diaries on courses, and to 'return the compliment' by putting together an edited version (we also note down things that we don't always wish to share: "Was X just being bloody-minded today or did (s)he really not understand the point?") which we then distribute to the group for *their* comments and questions. Here are samples of extracts from our diaries which were handed out for discussion and comment to a group of trainers on a postgraduate Masters trainer training programme:

Diary Extracts

Early October   "... don't like being late for the start of term and missing the case studies. I wonder what the students will be like? Not as many crises this year, I hope ...."

Mid October   "... It's a relief to be in and teaching. They seem to be a lively lot ... quite bright and involved. I wonder whether they'll start demanding input ..."

"I enjoyed the tutorials ... good to get to know them better ... especially the quiet ones ..."

Late October   "... one or two good sessions this week. They are working well in groups ... totally different atmosphere in Group B, somehow."

"I must keep more careful notes ... it's sometimes difficult to remember what I've covered in Group A and what in Group B ..."

"Those textbook images from Group A are still going round in my mind ... powerful stuff! Funny that Group B seem to see things so differently ..."

The first 7 weeks - reflections

I look back and see how much ground we've covered. I see a mass of images, mainly good, mainly positive ... in fact, I feel overwhelmingly positive at the moment when I think about the course and the group. I feel glad of the 'rest', too, during this reading week (a sort of catching up time for me - my desk looks like the wind's been at it). I'm often aware that I've only half fought through my paperwork - please let me spend more time in class, away from the paperwork, where I like to be. Being with the group energises me.

In sessions, I was most interested in the effect of the work on metaphors, visualising, music and shapes. I appreciated the patience and the trust (although I could also see the inevitable irritation and tension, too). I <u>know</u> more about the effect of these techniques now and I know that they work better than me telling anyone about what they mean. I felt at the time that it was risky - I could have been pursuing things too far. I felt good when several students asked to borrow the tape. I felt less good when the wall poster didn't work - perhaps that was going too far, too quickly? If I analyse that feeling, I see that perhaps I <u>was</u> asking too much - but then I put up my own summary and felt slightly guilty for imposing my own ideas. I know we can't win all the time!

During the session, I was aware of the growing confidence in exploring topics and issues, and a continuing intensity, as well as enjoyment. I need to find where funny bones are - I know I could spend hours just swapping jokes - one of life's pleasures.

This kind of disclosure is valuable to both sides. Participants' diaries often offer us insights which we may not gain in the 'hurly-burly' of group sessions, and our own diaries may help participants to gain a trainer's perspective on the course. Either way, they can play their part in moving a course forward and setting new learning priorities.

7.3.5 Discussion, Debate, Dialogue

One of the most common instructions in learning materials and in examination questions is 'discuss'. All of us familiar with 'discussing' points, but what do we really do? As a rule, we either present ideas or have them presented to us by peers. One by one we talk them through, usually eliminating them one by one until we are left with a 'solution' or 'answer'. It is the legacy of several centuries of intellectual activity that gives us this view of discussion - linear, problem solving, prone to points scoring and put-downs. Small wonder that training participants might not be too keen on 'discussion'. They associate it perhaps with 'debate', an essentially adversarial activity in which there is a winner and a loser. We do not think that these types of activity are particularly helpful in training courses, except where we might want participants to experience for themselves something of the flavour of an intellectual or professional struggle (see Chapter 8 for specific examples of activity) which involves an apparently clear 'choice' between two opposing points of view.

More productive, and associated with the types of exploratory talk we have discussed in 7.2.3, is the notion of 'dialogue. We are not referring to talk between two professionals here - rather a form of open and exploratory talk between a group of people who have agreed not to make any other contributions other than those which ADD to what has been said. The rules of debate are suspended so that talk expands, layer by layer, topic by topic, and allows different and perhaps radical and divergent points of view on a topic. The aim is not to reach consensus, rather it is to discover if alternatives do exist, if there are new and previously unthought-of approaches to a problem. This type of talk is likely to be problem posing rather than problem-solving. It is very difficult to take part in, and it is perhaps best developed on a voluntary basis.

However, there are times in a training course when it is valuable to suspend the rules of talk and to truly explore. As trainers, it is our responsibility to model effective behaviour in this mode - we may ourselves need training or at least opportunities to try out the form. Just to respond to a contribution in a new way can be very liberating, especially one we disagree with.

Some examples
DISCUSSION
Participant 1 - I think that a directive approach to supervision is very necessary. Young trainees can't think for themselves.
Participant 2 - That's nonsense. How can they learn to think for themselves under such circumstances?

DIALOGUE (same participants)
Participant 1 - I think that a directive approach to supervision is very necessary. Young trainees can't think for themselves.
Participant 2 - Yes, let's see what this might entail in practice.

Varying the modes of talk in our training sessions will open up a range of opportunities for development to our participants. It requires 'training' for both trainers and participants, but is a valuable adjunct to what is a potentially limiting mode of talk - 'discussion'.

7.3.6 Saying What We Mean

One issue we often face on training courses is of individuals taking ownership of ideas which they don't fully subscribe to. In the professional literature, this phenomenon is known as espousing theory. Practice is often not coherent with what is said. A typical example is of an individual who proclaims allegiance to interactive participatory learning, who, placed with a learning group, talks at them for most of the session, answers the tasks, provides right answers. A less extreme example might be of the individual trainer who carefully structures sessions so that participants end up saying what they wanted them to in the first place, despite professing 'learner-centeredness'.

This is not an unusual position. We noted in Chapter 6 that change is a long and often difficult process - a symptom of change is to espouse a principle but not practise it. A way of dealing with what might potentially be seen as a 'problem' is to acknowledge it and to create as many talking opportunities as possible in sessions. In such a way, individuals can have the opportunity to become aware of inconsistencies in their position on issues or between their principles and their practices. Activities such as 'micro-training' are ideal opportunities, provided we create space for participants to talk before and after actual training performance. The value of talk in training is to allow these dilemmas and inconsistencies to be expressed, and for an individual to make decisions about whether or not to modify their ideas or behaviour.

Summary

This chapter has brought together a number of related issues about talk in training - its purposes, types and the issues resulting from its use. Unplanned, spontaneous talk is potentially the most valuable of tools in training in our view. There are many dimensions to talk, and for us it is a major developmental area. However, once one has made the decision to open up talk in training there is no turning back, only a dynamic search for better ways of initiating and managing it. The resultant collaborative culture is of immense influence in the training process and beyond.

References

Brandes, D. and P. Ginnis (1990) The Student-Centred School. Hemel Hempstead: Simon Schuster.

Easen, P. (1985) Making School-Centred INSET Work. London: Routledge.

CHAPTER 8
CREATING MEANING: NEW LEARNING

Once course participants have become more aware of themselves and have begun to make sense of their experience, they are ready to learn more. This means gaining access to ideas from their peers and tutors, and to begin to select from the plethora of background literature those books and articles which have something to say to them. This can happen on courses of all lengths. Consider this coffee-time exchange, for example, on the fourth day of the one-week Austrian teachers' course referred to in Chapter 5:

> **Participant:** *Language Awareness is something new for me, but I want to find out more. Is there anything I can read after the course?*
> **Trainer:** *There's a lot. It depends which aspect of language you are most interested in.*
> **Participant:** *What I found useful was that activity on verb tenses. I didn't realise how many possibilities there are. I've always taught according to the rules in the coursebook.*
> **Trainer:** *OK. You might like to look at 'The English Verb' by Michael Lewis, and 'Meaning and the English Verb' by Geoffrey Leech. They're both in the Book Exhibition next door.*

This participant was already reconsidering his position in the light of the awareness-raising work which he had been exposed to for much of the first three days, and was expressing his desire to "find out more". It goes almost without saying that a trainer has to be in a position to respond to these individual 'moments of readiness' in participants. It is then that they reveal to us what they are thinking about and where a course is leading them. In a very real sense they are ready to begin creating their own meanings.

However, in our experience individual course participants reach this stage of readiness at different rates. While some are eager to push ahead and 'learn', others may need to continue exploring experience for longer, and others still may be 'blocked' in some way (e.g. by interpersonal conflict within the group, cultural alienation, by a clash between their preferred learning style and the procedures we have adopted as trainers). On longer courses, much of this can be resolved through individual tutorials, but on shorter courses it's not so easy to give much attention to individuals. As trainers, we have to 'take the temperature' regularly and respond sensitively, now pushing the group forward, now slowing down and reviewing the ground we have covered so far.

8.1 Activities and Ideas for Making Meaning
In this section, we shall review a number of activities which we employ to move participants from states of readiness to encounters with new ideas. They are complements to the activities we have described in Chapters 5 to 7, and represent the final pieces of a jigsaw of ideas which enable us as trainers to help participants make sense of training activity and learn from the experience.

8.1.1 Trainer suggestions
In Chapter 6.2.3 we discussed the value of 'thinking questions' as a way of helping groups and individuals to become more aware of the significance of their experience and of avenues for further exploration. We also use the same device in order to support participants in their quest for ways forward in a session, as follows:

EXAMPLES
(to an individual in a trainers' session on observation and professional support)
Perhaps you'd like to think a little more about which aspect of classroom supervision you'd like to find out more about.

(to a teachers' group in a session on correcting written work)
Now that we've explored each other's thinking on correcting written work fairly fully, which aspects would you like to read about .... there are plenty of references I could give you ... can you take a few minutes to discuss that?

At this stage in a training sequence, participants are usually confident enough to express a view on questions like these, and most would prefer to be consulted on reading priorities rather than to be given 'set texts'.

8.1.2 Professional Reading
There is no doubt that there is much for teachers and trainers to learn from reading. It has certainly contributed to our own development and we continue to benefit from it. On longer courses, participants have the luxury of time to read widely and to follow up their interests through references and bibliographies.

Teachers in-service have less time, and they can easily lose the habit of reading under the many pressures which surround their professional lives on a day-to-day basis. We see reading in much the same light as inputs from the trainer. Judiciously selected books and articles can help enormously in the processes of making sense of previous experience (how often we find reassurance and affirmation in our reading!) and of creating new meanings for ourselves as we consider the implications of new professional ideas for our future practice.

Course participants who may have lost the reading habit are often overawed by long reading lists and may not know where to start, and how to extract what they need from reading material. We see it as our responsibility to help them through guidance and tasks, and here we mention some ways in which we do this.

8.1.3 Seminars

We find that in-session discussion of key articles can be helpful and stimulating, and there are various ways in which we ask participants to prepare for these.

ACTIVITY 1	Presentation of ideas

The whole group is asked to read a key article, and two participants are given the task of identifying the main ideas and framing some questions in order to lead a seminar discussion in the next session. They are asked to work to a time limit and to round up with a summary of the key issues which emerge during the seminar. These are then reproduced on a handout which is distributed to the group.

This is a fairly traditional seminar procedure, but it is popular with participants as it gives them a chance, in the security of the group, to check their perceptions against those of others.

ACTIVITY 2	Debate

Copies of two articles with differing points of view on the same topic are distributed to participants. Examples of suitable pairs of articles are:

Widdowson (1985) and Swan (1985) *Communicative Language Teaching*
Allwright (1981) and O'Neill (1991) *Course Books*
Arnold (1998) and Gadd (1998) *Humanistic Language Teaching*

Creating Meaning: New Learning

> Half the participants are asked to read article A in depth and to skim article B. For the other half, this is reversed.
>
> In the seminar itself, all those who have focused on article A meet in one group and those who have been assigned article B meet in another. In these groups, they prepare for a debate by checking their understanding of the main points and trying to anticipate arguments and questions from the other side. (This may take 10-20 minutes, depending on the complexity and length of the articles).
>
> The remainder of the session is devoted to a debate, between the two sides, chaired by the tutor or a participant, in which participants are encouraged to speak 'in role', as though they were the author of 'their' article.

At the end, the chair sums up and notes the main issues on the board as 'food for thought'. A debriefing may be needed to allow participants to air their own views.

Debates like this are popular and animated events on our courses. Participants become very involved in defending the point of view assigned to them and in the discussion gain valuable practice in articulating ideas and familiarising themselves with professional terminology. At the same time, they inevitably begin to formulate their own thinking on the issues under debate, and with a little nudging, to see the limitations of polarised thinking.

> **ACTIVITY 3**   **Role Reading**
>
> Participants are asked to read an article from a particular point of view (e.g. as a learner, as a teacher in a particular context, as a school principal or head of English). One or two participants are asked to 'get inside the head' of the author as they read.
>
> In the seminar, the 'authors' respond to questions and comments from the audience, answering in the first person. One participant, or the tutor, chairs the discussion, sums up at the end and holds a debriefing discussion in which participants (as with all role plays) have an opportunity to 'talk down' the experience and express their own views.

Trainees and teachers often find it difficult to take up a critical stance when they read, especially if they come from cultures in which the printed word is highly respected. This kind of role-reading exercise helps to highlight other points of view, and to put

Creating Meaning: New Learning

the author's ideas under critical scrutiny in a useful and productive way.

ACTIVITY 4   Working For and With Authors

Participants are asked individually to read an article in depth. They then join a group and imagine they are a committee who are advertising a talk by the author based on the article. They have to produce a simple and striking advertising poster or 'flier' advertising the talk.

A variation is to imagine the author is on a 'panel' at a major conference and they have 5 questions they would like to ask in order to explore the article.

Good articles for this are those which are advocating a particular point of view or practice. Examples include:
Holliday (1994)
Eken (1999)
Brown (2000)

8.1.4 Reading Tasks

Professional reading is just one kind of reading, and we have found it useful to apply some of the principles of reading methodology in the design of tasks which can either be carried out individually, between sessions, or started individually and completed through discussion in the next session. A sample activity follows

---

ACTIVITY 5   Professional Reading

Reference: Brumfit, C. (1977) Correcting Written Work. *Modern English Teacher*, 10.

A.   Before reading the article, respond to these two tasks:

1.   Tick the statement nearest to your usual practice in correcting your learners' written work
   a)   I correct all the mistakes.
   b)   I correct some of the mistakes.
   c)   I indicate mistakes, using a code or identifying them.
   d)   I let learners correct their own.
   e)   Other (please specify)

Creating Meaning: New Learning

2.   Tick the statement nearest to your beliefs about written errors
a)   It is my responsibility as a teacher to correct my students' errors.
b)   Learners should take responsibility for correcting their own errors.
c)   Learners are not capable of correcting their own errors.
d)   Errors in written work are a sign of ineffective teaching or poor learning.
e)   Others (Please specify)

NOW READ THE ARTICLE

B.   Work in groups of 4

Brumfit lists 8 arguments in favour of students correcting their own work. Think of your own experience and state whether you agree with each of these arguments. Are there any arguments <u>against</u> this practice?

C.   Work in groups

Which of these theoretical positions can you recognize in the article?

a)   Prevention of errors is preferable to remedial work
b)   Students can learn from their errors
c)   Failure to correct errors will result in negative reinforcement
d)   Too much correction by the teacher will discourage learners
e)   Learners need to be trained to work effectively on their own errors

D.   Work in groups

Would Brumfit's ideas work in your teaching context? Give reasons for your response.

In this task, we start by activating participants' 'schemata' before moving on to invite them to analyse and interpret the writer's ideas, and finally to examine the implications of these ideas for practice. We find this kind of task-based approach to be useful on initial training courses and on other programmes where participants need support with their reading, especially in the early stages. Once again, the aim is to sharpen the critical reading ability of participants and to encourage them to be robust in comparing their own experience and opinions with those of an expert in the field. This, in turn, encourages 'theorising' in Ramani's (1987) sense of constructing personal theories.

8.1.5 Book and Article Reviews
This involves participants in reading and commenting on a book or article, and presenting their findings to the group in one of three ways:
- a poster for display in the training room
- a talk given to the group
- a written review which may be copies and distributed to fellow-participants

There are a number of possible benefits in these reviews:
- an incentive to read a relevant book or article
- a way of introducing a reading which may be of value to others in the group
- sharpening of critical reading skills
- 'public' articulation of ideas and a chance to receive feedback on them from participants and tutors
- practice in writing for publication

8.1.6 Quotes
A further way to promote reflective and conceptual thinking is to put up on the training room wall a selection of short quotes about the topic we are dealing with. We don't actually make direct reference to these unless we feel it is necessary. Rather, they are left to catch the wandering eye of a student, or to read while waiting for a session to begin. We have often found students adding to these or starting their own collections with quotes that are meaningful to them, too. Whatever the case, we find that the conceptual world of the training room is enriched by these 'subliminal' messages. Here is a sample which Tony has used in sessions on change in education:

THE IMPACT OF RESEARCH KNOWLEDGE UPON PRACTICE IS ROOTED IN THE ABILITY OF INDIVIDUAL PROFESSIONALS TO CHANGE <u>WHAT THEY DO</u> AND <u>HOW THEY THINK</u>. (Bridget Somekh)

> CHANGE IS NOT MADE WITHOUT INCONVENIENCE. EVEN FROM WORSE TO BETTER (Robert Hooker)

> THERE IS NOTHING IN THIS WORLD CONSTANT BUT INCONSTANCY (Jonathan Swift)
> AN ACROBAT ON THE HIGH WIRE MAINTAINS HIS STABILITY BY CONTINUAL CORRECTION OF HIS IMBALANCE (Gregory Bateson)

> IT IS VERY DIFFICULT FOR US TO PERCEIVE CHANGES IN OUR OWN SOCIAL AFFAIRS IN THE ECOLOGY AROUND US (Thomas Kuhn)

> TIME MAY CHANGE ME
> BUT I CAN'T CHANGE TIME (David Bowie)

> WE DO NOT NEED TO CHANGE THE WORLD. TO NUDGE A LITTLE BIT OF IT ALONG WILL BE ENOUGH (Charles Handy)

> CHANGE COMES FROM SMALL INITIATIVES WHICH WORK, INITIATIVES WHICH, IMITATED, BECOME THE FASHION (Charles Handy)

An additional activity featuring quotes is to ask individuals to identify **'quotable quotes'** from articles or sections of text which the group are currently reading, to translate them onto A4 paper so that all the group can see them and to mount a display in the training room. This can be the focus for exploratory talk, or could be used to invite students to justify their choices, and to say why they resonate so much with them.

8.1.7 Diagrams

All standard textbooks, and most articles feature diagrams. Very often the diagrams confuse or intimidate rather than illuminate. There are several exercises we can use with diagrams. Here is one which we have used to help participants (a) see relationships between elements of a teaching/learning situation and (b) demystify diagrams.

Creating Meaning: New Learning

ACTIVITY 6   **Build A Diagram**

1. On large cards (lettering 2/3 ins high) write the following

| LANGUAGE | LEARNING | TEACHING |

2. Show each one to the group in turn, inviting them to jot down what each one might mean to them.
3. Stick them to the board at random. Invite individuals to come to the board and arrange them in a way which seems to capture the essence of the relationships between them. Board markers are available to draw connections, arrows etc. Individuals talk through the relationships as they see them, and answer queries from the group.
4. Form group into pairs and invite them to construct a diagram, with as much detail as they wish, of their own, and to (a) write a caption and (b) write a short explanatory paragraph. (This step has the important additional benefit of practising specific writing and presentation skills). Allow an hour for this step. Advise the pairs to work with a set of 3 slips of paper, so that they can move them around and explore alternatives.
5. Collect in the diagrams and copy them for the next step. Pairs split up and form new pairs to share their diagrams.
6. Finish with a plenary and focus on (a) what participants have learned about the relationships between the three elements (b) what they would like to know more about (c) What they have discovered about diagrams.

The value of this type of exercise is that there is no correct answer - this may be problematic for the members of the group who need closure - and that it invites exploration and experimentation. It also has a tactile element, as individuals can physically move the elements and 'see' the relationships. A similar activity can be set up using modelling materials (card, Plasticine, string etc.) if the group are more kinaesthetically inclined.

8.1.8 'Mapping'

An extension of the diagram ideas is the concept of a 'mental map'. An exercise we have used with some success as a way of pulling together a series of issues on a programme or to enable a group to review 'where they're at' after an extended sequence of training experiences we call 'Mapping'.

There are a number of ways to do this exercise; here's one that seems to work.

Creating Meaning: New Learning

> **ACTIVITY 7   Maps**
>
> 1. Collect a series of maps of the locality where the training course is taking place. Usually there will be a regional map, a town or city map and possibly even a site map of the institution in which the programme is taking place. Add to these national, continental, world maps, and even a diagram of the solar system. If you can, find some old maps of the locality or country (ones with pictures etc.) on, and maps from novels, satellite photos - any visual representation of Earth or localities, in fact.
>
> 2. Tell the group that the aim of the session is, for example, to consolidate what they have done with regard to the topic over a period of time. Let's say that the topic is training course design. Tell them that you are going to invite them to create a 'map' of what they know (a) as a way of reviewing and (b) to examine the idea of 'mental maps' as a way humans store information and organise it.
>
> 3. Show the group a sequence of maps from the solar system down, if possible to the building plan. Talk about the notions of SCALE and DETAIL. Invite comments and questions.
>
> 4. Show the group other maps and representations, commenting on what they show and how. Talk about the idea of the map and the territory.
>
> 5. Invite discussion of the issues raised by the presentation. Then invite the group to focus on the topic - teacher training course design, and to jot down ideas, individually, on what might be features of a map of this territory.
>
> 6. Form them into pairs and groups - some may want to do this activity individually and they should be allowed to do this - and ask them to construct, on a poster-size piece of paper, a map. They should be prepared to give other group members a guided tour, using the map. They can choose to work at any scale, any level of detail and with any representation system that they want to. Allow at least 2 hours for this stage.
>
> 7. When the maps are complete, mount a display, and initiate a series of guided tours, led by the creators of the maps.
>
> 8. Plenary session focussing on (a) what the group have learnt about their current state of knowledge on the topic and what they discovered in the activity (b) what they have discovered about the notion of 'mental maps'.

This activity has proved to be a very effective means of reviewing topics, for finding out what current states of knowledge are (less successful, as most participants are not visually 'primed' at the

Creating Meaning: New Learning

outset of a course) and for exploring how memory and cognition and learning work. It also seems to lower inhibitions so many participants have about their 'artistic ability' - non-judgemental activity like this can restore confidence and show that visual work is enjoyable, and potentially liberating.

8.1.9 Some Further Thinking Tools

Another way in which we can try to help participants conceptualise is to provide them with strong models or images to work with at the exploring ideas/conceptualising stage of a training sequence. Here are two we have found extremely effective.

ACTIVITY 8	**Membrane**

1. Tell the group that you will talk through an idea about learning and the learning process. Put the following simple diagram on the board or OHP:

What we already know
_____
What we don't know

2. Ask the group to imagine that the line between what we know and what we don't know is a membrane. It can be opaque or transparent, porous or solid. So it's possible to come up against a barrier to learning, or to accidentally find oneself in new 'territory' (going through a hole in the opaque membrane). Sometimes we can see through, but not move through, and sometimes we can both see and move through.

3. Ask the group, individually, to try to remember an instance in their own learning of each of the four possibilities, and after, say, 5 minutes' reflection time, to share these ideas with a small group for 10/15 minutes.

4. The plenary should collect together the ideas offered by the group (a recorder will help, so that you can be free to facilitate the discussion).

5. Copy the list of ideas and either in a subsequent class or the same one, distribute copies of the list with the instruction:

Look through the list of experiences of learning that the group remembered. Try to find patterns in them. Can you see any underlying trends in these experiences?

Also consider the relevance of these experiences to your current training experience. Take a new topic and ask yourself if you think you have passed through the membrane. What has helped you pass through? What was the role of exploring your own experience and images in this process?

6. Following group discussion, again hold a plenary to establish patterns and common themes. You may, if the group don't mention it, want to talk about
- mental models, assumptions and theories
- the role of awareness-raising in 'cleaning the membrane'
- the value of group discussion in a) cleaning the membrane and b) helping individuals pass through the membrane.

ACTIVITY 9   'Ant Hill'

This is a variation on the well-known image of Freud's 'iceberg', with the bulk under water and out of view. This can be used, of course, but may be familiar to a group. This is an alternative (same instructions apply if you want to use 'iceberg') which can assist a group in seeing the psychological territory of learning and teaching.

1. Tell the group that you are going to talk about an image of how our mind works and is organised. They should think, as they are listening, about what it means to them and whether they have a similar image.

2. Show them this picture either on a card or on the OHT.
Tell the group that this is a tropical termite mound. The part above the surface of the ground acts as part of the cooling and ventilation system for a huge underground system of chambers where the termites live. Explain that this is rather like the human mind. The part above the surface or active consciousness is relatively small although quite prominent. Below the surface is a vast, to some extent unknown, system, which we could liken to the unconscious mind, containing values, attitudes and beliefs, emotional/feeling centres, memory and so on. The inter-level at the surface can be likened to a 'thinking' level linking the inner and outer, or an active decision-making system.

The evidence of learning is in the shape and structure of what you see above the surface (behaviour in humans). Learning experiences, like rain or animal interference, can change the shape of the outer structure - but the termites quickly repair the damage, although not exactly as it was before. To have an influence on what is below ground means perhaps changing the conditions at the surface (raised temperature, for example) or perhaps something much more drastic, like a fire.

> 3. Ask the group to think about the image for a short period (5 minutes) and to share impressions with a neighbour. Invite general comments in plenary. Probe with questions like 'What relevance does the image have for the course you are currently doing, or previous learning experiences you have had?' 'Can we influence values, attitudes and beliefs? Why might it be necessary to do so in teacher education?'

You might want to work with the model we have discussed in Chapter 6, adapted from Handal and Lauvas (1987) as a way of focusing the discussion.

CLASSROOM PRACTICE

ACTIVE DECISION-MAKING

VALUES, ATTITUDES and BELIEFS

This type of work, and metaphor work described in Chapter 4, is valuable as a means of helping participants conceptualise, visualise, make sense and form principles. It takes individuals beyond the concrete, sensory world into the world of images, ideas and abstractions, the basis for our principles of action.

8.2 New Learning: Issues and Implications

In 8.1, we outlined some of the ways in which we attempt to enable training groups to move from concrete experience and immediate reflection to more abstract and 'conceptual' thinking patterns, to a point where principles may be formulated or refashioned, the point at which new learning is possible. This section reviews some of key issues in this part of the training process - types of thinking; the role of 'theory' and notions of 'expertise' and 'knowledge bases'. In this discussion we shall mention training issues, such as the role of professional reading.

8.2.1 Types of Thinking

A major goal of any training course must be to assist in the development of participants' thinking skills. Thinking and action - conscious and unconscious - are complementary elements of the trainer's and the teacher's working lives. Teacher and trainer development initiatives provide unique opportunities to explore thinking types and styles, and to develop our thinking about professional issues and practices. In this section we look at how we try to promote different types of thinking in professional development and training programmes. The essence of our practice in this area of training is to provide opportunities for participants to explore the thinking which underlies action in teaching and training.

Ritsuko's diary entry which follows illustrates some of the different types of thinking that a course can activate.

> 'In the core studies we used a lot of metaphors. The following is one of my comments on metaphors in my diary:
> Unlike brainstorming, my thinking comes from my deep deep mind. I can explore myself, what I am thinking about a topic, and I think it is fun to go into the deep thoughts and to discover the little things I usually miss (...), I can clarify my thinking - concentrating the picture would make me think more and more deeply.' (Ritsuko)

THEORISING

We have already alluded in this chapter to the value of theorising, the formation of principles, the development of concepts. We do this naturally enough - it is unfortunate that so many professionals associate 'theorising' with the sort of high-level conceptual thought processes of the mathematician or physicist. We can theorise about anything as soon as we begin to ask 'Why is it like that?' 'Why did she do that?' 'What's behind that statement?' In searching for responses to the questions we are forced to examine the evidence our senses provide us and to articulate some sort of 'reason'. This sort of practical reasoning is at the base of all professionals' decision-making processes.

In training, as well as the activities in 8.1, we can encourage participants to make explicit their theorising by engaging them in activities such as micro-training or materials production where they have to justify their actions or the content of the products. Better still that the participants ask each other the questions to explore each other's theorising.

PROBLEM SOLVING/PROBLEM POSING

This type of practical thinking skill is extremely useful for professionals, much of whose working life is spent 'problem-solving'. Problem-solving involves various analytical and creative thinking processes, and is more a stance towards professional realities than a mode of thinking per se. Teaching and training are very problematic activities and again the act of articulating one's thought processes is a valuable way of clarifying why we take certain courses of action.

Of potentially more value is the process of problem-posing or 'critical thinking' as it is sometimes called. In this process training participants are invited to explore their assumptions about professional practice. Activities such as critical incident analysis where value systems are brought to the surface, prejudices exposed and inconsistencies in thinking illuminated are of real value in training. Critical thinking skills enable professionals to examine their work with a view to developing and changing practices, to become more flexible in response to professional issues. Thus, problem-posing, the activity of setting up and identifying situations and contexts for critical thinking is a necessary counterpoint to problem-solving. Often a great deal of effort is wasted solving problems which have been inadequately framed, or chasing shadows of problems which don't exist 'out there', but rather 'in here', in the thought processes of the participants themselves.

REFLECTIVE - EXPLORATORY/INTROSPECTIVE

> *'After reviewing my diary, I have come to the conclusion that my training has nothing to do with pure theory. It is based on reflections and practice.' (Fatima)*

Many training activities invite participants to examine their own experiences and thoughts in a systematic, structured and supported way. Reflective thinking encourages review of experience - of feelings before, during and after experiences; of the events and stages of an experience. This material, when distilled further, is then available for principle formation. There are a number of ways of encouraging reflective thinking - diary writing and 'creative reviews' are two commonly used methods. Less commonly used, but nonetheless highly effective, are 'grids' (see Chapter 5). Reflective thinking consists of structured ways of looking at personal and collective experience, and asking questions such as 'What exactly happened?' 'How did I feel?' It is the basis of reflective practice, and lays the foundation for learning from experience.

CONCEPTUAL

> *'I'm still worried about diagrams. I'm not sure how far these two-dimensional representations of ideas, systems and processes actually clarify things for people from such varied backgrounds. I must keep checking on this ...' (Rod)*

> *'For diagrams, I did not have any special feeling for them. I myself had seldom used them before. (...) I felt more comfortable to express myself in writing. Diagrams disturbed my thinking.' (Qiyan)*

This type of thinking intimidates many of us. Not many of us are by nature 'theorists' in the mathematical/scientific sense, thinking putting our thoughts into formulae or principles. It is the type of thinking that enables its user to grasp 'the whole picture' or to see the pattern in an otherwise random sequence of events. It is cerebral, often austere, often hard to put into words. It is at the centre of Western scientific thought. It is also a very valuable set of thinking processes - it encourages rigour and being systematic. It helps us to organise what might otherwise be random sets of information. It is above all a tool for taming vast amounts of information and subjecting them to classification, connection and categorisation. As long as we don't think that all our problems are solved by this way of thinking we are in control of a powerful instrument for making meaning from the world. A further value of this way of thinking is its use in writing, structuring our thoughts on paper. Conceptual thinking also helps us to interpret diagrams, other professionals' writings and professional ideas, build models of what we do and could do.

In this brief section, we have mentioned the main types of thinking that we believe are important for trainers and teachers to experience on training courses. These are in addition to creative and lateral thinking (Chapter 4) 'emotional' thinking and sensitivity (Chapter 6). Thinking enables us to explore our assumptions; understand our experience, and learn from it; create schematic representations of our work - through, for example diagrams; to visualise, to 'hear' and to create new ways of doing; plan for future action; deal with large amounts of information; understand the thoughts of colleagues and writers. Thinking professionals are people who are always in a position to develop their practices and move forward in their own thinking.

8.2.2 Theory/Practice Relationships

> *'The (training) route is usually from the introduction of an important topic or issue to group or class discussion and then to practice. (...) This mode of combining theory with practice is very helpful. Learning, thinking and practice deepen or understanding of teaching and training issues.' (Ying)*
>
> *'I really like the way that our awareness of how we think about various aspects of our teaching is being raised by doing thinking tasks and getting us to extract principles from the task.' (Rose)*

> 'Many a time and during group work, we reflect on our own experiences, trying to devise new criteria, principles etc. (...) These things strengthen my belief that practice precedes theory' (Sadek)

All professional work generates theory, working theory (or *practical theory*) - the work of teachers and trainers is typical of this process. The three diary entries capture the essence of how participants have experienced our approach to theory and practice. The work of professionals is also informed by others' conceptualisations of teaching, learning and training (some call this *received knowledge*). In our work with teachers and trainers, we seek actively to encourage participants to develop thinking skills and experience thinking processes to enable them to confidently forge links between practice and theory and vice versa. A training course is a unique opportunity for busy professionals in service to gain space to think and to examine relationships between their practices and the theories underlying them. Many see it as a chance to step back from their work and to 'take stock' and think through the meaning of their often crowded lives. For the aspiring professional, an initial programme of training is an opportunity for beginning to forge dynamic, creative, lifelong links between theory and practice. We believe that there are at least three levels of theory which we can address in training; we shall call them Theory 1, Theory 2 and Theory 3.

1. THEORY 1

In Chapter 4, we discussed the role of participants' previous experience in training, and referred to 'personal theory'. This is 'Theory 1'. Participants' immediate working principles, the sort that inform methodological choices in training are examples of Theory 1. Experienced teachers and trainers have often well-developed and well-thought-out **personal theories** on teaching, learning, people and so on. These personal theories inform action and reaction. They are usually developed, maintained and used unconsciously. Their development comes from a natural predisposition that people have for **theorising**, or attempting either to predict, speculate or explain what is happening around them. Successful learners have a store of 'tips' they can offer others trying to emulate them - the 'tips' are an articulation of personal theories. Teachers draw upon a store of theories and actively theorise about their work as a way of trying to understand and monitor the effects of their actions on learners. Training that explicitly draws upon participants' personal theories and the capacity to theorise is likely to be perceived as more 'relevant' by participants. Training courses, as we discussed in Chapter 4, are venues for opening up exploration of Theory 1. A specific time when we can do this is when exploring training or teaching experiences. First 'how did you feel about the experience?'. Next, 'what exactly happened?' Then 'what themes or patterns emerge from individual and collective experience?' These questions form the basis for creating meaning from the experience. The 'meaning' is often expressed in a set of principles which emerge from structured discussion of the questions. Further, by regularly inviting (sometimes challenging!) participants to articulate their rationale for choices in practice, or for adopting new practices, or changing current ones in significant ways we are assisting them in developing Theory 1. Back in the classroom or training room, it is the only theory that ultimately matters to practitioners as they face the complexity and 'fuzziness' of teaching and learning contexts.

2. THEORY 2

It is unlikely, although by no means impossible, for practitioners to develop their own teaching or training principles without either guidance or reference to outside sources. There are also theories 'out there' which we find useful and exciting. We call these collectively 'Theory 2'. For example, change theory is interesting and relevant to our work, and so too are theories of professional development and learning such as Kolb's and Schön's. Professionals have been thinking about these issues for many generations. They offer ideas derived from their own practices and experiences for us to tap into. These ideas live through our work. We acknowledge their influence, and strive to make them available to participants, when our judgement and their desires coincide.

Transmission training takes Theory 2 as its starting point. Theory 2 has the authority of publication and the respect of academia. It can be delivered through lectures and reading as a body of knowledge. This has the attraction of enabling the trainer to 'present' ideas, and it can save time. It can also cement the position of trainer as expert and source of theoretical knowledge. We do not see Theory 2 as a body of knowledge, however. These are theories which we need to engage with and understand for what they are - ideas. They are evolving in professional debate and experimentation. There is, however, no guarantee that they *mean* anything to participants unless their own schemata have been activated first, and their own experience explored. Participants need time to reflect - processing time in reflective mode is not lost time, rather it can prepare the way for deeper conceptual learning and principle formation, where participants' and received knowledge can blend. We need hooks to hang new ideas on. It seems more productive to work in ways which **lead to** exploration and understanding of received knowledge rather than being driven by it. The bigger questions and ideas which inform practice have their place in training, but as a landmark rather than a destination per se in the learning process.

An alternative strategy is to invite participants to 'personalise' received knowledge during training, where abstract notions can be brought alive through connection with participants' lives and experiences. We have tried to illustrate this principle in this and other chapters in the book.. Better to begin sequences of training with generative questions and activities which raise material to the surface, than to present participants with ready-made answers from the key texts and ask them to relate these to their own experience. We would suggest saving the latter type of activity until later in a training sequence, as we have suggested in this chapter, for example, with our ideas on reading activities.

3. THEORY 3

This is 'trainer or teacher theory' - our principles. For many years we have wrestled with the issue of when and how, if at all, we should reveal our own principles in training. One position says we should let our practice do the talking for us. The messages are there if you care to look. Another says we should always let training groups know what we're up to, why we're doing certain activities. Another says we should give our opinions about issues.

We are aware of the dangers of swamping participants with 'our answers', of risking 'cloning'. There is no doubt that we model practices, and it seems to be clear that many messages of training and teaching are unconsciously 'picked up' through experience of a trainer's style and practice. We have had bad experiences when we have not revealed our rationale for activities - we lay ourselves open to accusations of manipulation at worst, and of at least confusing a group when we don't orientate them to activities. We can be guilty of patronising participants by not engaging in debate with them over issues.

With trainers' groups, we have to come clean. Part of a training course for trainers must involve an understanding of what theories (1 and 2) motivate *this trainer who's in front of the group NOW*. This is a difficult area for us, as we are committed to training experiences which focus on participants' theories, derived as far as possible from their own experiences either in previous

Creating Meaning: New Learning

training or teaching, or in the training room as they experience the course. Participants are entitled to ask 'why are we doing this?' They are not always going to ask this question when we'd like them to, at the 'right point' in a training sequence. So do we give the game away and give the rationale at the outset, in its entirety? Or do we withhold it, and meet with frustration and irritation? The danger of giving 'our point of view' at the outset is that it blocks participants' thinking, particularly participants who have a 'shopping list' approach to training, and profess to wanting only information. Participants like this give the impression of keenness, but really do not want to change or develop in fundamental ways. Do we then challenge them with an alternative? And run the risk of being accused of denying them knowledge, or not meeting their needs, or being seen as ignorant or incompetent ourselves? After all, trainers are 'experts', or purportedly so.

What we have just rehearsed here in fact matches fairly closely to the line we take when discussing these issues with trainers. For us, this is a key training issue. Because trainers have a position of power and given authority, their principles are inevitably going to have currency among participants, particularly in the uncertain early days of a programme. By deliberately avoiding an explicit statement of our Theory 3 about an activity, we believe we can create space for participants to gain sufficient confidence to begin to address their own principles. By beginning with experience, signposted for participants to give them a sense of direction, we believe we can contribute to the conditions which will encourage creative, honest and critical exploration of principles by participants.

Our own contributions are also crucial, too. We believe that a statement of working principles for a course (see Chapter 3) can help to orientate a group of participants to a course and to give them a preview of what will happen. We hope, also, to avoid the tendency to 'hunt the answer' which some participants, unsure of their own stance, indulge in. At these times, trainers come under intense pressure to 'reveal all'. Beneath this desire lies a fundamental belief about teaching and learning, a transmission view. But you cannot transmit to a receiver which is not tuned in. We would be foolish to pretend that we didn't have a 'message' about training, but the message is more about process and learning than teaching and product. Sometimes we must teach in the conventional sense, but only when the group is 'ready', and readiness comes, we believe, as a result of the process of developing thinking skills and processes during the training experience.

To sum up, we believe the theory/practice relationship is a fulcrum of a training course - there would be little point in doing a course unless practice was informed by 'theory' or new ideas. We want participants to become better practitioners, and that means being more 'principled', more thinking as well as better informed. Thus we would always seek to build theory with, not to deliver theory to participants. In practice, this means finding the best possible combination of theories 1, 2 and 3, and finding the right moment to bring them into play in the training process.

8.2.3 Knowledge in Training

> *'Attending to the training sessions and taking in the messages presented may be compared to a scattering of seeds: some will be working right away; some will stimulate processes in the unconscious; some will need to rest for a long time until the mind has reached a state suitable for their germination. Those seeds which have fallen on the right soil will grow into beautiful flowers and sturdy trees.*
>
> *At this stage the corresponding system is trying to create order and meaning from lots of messages' (Shu Wei)*

Training programmes for teacher and trainers have explicit learning goals - new skills, awareness and knowledge, as well as the potential transformation of existing knowledge, skills and levels of awareness. Training programmes may also explicitly desire to help participants develop ways of learning about learning itself. Shu Wei's diary entry points out the relative slowness with which trainees process new ideas, and also the IMPLICIT messages behind many training experiences. This section explores the nature of knowledge in training, in particular the 'knowledge bases' that training is attempting to influence.

Knowledge Bases: Expertise for Trainers

> *'I would like to mention that I have not only enjoyed the sessions, but also learnt about peoples' attitudes and behaviour. This has helped me to think about the reactions I will receive from my colleagues back home.' (Johana)*
>
> *'I have learnt and become more sensitive to my own role as a trainer to young trainees. I've confirmed my belief in the importance of:*
> *- psychology in training*
> *- counselling skills*
> *- practising what you preach' (Gertrude)*

Both Johana and Gertrude, in the comments above, acknowledge the importance of non-theoretical knowledge in training. When deciding on the content, shape and balance of a training programme, we are forced to consider the issue of what knowledge we wish our participants to gain. In part, this depends on factors such as their needs and wants, but also appeals to a stronger definition of what we believe to be relevant knowledge for trainers and teachers. We shall concentrate on trainers' knowledge in this section, but with an eye on what the knowledge base for a language teacher may also be, as it forms part of the knowledge of the trainer.

In a transmission view of training, the key knowledge base is the 'content' knowledge base. If one is a trainer of EFL teachers, this knowledge base will consist of

- knowledge about language
- knowledge about methodology at classroom level (procedural knowledge - Allwright 1981)
- knowledge about how people learn
- knowledge about wider political and social issues involved in language teaching

This knowledge may be broken down into even smaller units, such as , in language, phonology, grammar and so on. On a course, the different segments may conform to different 'specialisations', and therefore, different teaching personnel may be required the more specialised it becomes. Trainers must therefore 'know their stuff' (content knowledge base) and deliver it, typically through a diet of lectures and reading, to training participants who will then put it into practice. This will be a fairly familiar picture to many readers. (An early exposition can be found in Strevens (1974))

But let us also address the business of training *trainers*. Would the sort of knowledge base outlined above enable a person to train others to engage in training itself. We could say, yes - there is no need to address the issue. As long as you know your stuff, you don't need training. This is not an argument which would cut much ice in management training, or training for the caring professions such as counselling, social work or occupational therapy. There is a clearly recognised need in these and other aspects of professional work involving contact with people that there is a wider set of knowledge bases which training should make available.

Once one moves away from a transmission view of training, and opens up a range of new possibilities for interaction and engagement with knowledge, issues and questions, new areas of knowledge are required. We believe that appropriate knowledge bases for trainers include the following three linked knowledge bases:

- interpersonal skills and leadership skills (including supervision and feedback skills; conflict management and so on)
- group processes (including group formation, group dysfunction, and individuals' behaviour and response to working with others)
- knowledge of change and development processes from personal and professional perspectives

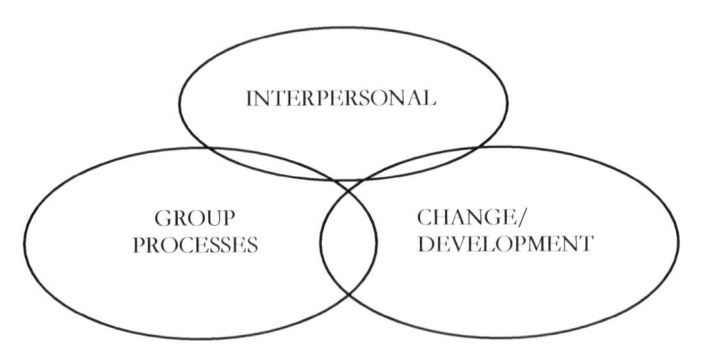

Figure. 8.1 : Knowledge bases for trainers

All three main knowledge bases require the development and potential for development of **skills**, such as
- effective listening (interpersonal)
- setting tasks and goals (interpersonal)
- developing participants' group organisational skills (group)
- helping individuals and groups adopt strategies for dealing with change (change/development)
- monitor and gather/interpret data from learning situations (change/development).

In addition, there is a strong underlying current of individual **awareness** for each knowledge base to be brought alive. In this lies the potential for development of the trainer in personal awareness of training style and its strengths and weaknesses, as organisers and managers, and one's own capacities and limitations as a change agent. This is a set of interlinked knowledge bases which provides a trainer with the knowledge, and associated skills and awareness to put them into practice in training situations, both formally on training courses, and more informally, on the job.

8.2.4 Professional Reading
We presented a series of activities to enable course participants to make the most of their professional reading in 8.1. In this section we shall discuss some of the issues which derive from the role of professional reading in training in assisting participants to create meaning and form principles, such as the timing and amount of reading.

READING OVERLOAD
It is the beginning of a taught postgraduate course for trainers. The course handbooks provide indicative reading lists. The tutors for the course carefully and rigorously explain the purpose of the reading lists, and advise moderation and focus in the initial stages, in order to avoid overload for the participants. the scene switches quickly to the library and a group of postgraduate students feverishly combing the shelves looking for titles on the indicative reading lists. In tutorial a few days later, participants complain of not being able to make sense of the reading. 'Too theoretical.' 'Nothing to do with my context.' 'Frightening amounts to read.' These are just some of the anguished comments of participants at this stage of the programme. Yijie's retrospective comments are instructive as they illustrate well the problem of a course participant in making sense of reading. Perhaps we could have helped more in tutorials or in training sessions? Perhaps she was reading before she was 'ready', hoping that the books would help her sort out her confusion?

> *'I enjoyed talking and listening to the other course mates. But I thought we couldn't create anything new; the points we made were so self-evident; there were countless books and articles to refer to which would be more thorough and deeper than what we did. I did do some reading but it seemed so remote from what we were doing and talking about. It seemed I could make sense of what was said in the books and articles, but the more I read the more I got confused: different writers, different opinions. Who is right? Who is to follow?'*
> *(Yijie)*

They have run into the phenomenon we have come to know as 'reading overload'. It happens for a variety of reasons - the desire among many to 'be ahead' of their peers on the programme; the desire to get into 'the study habit'; panic at the commencement of a major challenge; expectations - people traditionally 'read' for degrees. We have no direct answers to any of the puzzles posed by this phenomenon, except to say that, with careful and supportive tutorial guidance, above all listening to participants' problems, doubts and fears, we can wean participants off the overload. By targeting reading, by building up the reading load to match the complexity and depth of ideas being covered on a course from article or short section length, by giving reading tasks an instant pay-off in terms of training activity such as those in 8.1, we can move away from the problems we have outlined above. We can't stop the stampede for the library, but we can provide alternatives and support. After all, one of the trainer's key areas of expertise will be in knowing what participants need to read in the early stages of a training course.

DO and THINK FIRST - READ LATER

> *'The biggest change that happened at this stage ('making strangers into friends') is in my reading. I could understand my reading. I remember how those words which had been so strange to me had become friends. The messages were meaningful to me.' (Qiyan)*

Qiyan's comments are revealing - how reading begins to make sense. How concepts form and are mirrored in texts. Conventionally, reading and lectures complement each other on training courses. Reading is for either follow-up on a lecture, or in advance, to 'prepare' participants for what they will receive in the coming lecture. Sometimes this may be appropriate - if the participants are prepared in some way, by previous engagement of their experience and knowledge to 'prepare the ground'. We are most interested in what happens before 'the lecture' and the 'reading assignment'. Our experience of training programmes reminds us that the most appropriate time to read is often **after** activity and reflection in the training room. This is not to exclude 'mini-readings' (very short and carefully selected items which act as input to an activity); this strategy is all about using reading to deepen participants' conceptualisation of issues and procedures, to introduce relevant new ideas (in small doses), and to provide a more structured and robust framework for discussion in the abstract as well as based on concrete examples. We cannot remember how often participants have said to us 'I want to read now. Now I know what I want to read.' and 'It was great reading these articles - I constantly found myself saying "yes" as I went through them. It sort of reminded me of what I already knew.'

For us, these comments epitomise reactions to effective professional reading assignments. Reading which confirms, and assists in the conceptualisation process (we also find that participants' writing is affected positively by extensive and relevant reading - we examine this in Ch. 9.) is vital on training course. It also opens up participants to the wider world of professional debate and dialogue and the broader world of ideas. In an international context this is particularly important, as it seems to pay to be able to hear all the different professional voices, and to begin to discern differences in approach, philosophy and style. This is particularly acute in ELT, where it helps to know that North American writing on a range of training issues has a very different root from, say, British writing in the same fields.

GUIDANCE

It often helps to have guidance in reading tasks. It can also help if participants can use supportive frameworks in their reading. Here again, trainers can help by providing 'maps' and pointers. We are aware that we are in danger of imposing a reading strategy on participants - there are times, though, when this is necessary; when, in our judgement, there are certain texts and articles which are 'musts'. We will usually signal these in specially prepared, annotated reading lists, for example:

Suggested Follow-up Reading: Training Activities and Procedures

Baldwin, J. and H. Williams (1988) *Active Learning: A Trainer's Guide* Oxford: Blackwell
(excellent first hand personalised account of issues facing trainers in running training courses and sessions)

Bentley, T. (1994) *Facilitation* London: McGraw-Hill
(comprehensive account of the work of facilitators)

Boud, D., R.Keogh and D. Walker (eds) (1985) *Reflection: Turning Experience Into Action* London: Kogan-Page
(collection of articles on various aspects of 'reflection'. Not always easy to read but full of interesting insights and practical ideas)

Dennison, B. and R. Kirk (1989) *Do, Review, Learn, Apply* Oxford: Blackwell
(readable manual on using Kolb cycles in secondary teaching)

Jacques, D. (1991) *Learning in Groups* London: Kogan Page
(excellent 'standard' account of students' and tutors experiences of working in groups)

> Kolb, D.A. (1984) *Experiential Learning* Englewood Cliffs, NJ: Prentice-Hall
> (a classic in professional learning literature. Hugely influential in training circles. Not that easy to read.)
> McGill, I and L. Beaty (1993) *Action Learning* London:Kogan-Page
> (clearly written account of how experiential learning can take place on courses and in sessions)
> Schön, D.A. (1983) *The Reflective Practitioner: How Professionals Think in Action* London: Temple-Smith
> (very influential book on the nature of professional learning and action. NOT ELT!)
> Schön, D.A. (1987) *Educating the Reflective Practitioner* London: Jossey-Bass
> (Recounts the essence of 'The Reflective Practitioner' and provides case studies of various professional learning and coaching situations)

Another way in which we have successfully supported participants' reading is with a genealogical map or 'tree' of a particular aspect of knowledge or practice. The 'tree' of language teaching which appears below was originally devised to assist a group of experienced and well-read, but hitherto isolated Central European trainers in coming to grips with 'new' developments in ELT in Britain and the USA. It was designed to enable them to see where they might have gaps in knowledge and where they felt comfortable, and also to enable them to pose questions about the ELT ideas which were finding their way increasingly into their country in the post-1989 period.

A RICH DIET

Although our background is in ELT, we find ourselves increasingly drawn to fields outside our own in search of relevant training literature. A glance at our own suggestions for reading will make that much apparent. Working with trainers especially, and addressing the needs of the knowledge bases mentioned in 8.2.4, we like to cast our net wide. Participants also cast their nets widely once they see the possibilities, and many a time we have been recommended books and articles by course participants, reflecting their own interests and agendas, but also feeding from the pool of ideas that informs trainers in their practices.

And it is not only the professional literature that is of value to us. Novels, poetry, titles on spiritual questions and social issues can all contribute. The trainer does not only read about training, although this might be the mainstay of the diet. Training raises more fundamental issues about the human condition, about which the novelist and the sage may have at least as much to contribute as the fellow professional. This reading is, however, not prescribed. Its presence is made known - the trainer's job again - its use can liberate the individual from narrow thought processes, and help to create connections between apparently un-related areas of knowledge. These in themselves are reasons enough for reading. They can also help to locate individuals in the world of training. Books are tools for making sense of the emerging map of professional life and for identifying where the personal and professional overlap.

PROFESSIONAL BOOKSHELF

All trainers have a selection of books, articles and materials to which they refer when planning training sessions, or following up on issues raised in training. Part of the process of training should be to enable participants to select and add to their bookshelf titles which they find useful. Again, trainers can guide and suggest, but the ultimate test for the participant must be if the ideas or procedures suggested in a particular book 'speak to them'. Only by incorporating ideas from the professional literature in their own emerging conceptualisation of training practices will participants see their relevance and future potential. Thus we propose that if participants are required to submit written work for assessment on award-bearing courses, that the written work be first and foremost *practical*, but supported by evidence of appropriate professional reading. In this way, participants can see the relevance of particular titles in supporting their practical ideas. In this way, too, the links between theory and practice are sought out and reinforced.

THE TIME FACTOR

In our busy working lives we do not often have the privilege of time allocated for reading, and yet most teachers and trainers would single out reading as one of the most important ways in which they can equip themselves with new knowledge and to explore questions that concern them. Any programme of INSET activities must include reading for precisely these reasons. Reading has a calming effect if the material is easy to process; it can also excite and inspire. There is a certain degree of comfort to be drawn from finding writers with similar interests and dilemmas to our own, and of hearing voices with the same cadences as our own. Thus the choice and amount of reading for INSET participants are of critical importance - time is tight, so the reading must be relevant and have immediate or fairly immediate pay-offs in order for it to have an impact. It must also have a potential to expand horizons and connect with the professional's working and personal lives. We offer suggestions at the end of this chapter and in the section on 'Resources' for the type of reading which may be suitable.

Professional reading has a vital part to play in teacher and trainer development. It is an opportunity to be alone with ideas, to make connections, to find support, to open horizons, to excite, to inspire, to consolidate and to help gain ownership of ideas. For once a concept is understood and internalised, it is owned. Reading can help to capture and systematise what we have struggled to articulate orally. Reading is best undertaken when we are 'ready', particularly when the concepts are difficult to grasp. There can be little worse for the keen reader to find that what they are reading is nothing more than a stream of words with increasingly less meaning as it continues. On the other hand, there can be few more intellectually rewarding experiences than building up a picture of what people have said and done in a professional field, the sort of reading that goes on when a course participant is preparing to produce a 'dissertation' or similarly extended piece of writing.

Summary

In this Chapter, we have focused on some of the ways in which we attempted to help course participants create meaning from their training experiences. In many ways, the struggle to 'create meaning' and to articulate emerging personal theories is one of the most challenging phases of any training course. Yet it is an essential stage in professional development and one for which we, as trainers, have to take our share of responsibility. When overseas teachers return to their posts, or when our trainees take up their first teaching appointments, it is essential that they are equipped to argue their case from a principled position. A practical idea, however good, without a rationale to underpin it, is easy to shoot down.

References

Allwright, D. (1981) What do we want teaching materials for? ELT Journal,

Brown, R. (2000) Cultural continuity and ELT teacher training. ELT Journal, 54/3.

Brumfit, C. (1977) Correcting Written Work. Modern English Teacher, 10.

Eken, D. (1999) Through the eyes of the learner. ELT Journal, 53/4.

Handal, G. and P. Lauvas (1987) Promoting Reflective Teaching: Supervision in Action Milton Keynes: Open University Press

Holliday, A. (1994) The house of TESEP and the communicative approach: the special needs of state English language education. ELT Journal, 48/1

Lewis, M (1993) The Lexical Approach. Hove: LTP.

Leech, G. (2004) Meaning and the English Verb. Harlow: Longman. 3rd edition.

O'Neill, R. (1991) The plausible myth of learner-centredness: or the importance of doing ordinary things well. ELT Journal, 45/4.

Ramani, E. (1987) Theorizing from the classroom. ELT Journal, 41/1

Strevens, P. (1974) Some basic principles of teacher training. ELT Journal, 29/1.

CHAPTER 9
PLANNING FOR ACTION

As a course draws to an end, whatever its length, participants' thoughts inevitably turn towards their return to teaching or training. Our aim is always to try to pace our courses in such a way as to allow time and opportunity for participants to plan for this towards the end of their course by bringing together the ideas they have accumulated and putting them into some kind of organised framework for implementation on their return to work. The end of the course also signifies the move back from group support to the individual decision-making and action which characterises the careers of most of those involved in education. For these reasons, the tasks and activities which we set at this stage of our courses tend to be 'synthetic' in nature, requiring the integration of several strands of thinking and learning, and we present some examples here:

9.1 Activities for Linking and Action Planning

The activities we present in this section are all designed to assist participants in linking new or revised knowledge with real teaching and training situations. It is a step that is all too easy to omit from a training programme, and one that poses unique challenges.

9.1.1 Materials Design

Designing or adapting teaching or training materials for a known context, based on new design principles is a productive activity.

SAMPLE ACTIVITY
Option in Materials Writing
Materials writing: Guidelines for individual projects

Identify a specific training/teaching context in which you may need to develop materials, or revise existing materials. Formulate *a learning pack/sequence of materials/sample materials* which could be implemented in a training teaching context of your choice.

The materials should ideally be self-contained and sufficiently accessible for a colleague to use.

Your final submission should include:
- a brief statement of your context
- the rationale for your materials
- the materials themselves, divided into teachable units
- a commentary to the teacher/trainer who will use the materials, explaining the aims of each section, and intended outcomes.

TOTAL: 3,000 words or equivalent

> **Criteria for assessment**
> "clear information paths which help learners and the teacher/trainer to understand the relationship between the sources and the tasks" (M & P Ellis)
>
> - clarity of goals
> - relevance of the teaching/training materials to the proposed context of use
> - materials that clearly reflect goals
> - materials that are realistic and practical
> - clear identification of issues and concerns which would be relevant to the user of the materials
> - clarity of instructions and procedures

The writing of materials for teaching or training raises almost every issue of importance in professional practice at the level of approach, method and implementation. Decisions to be taken during the completion of a task like this include:
- whether to use an inductive or a deductive approach
- how to tailor the materials to meet the needs of learners or trainees
- whether to supply an answer key
- whether to write teacher's/trainer's notes, and if so, how close the guidance should be
- whether and how to trial the materials

In addition, the task will give practice in:
- exploring the topic of the materials thoroughly through reference books, background reading etc.
- producing the materials in a classroom-ready form
- producing the materials to an acceptable quality (in terms of layout, graphics etc)
- writing good, clear instructions and rubrics
- visualising the materials in use

An additional aspect of this type of task is to build in peer review of materials before the write-up. This is a useful substitute for piloting in real classrooms if access is difficult.

9.1.2 Course Design

We usually build in a course design project just before the end of our courses for trainers. Many trainers have to design, or assist in the design of, in-service courses or components of initial training courses at some point in their careers, and this is often a complex and multi-layered procedure calling for the ability to conceptualise and to manage resources as well as to function successfully in the training room. For a sample course design assignment, see Chapter 11.

Planning For Action

Typically, in this kind of assignment, participants work on areas such as these:
- matching course content to trainees' needs
- principles of course/syllabus design
- approaches to training
- deploying and managing staff and resources
- budgeting
- evaluation, validation, and assessment procedures

and they gain valuable practice in:
- preparing extensive documentation for courses
- timetabling
- teamwork
- working from concepts towards practice
- giving oral presentations
- giving and receiving feedback

9.1.3 Research and Action Research

Another very valuable way to provide trainees with opportunities to link a training course and their context is through classroom research or classroom action research. The experience of examining their own or others' educational experiences is also a potential trigger for fresh insights and new learning, with the advantage that any new or revised theory is developed from close investigation of practice, and that any insights are put into action. In effect, it is an activity which has the potential to 'pull things together'. Here is a typical sequence of research activities.

Activity 1   QUESTIONS ABOUT MY CLASSROOM
(Time required: approx 45 mins.)

1. Tell the training group that they are going to have the opportunity to address questions they have about their own teaching or teaching/learning situations. Starting question:
What would you change about your classroom if you could?
2. Participants have a few minutes to think of 2 or 3 things which they would change if they had the opportunity, and then discuss with a partner. Plenary feedback can follow, with main points written on the board.
3. Working with the points on the board, participants identify themes and issues which are either problematic or puzzling. From the themes, working in small groups, participants can now identify questions which intrigue them.
4. Participants write the questions, and then consider 'how' they might be investigated, and 'why' it would be useful to inquire.

Here is an extract from a summary of the responses of one training group to this task:

INVESTIGATORS' QUESTIONS
Below you will find a compilation of the questions you asked about your own classrooms. They are followed by a series of thinking questions to enable you to review the material. Each investigative question is followed by ideas on how and why to investigate it.

1. *Does participation in an activity mean learning is taking place?*
HOW: approaching learners - interviewing learners/filling in questionnaires
observing classrooms
learner's profiles
WHY: to find out about the personality of the learner
to find out which activities affect learning
to make our own teaching effective

2. *What can a teacher do about reducing mother tongue input (conversation) during group work activities?*
HOW: observe students during group work activities and the way the teacher monitors them
(use recorder if not too obtrusive)
WHY: aiming for as much free production of the target language as possible

3. *Why are some teachers not very good at timing? What kinds of things prevent a teacher from timing sessions well?*
HOW: Look at the lesson plan first and then observe the lesson
WHY: It is a problem which affects both very good and less competent teachers

4. *Is the lesson skill-focused?*
HOW: observe the class and listen to what is going on in the class
WHY: every lesson should aim to integrate the four skills

THINKING QUESTIONS
1. Which questions appear to you to be rather 'broad'? Why might this type of question be of less value to a teacher/investigator than a tightly focused question?
2. How many of the purposes behind the questions point towards 'Action Research' i.e. teachers investigating in order to deal with their own problems in their own classrooms? How many are 'pure' research questions, which don't imply action? How do you decide whether to act or not?
3. What are the links between teaching methodology and classroom investigation as revealed by these questions?

Planning For Action

> 4. Note any terminology - either methodological or investigation - that you are unfamiliar with. Check out meanings in key texts

---

Activity 2   PLANNING AN INVESTIGATION

Participants decide on a question to investigate, having first been through the thinking questions, and plan out the actual investigation either in their own classrooms (if in-service) or in classrooms/training rooms that are available (initial training). They then conduct the investigation over a period of time agreed with the course tutors, and agree a format for presenting the results their peers.

Here are the questions which emerged from a series of investigations, collected from the questions participants asked each other in the presentation phase of the work:

a. What are the problems resulting from interviewing teachers and students?
b. What is the value of recording classroom talk? What are the difficulties?
c. Would questionnaires have helped in any of your investigations?
d. What would you do differently next time?
e. Would your investigation be suitable for following up with action in the classroom?

RESEARCH ISSUES

For many participants on training courses, the very idea of doing 'research' might be anathema. 'We're only teachers' is an oft-repeated protest. In this section we discuss some of the issues that 'research' activity in training has raised. The three student reactions which follow are indicative of successful outcomes to this type of work on training courses, overcoming the barriers that are so common.

> *'it is very practical for the course to have provided the rationale for doing classroom investigations like baseline studies of the changes and innovations in courses at my University. It will certainly contribute to the development of courses as well as tutors.'* (Han Ping)
>
> *'Classroom studies is an area in which I have interest but have always feared to tread too deeply into it. Perhaps because I was scared that I might reveal my own ignorance of the subject. Through this course I think I have gained some confidence in my own worth. I believe I would be able to carry out some classroom studies/research when I get back to my institution, and speak more confidently about it.'* (Elizabeth)
>
> *'CLASSROOM INVESTIGATION: this subject contains all the working principles for professional development.'* (Agung)

On our programmes, either directly through the types of activity outlined above, or indirectly, through regular and focused reflection on the training process, we aim to encourage the stance of an 'inquiring teacher'. We prefer the term to 'action research' because of the pseudo-scientific connotations of the phrase, which has unfortunately been appropriated by authorities and bolted on to the superstructure of Research (with a big 'R'). We prefer to refer to the stance of inquiry because of its connotations with exploration, experience, discovery, unpacking ideas and experiences, because it integrates the cognitive, social and emotional.

Many of the training processes and their attendant issues and problems that we have described encourage active questioning, active processing and analysis of information - ranging from body language and gesture, to the language we use when asking questions. It is from this mass of information that we seek to derive principles to structure and order experience, so that training is not a guessing game, or an open-ended free for all. Without principles we cannot act responsibly.

It seems natural to run training programmes in cycles which invite participation from trainers and teachers, and which, as far as possible, invite inquiry into the process itself. With some groups, we have found that this is the agenda - to inquire into the process of training which they are currently taking part in. All the thinking skills, questioning, communication and interaction skills we have discussed are a part of this overall process. Ultimately, we are in the business of trying to help people learn new knowledge and skills, and develop corresponding awarenesses. What better venue for learning about learning than the process itself, the immediate experience? Action research can be both cyclical and act as a way of integrating components.

Increasingly, on training courses we run, there is an overt component on inquiry, with an emphasis on the following aspects of inquiry:

- observation and recording in educational settings
- asking questions (interviewing, questionnaires)
- analysis of information and drawing out of patterns
- drawing conclusions from analysis
- presenting of inquiry and findings (oral/written etc.)

The cycles of activity we describe follow very closely the overall cycle described in detail in Chapter 2. For inquiry purposes, it can be recast as follows:

Planning For Action

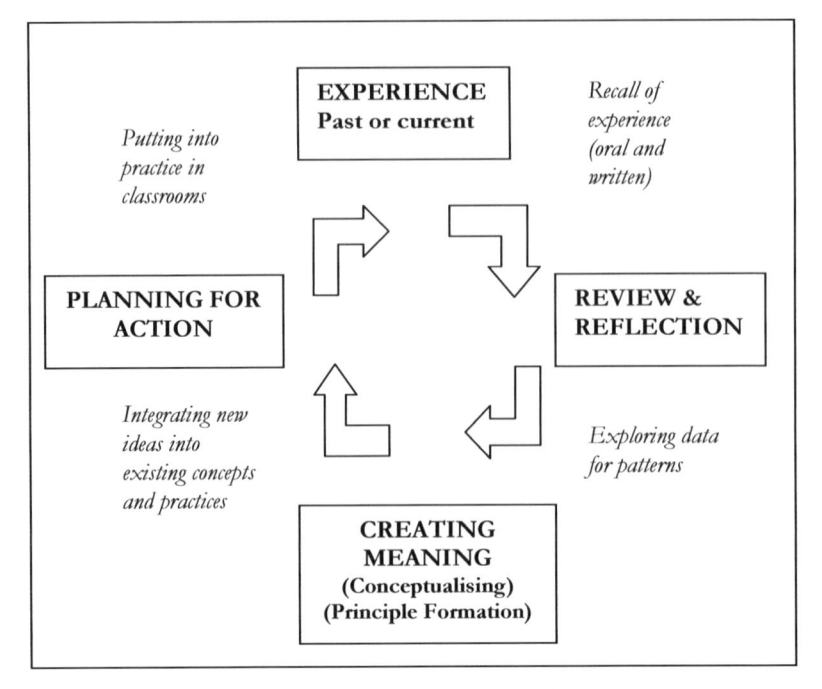

```
                    EXPERIENCE           Recall of
                    Past or current      experience
   Putting into                          (oral and
   practice in                           written)
   classrooms

   PLANNING FOR                          REVIEW &
   ACTION                                REFLECTION

   Integrating new                       Exploring data
   ideas into                            for patterns
   existing concepts
   and practices
                    CREATING
                    MEANING
                    (Conceptualising)
                    (Principle Formation)
```

Fig. 9.1 A cycle of activity for the inquiring teacher

In job-related INSET programmes, these processes are invaluable as tools for participants to use in future working contexts as well as tools with which to examine the training process itself, and teaching contexts. Major outcomes are

- better understanding of training and classroom processes
- enhanced awareness
- acquisition of specific skills

We deliberately focus on the interpersonal aspects of inquiry, as we find these complement other aspects of the training process well and are ways in which participants can practice and develop their skills in communicating with others.

> *'... there has never been an occasion in which I had to look at my practice in the classroom and try to understand what I was doing and why. Neither had I thought that my beliefs and practice have probably been sharpened by people at work or in the classroom as a student. Classroom Studies has provided this opportunity.' (Modesto)*

Far from seeing 'research' as distant, we see it as an integral part of the training process, providing input and enrichment to *all* participants, trainers included.

9.1.4 Personal Action Plans

Often, we hear of, or from, participants who return home after a course full of idealism and good intentions only to be confronted with resistance to their plans to "change the world". In such cases, the personal energy with which they have returned from the course can be dissipated all too quickly, and disillusionment can set in. For this reason, we see it as important, whenever possible, to help participants to plan realistically for their return. A typical activity will involve a certain amount of reflection and introspection, based on recent experience on the course as the basis for future action. Here is an activity we have found useful at different stages of a course, as well as at the 'linking' stage of the inquiry cycle, where participants consider ways of connecting new knowledge or skills to their practices:

ACTIVITY 3   Interpersonal Skills: Working in a Group

A(i) Make a few notes about your contribution to the training group

1. as a course participant in general terms.
2...... as a thinker about ELT and about education.
3...... socially.
4...... in any other way you'd care to mention.

(ii) Check your perception of yourself with a partner

B(i) As far as your work in the training group is concerned consider how you would like to develop during the weeks ahead in the areas listed below. Suggest for yourself a specific example for each area.

   One way in which I would like to develop ....

1...... in managing myself.
2...... in clarifying my personal goals and/or value system.
3...... in being an effective group member.
4...... in continuing my own personal and professional development.
5...... in managing my own time.
6...... in using class time more effectively.
7...... in my levels of openness and frankness with others.
8...... in my ways of thinking.

(ii) Share some of these ideas with a partner

C(i) Three things that I propose to do as a result of this activity.
1.
2.

Planning For Action

> **3.**
> **(ii)** Consider your three proposals and examine the implications and possible outcomes by using this diagram.
>
> | | **FOR YOU** | **FOR OTHERS** |
> |---|---|---|
> | **SACRIFICES** | | |
> | **PAY-OFFS** | | |
>
> **(iii)** Share your findings with a partner.
>
> [adapted from Gibbs and Habeshaw (1989)]

Activities such as these, involving discussion and clarification with tutors and peers, can help to ease the way back for participants, to prioritize their proposals, and to develop workable strategies for implementation.

9.1.5 Dissertations and Projects

On our award-bearing (degree) programmes, the writing of the dissertation often performs the valuable function of helping participants to build a 'bridge' back home. They are usually encouraged to tackle a topic which will be of practical value in their own contexts. This may involve tasks like designing a course, setting up a training scheme, writing a syllabus for an ESP programme or working on assessment criteria for language testing. Whichever they may choose, they will reach the stage where they have to consider the implementation of their ideas, and this is sure to engage them in thinking about their own role as innovators or as agents of change.

The writing of a dissertation is an individual (and sometimes lonely!) undertaking, no matter how much support is available through tutorials or informal exchanges with peers. Coming, as it does, at the end of a course, it helps participants to "leave" the group and to re-learn how to be responsible for their own actions. In Britten's (1988) terms, it is the last step in the move from group or peer-dependence to autonomy.

9.1.6 Futures Projection (What If... Activities)
Less instrumentally focussed, but nonetheless valuable, are activities which invite participants to construct a 'future scenario', in which they are implementing a new idea they have learnt on a course. This type of activity helps to integrate the activity more closely with practice, and also to explore its implications more deeply.

ACTIVITY 4   Planning for Innovation

1. Divide the training group into smaller working groups. Outline the activity and its purposes. Tell each group to choose one member's proposed course of action in the future, and to devise an implementation plan with a time-scale, including personnel involved, and potential risks and assumptions that the innovation is dependent on. One group member is therefore the 'insider' and the others consultants.

2. Groups have up to 2 hours in which to come up with a graphic representation of their work plan (on poster paper if necessary) of how they would implement their colleague's plan. This could be a literal representation of the plan in the form of a 'flow chart', or an advertisement which highlights the main features of the innovation for a selected target group.

3. Plans are exhibited and groups move around from poster to poster, depositing questions and comments next to the posters. Allow 20/30 mins. for this phase.

4. Groups gather up their questions and comments and sort them out. They can, for example, choose the 3 most useful in pushing their thinking forward, or for seeing the unforseen.

5. Plenary to share themes coming from the activity in terms of (a) the innovation process (b) the value of action planning.

9.2 Issues in Action Planning and Linking
We mentioned earlier in this chapter that this is an often neglected aspect of the training process. It is, perhaps, tempting to enjoy the buzz of activities or the intensity of reflection and exploration, or the ether of abstract thinking. This final phase in the training process is a very practical affair, and it may be tied up with feelings of loss or closure with groups departing. There may be a tendency to avoid these issues, quite unintentionally. And yet, for many participants, reconnecting with their professional world is of crucial importance. This section examines some of the issues related to this phase of the training process.

9.2.1 Coming Home: Reconnecting with the professional world after a course or other training event

Linking and action planning entail transition, and the activities we have outlined in 9.1 are ways of easing the transition for participants. Courses can sometimes lead participants to change before they have finished - they need time to reorientate themselves to their worlds before returning, worlds which will not have changed so significantly in their absence. One to one tutorials can help to ease the transition, and considered forethought can second-guess many problems facing the returnee. Sessions on managing personal change are appropriate at this juncture, although they may not be necessary for all participants. They are best left as voluntary.

We can easily forget the strains on a course participant whose worldview has been disturbed to the point that they are still in flux when the course is finishing. We cannot bring the process to a close, however. We can, if we have the opportunity, agree to stay in touch with group members after they have left, to act as a neutral ear for any problems they may be having back at home.

Action planning is essentially an individual matter. The individual is leaving the supportive atmosphere of the group and returning to what may be a lone existence once more. In order to ease the often painful transition, we try to phase in individual work together with group and paired activities, so that the individual has someone to give them feedback on plans and to listen to their doubts and problems. As we mentioned, the final piece of work on a course is often some sort of individual project - these projects are done better if there is support around from both tutors and peers.

The collaborative culture of the course is both a support and an obstacle to individuals who may have to work in highly individualistic institutional cultures on their return. Group exploration of these issues can be of immense value. Very often, the most important learning has concerned group processes. Maintaining the course culture can strengthen individuals' resolve to work more collaboratively on their return to work.

9.2.2 The importance of 'linking'

One indicator of a successful training course is that ideas gained on the course are transferred into action in participants' home classrooms or training courses. The question of transfer has been at the heart of much professional debate about training for many years. There is no guarantee that transfer will take place, that participants will change and develop, and adopt new principles, and put them into practice. This is why we see linking activities as so important, both as part of the overall cycle of training and learning, and as a prelude to action planning.

We have found that good linking activities share some or all of the following features:

- they involve producing something - materials, plans, courses - 'concrete'
- they require the activation of new principles encountered on the course
- they involve consideration of the participants' working contexts
- they draw on both received and personal knowledge, individual and collective
- they require both individual and collaborative action
- they are, to all intents and purposes, managed by the participants
- trainers play a supportive and low-key role

An example of a successful linking activity is to invite participants to analyse classroom teaching materials for a grammar point on which they have previously done their own language awareness exercises, and established pedagogic principles. Rather than just looking at language, the linking activity has the effect of bringing the worlds of abstraction and the classroom into creative contact. A sequel to this activity might involve a trainee preparing a lesson, using some of the materials analysed, supplemented by some original material devised to introduce students to new features of the grammar item.

Linking activities form the bridge between the world of thinking and the world of doing. Training experiences can begin with doing and move to thinking. Linking activity reverses the process. Participants should now have new knowledge, skills and awareness to activate if the course has done its work. Now it's time for action and experimentation. We need to support and nurture this process through linking and action planning.

9.2.3 Professional Writing As A Link To The Professional World

'What is never far from me, and will take much (more) effort on my part, is the written work that develops the sessions. I have never worked on essays and assignments that have such academic weighting and this is something I have to address.' (Rose)

'I cannot help but notice that everyone seems fully involved in doing the assignments. (...) It really motivates me as well as frightens me. This extreme external pressure in some way has pushed me into making a change. I started to realise how ineffective I had been in managing my time before.' (Agung)

'A very significant factor, that has cropped up after completing the assignments is the fact that things always seem much clearer after completion of the assignment than before or during.' (Zubaida and Shanti)

Three perspectives on writing on training courses: pressurising, developmental and consolidating or clarifying, all necessary parts of the learning process. On award-bearing courses, without doubt the most demanding activity for the great majority of participants is writing. It is difficult, demanding, and yet potentially very rewarding, in part because of the tacit links between thinking and writing, we alluded to in Chapter 8.

Professionals need to be able to write effectively for a range of purposes, and in a variety of forms. Education professionals, above all, seem to thrive on the writing habit. We notice that when things seem to be out of focus, or unclear in some way, that writing things down brings everything back into focus and may even help to locate responses to problems. Even the simplest and perhaps most basic form of writing - listing - is valuable. What, then, constitutes professional writing? What can we train course participants to write? What are effective ways we have found of offering support to this, possibly the most difficult aspect of professional life and training?

FORMAL WRITING

We see writing activities falling into two broad groups: professional writing of a more formal type, and the less formal, but no less relevant or important. On the formal front, core activities for trainers are

- writing proposals for programmes and courses,
- producing reports of courses, programmes and other professional activity
- adapting and writing training materials and other professional documentation with users' guides (e.g. observation and supervision guidelines; monitoring and evaluation instruments).

Over and above this core is the production of articles and reports for local newsletters, and ultimately, articles on professional issues for national or international audiences. We also include conference presentations and papers in this group of professional writing tasks. Training programmes can provide opportunities for participants to practice these forms of writing within the framework of the course itself, writing reports, evaluations and short articles and so on for audiences including peers and trainers. In this way, the process of professional writing, and the necessary work of 'tinkering', 'fine tuning' and developing that goes on can be encouraged. Practice in drafting and editing is important, as is the opportunity to articulate orally what one wishes to say before committing it to paper. Here, the learning group can be of great assistance, providing feedback and support to individual writers, and also providing the all-important feel for audience which guides all formal professional writing. Practice in 'team writing' is also a helpful way of encouraging talk about writing, and developing feedback and support skills.

WRITING AS A PERSONAL THINKING TOOL

Less formal writing, usually of a more personal nature, intended for a more limited audience, even no external audience at all, is also important in a number of ways. Writing diary entries, for example, no matter how cryptic and arcane, is a way of capturing one's thoughts and feelings. Just to be able to do this regularly is useful - the habit of recording and perhaps later referring back to material is generative and productive in the reflective process. Informal material of this type can also be the basis of more formal writing.

We need to escape form the belief that writing always needs to be polished, that it must strive to attain the finish of formal writing. But that is to misconstrue its purpose, Writing is an aid to thinking above all, and just as there are many types and processes involved in thinking, so too are there in writing. We also encourage our course participants to write reviews of their experiences as learners. Systematic writing, of an informal nature, not assessed in any way, has helped participants isolate development issues and problems in their training programmes, has provided important feedback to us as trainers, and has been another opportunity to keep up the writing habit.

We have drawn on this type of writing in the preparation of this book, using both our own and participants' writing as a starting point for many ideas. An example rubric for a 'process report' (or review) follows below.

ACTIVITY 5   Process Review

We hope you have been keeping some sort of diary or log of our work over the past 5/6 weeks. It is now time to start looking at certain areas of our coursework as you have experienced them in the first part of the course.

Please go back over your diary/log and note what for you have been the main features of this course so far. You might like to consider all or some of these:
- the training processes you have experienced
- the training styles you have experienced
- the learning process as you have experienced it

As well as our work in class sessions, note any features of the rest of the course - library, group life etc. - that have made a significant contribution to your work on the course so far. As a final point of reference, look back at the principles of professional development that we looked at in Week 1. How far have these been realised for you so far?

Write up your review(1/2 pages max.) and hand it in next week.

Some participants, unable to find time for a face-to-face tutorial, write us notes and letters. Again, these are good opportunities for capturing thoughts, being clear, specific and unambiguous. Perhaps it is this direct type of writing which is ultimately of most value to participants.

A further type of writing which we encourage is to invite members of a training group to write summaries of sessions, and add their own review and thinking questions. For trainers, this is a valuable skill development process in itself. Often their thinking questions can become the basis of group discussion, or the basis of a workshop on question writing.

WHAT OTHERS SAY
Incorporating the ideas of fellow professionals into our writing is never easy, an art form in itself, some might say. A simple rule we follow is to encourage participants to use what others say in the professional literature to *support* what they themselves want to say. We believe that what others say is of value to one's own writing only insofar as it develops, underpins or inspires our own ideas. Professional work is action-oriented. Writing is one form of action, and for it to be coherent with other forms of professional activity, it too needs principles and rationale. Writing itself is potentially the most efficient vehicle for articulating theory, and for connecting one's own ideas with those of others.

QUESTIONS OF STYLE
Writing things down tends to objectify them anyway, and we regard it as an obligation to make our experience as clear as we can for our readers, not to hide behind formal style. We encourage professional writing that is direct and as uncluttered as possible, regardless of the formality of the task itself. There is a hidden scale of personal and formal which seems to work in this way: the more formal the less personal, and vice versa. This should not, however, deter writers from owning opinions and beliefs. Directness of this type, whether in reports or proposals, is relatively constant. Knowing how to be guarded, in the right circumstances, is also an art. But guardedness should not mean convolution. Finally, being as *consistent* as possible is a further criterion for evaluating professional style.

Summary
Preparing for the end of a course, especially if it has been successful, is never easy, either for participants or for the trainers. We have to try to view it from the perspective of our course members and treat it as preparation for the next phase in their professional lives. For them, a course may be simply a milestone or a staging post, a chance to re-charge their batteries. At best, it may even be a turning point. Whatever its function, we realise that they will benefit if they can go back to work not only with renewed vigour and zeal, but with usable materials and plans, and a clear notion of what they might achieve. It is our duty to help them to reach that point. Action planning and linking activities can help to achieve this.

References
Britten, D. (1988) Three stages in teacher training. ELT Journal, 42/1.
Gibbs, G. and T. Habeshaw (1989) Preparing to Teach. Bristol: TES.

CHAPTER 10
FEEDBACK, ASSESSMENT and EVALUATION IN TRAINING

> *'Feedback contributes to my improvement. I work on all the feedback I get. It helps me remember and review issues I'm not sure of or which I lack understanding of.' (Maliki)*

This chapter focuses on the frequently problematical area of finding out if a training course is having an impact on participants' thinking and practices, and whether what is happening in a programme is worthwhile from the points of view of participants and trainers alike. We look at the complementary fields of assessment and evaluation in the context of the contribution of feedback to the training process, the spirit of which is captured by the extract from Maliki's diary which opens the chapter. We believe that the basis of a developmental assessment and evaluation system is the effective communication of intents, purposes, processes and outcomes. The basis of communication on a training course is the **feedback** which the participants give and receive on what they have done, are doing and intend to do. The quality of feedback can tell us a great deal about the nature of relationships between trainers and participants, and among participants themselves.

First we outline various activities we use to elicit feedback from participants, and means by which we provide feedback to participants. These include evaluation, assessment and feedback activities (there is considerable overlap, as we discuss in the second part of the chapter), both formal and informal. In the second part of the chapter we discuss issues which have challenged us in our experience as trainers, and share some of our emergent thinking about these issues.

10.1 Activities and Procedures for Giving Feedback
In this section we divide activities into those which we use DURING a course or training programme, and those which we use at the END or after a training programme has finished.

10.1.1 During a Course: Formative Feedback
PERIODIC FEEDBACK
On longer programmes (more than 2 weeks in duration), we undertake periodic reviews of components or key parts of a programme. The use of a learning log (or 'process diary') is a key

means of doing this. The opportunity to review a programme at regular intervals not only allows participants to put things into perspective, it also contributes to their learning and provides opportunities for review and reflection.

We also elicit feedback from participants, informally and formally. The informal post-session chat is a way of keeping channels open, for example. When channels close up, as they have for us from time to time, difficulties emerge. Suspicion is usually the first visitor in such circumstances. We are reminded that open communication is the secret of successful assessment systems, and that this is grounded in good two-way feedback. It is a trainer's responsibility in the first instance to keep the channels open, and to show participants that what they say counts. Participants won't necessarily take on any responsibility for giving feedback unless they see that it is worthwhile.

Here are some extracts taken from a collection of feedback comments to us after 4 weeks of a course:

- *Sometimes there are too many tasks at one time.*
- *How much attention is paid to individuals' experiences on this course?*
- *Within a very short time we have come up with a lot of things but not in a very clear order.*
- *At least the tutors should have given us their point of view.*

This sort of feedback is very valuable for us as trainers and helps us to regulate our contributions in a number of ways: for example, the volume or pace of work. We have also on occasion created compilations of participants' comments for group discussion, with the permission of the participants. The discussions have been a valuable means of unblocking communication channels and removing obstacles to learning. They are also a valuable starting point for reviewing and reflecting on the learning process.

WRITTEN ASSIGNMENTS

'Writing assignments is difficult for me. However through reading and reflecting on what we've learnt my thoughts have become more consolidated and I have also felt more confident about what I want to say.' (Jing-Yu)

On award-bearing courses, written assignments are inevitably a part of the training landscape. In Chapter 9 we discussed the value of writing as a 'linking' activity and showed that we believe professional rather than 'academic' assignments are both productive and relevant for trainees. These assignments

- develop specific professional skills

- encourage explicit statement of principles and reference to relevant professional literature
- have concrete and usable products - particularly important when the assignment is undertaken as part of an in-service, on-the-job programme, as realistic evaluation of products can be built into the process of the assignment
- build on work already undertaken on the programme

On training courses, assignments should have professional face validity. Often, however, we find ourselves having to 'sell' this type of work to sponsors and participants on award-bearing courses, who are expecting 'academic essays'. It is our responsibility to introduce them to the novel format, and to help them come to terms with it. Quite often participants are overcome by the detailed specification of tasks and products, having previously been used to the 'discuss a proposition' type of written assignments. Properly conceived, assignments on training programmes can help to develop professional writing skills (a long-term benefit in a profession that needs to express itself coherently), as well as providing evidence of progress. We see them as opportunities for training in writing and in the presentation of ideas and proposals.

We also see it as important for trainers in training to work out their own criteria for good professional writing, both for self-evaluation purposes and as a basis for evaluating their own course participants' work in future.

COURSE COMPONENTS

On trainers' courses, we include components which explicitly address issues of assessment and evaluation of training, including discussion of modes such as unseen examinations, and coursework/continuous assessment. In this work, participants can be encouraged to talk about their own constructs regarding the feedback process through appropriately chosen activities. A typical activity would invite participants to 'mark' student work.

Trainers in training also need to develop an appreciation of assignment types which can be used on programmes they are responsible for. The development of criteria for choice and appropriacy is thus a vital part of this aspect of the training.

FORMATIVE FEEDBACK

We are committed to giving feedback on assignments (written or otherwise) which is formative, and contributes to the development of a participant's skills, knowledge and awareness. In Appendix III we have put a typical page of comments which we might write about a participant's work.

We tend to give a lot of feedback on written work, on content above all, but also on issues of content, presentation (layout etc.), and use of language. In addition, we like to point out where a writer has put a point well, used a source well and so on. We might also suggest further sources to go to, how to tidy up presentation, improve layout (especially important in training or teaching materials). Where we do detect a problem, we tend to ask a question rather than make a bald statement of the problem to try to move the writer forward by addressing the question and coming to their own solution, rather than directly criticise, which may have the effect of 'blocking' learning.

After all, we are concerned with improvement. Writing is a developmental process, in the same way that training and learning are, and a professional's skills are developed through a process of planning, drafting and development (although not necessarily in that order), aided by supportive feedback from peers and tutors. With longer pieces of written work like projects and 'dissertations', we use formative feedback to help participants work from draft to final versions, and as the basis for discussion in tutorials. There is a great deal of pleasure to be gained from watching a longer piece of writing develop and grow. The tutor's role is to help shape it. The tool is feedback, written and spoken.

COLLABORATIVE WORK

Formative feedback invites dialogue, both internal and with trainers and peers. We actively encourage participants to share their work at the drafting and development stages, and to practise offering feedback and suggestions to each other if they are solicited. Most trainers need to develop 'tutorial' skills as part of their professional repertoire, and we take it as axiomatic that 'sheltered' practice in course sessions can help to develop confidence in this key area. We provide guidance in group sessions in which agendas and ground rules may be set, and we also deliberately foster this process through, for example, peer training sessions where we ask participants to work closely as teams and provide each other with support and feedback.

Formative feedback encourages reflection, and deeper thinking. It demands time and commitment, but the time spent engaged in the process can be of more long-term value than many other training activities. It also helps develop writing, itself a definitive aid to thinking. Interpersonal engagement encourages honesty and openness, and because it is peer-to-peer, and sometimes even outside the training sessions, can be conducted in a secure environment. In Chapter 11 there are examples of how the formative feedback process works in practice through our discussion of a course component on a course for trainers.

10.1.2 At the End of a Course
The last days or sessions of any course are busy for tutors and participants alike. Participants often have heavy extra-curricular agendas, including packing, shopping, returning library books, saying their farewells, and so on. We are often tied up with returning assignments, tidying up resources, dealing with paperwork and (all too often!) planning for the next course. Such an atmosphere is often not conducive to cool and objective evaluation. For one thing, time is at a premium, and for another, everyone is still in some way emotionally entangled in the 'web' of course. Many will not really know what the course means to them until long after it is over, and they have had time to digest all the 'lessons' they have learned and to try out their ideas in practice. For this reason, we usually ask participants on our longer courses to complete and return a course evaluation questionnaire six months after they have gone back. It gives us more useful balanced feedback then we could ever get through reviewing the course formally on the final day, which would not tell us anything we had not already found out through all the ongoing feedback procedures we employ during the course. (An example questionnaire appears in Appendix III)

However, in an educational culture which seems, increasingly, to demand evaluation of everything that moves, with back-up statistics if possible, we do have to evaluate many of our courses on the final day, while we have our participants as a 'captive audience'. We use a number of procedures to do this:

NEGOTIATED EVALUATION
In this procedure we reach agreement with a group on the questions and criteria against which the course should be evaluated. This may be achieved by a pyramid discussion or through talk with the whole group. Then, either the group or we draft a questionnaire for everyone to complete and hand in. This is very valuable on a short intensive course and is a way in which course content can be covered practically and with real relevance.

The obvious advantage of this procedure is that participants have a stake in deciding the basis for evaluating their own course. Negotiated evaluation also reminds us of participants' perspectives on a course: they don't always see it as we do, nor do they always accord priority to the same issues as we do. Their questions are often directed towards group issues, or contain a strong self-evaluative element, as the examples below show:

Example 1
How do you rate the experience of working in this group?

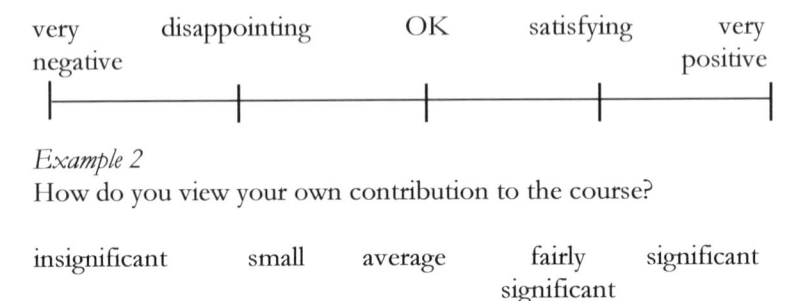

very negative	disappointing	OK	satisfying	very positive
⊢	⊢	⊢	⊢	⊣

Example 2
How do you view your own contribution to the course?

insignificant	small	average	fairly significant	significant
⊢	⊢	⊢	⊢	⊣

STANDARD QUESTIONNAIRES
When time is very short, we make use of one of a number of standard end-of-course evaluation instruments, like the example in Appendix III. Questionnaires like this one are designed to fulfil the requirements to evaluate and to gather data as quickly and efficiently as possible. One drawback is that participants often view them as nothing more than a necessary formality, and they devote correspondingly little time and attention to completing them. Nevertheless, we do use the qualitative comments, when participants take the trouble to write something, to help us review our courses.

GROUP-LED EVALUATION
This procedure involves inviting the group to manage its own evaluation process with or without the tutors' presence. The group, in discussion, agrees on key points to refer to the tutors, perhaps in the form of advice for future courses, and feeds them back either orally or in writing.

This kind of evaluation tends to be qualitative in nature and has the drawback that the data which emerges is difficult to quantify and record. However, like negotiated evaluation, it gives participants the opportunity to set their own evaluation agenda, and there is always much for tutors to learn from this type of feedback.

'EXTERNAL' EVALUATION

This procedure is supplementary to other methods on award-bearing courses, and it involves a session with an external examiner, at the end of the course, during which issues arising from the course are raised and recorded for inclusion in the examiner's report. This kind of procedure is formal and yet valuable as long as the external examiner is prepared to play the 'honest broker' role in an even-handed way. We find it useful as a more objective and 'distanced' mode of evaluation on courses in which we often establish a very close relationship with our students. The procedure can be open to abuse when, as occasionally happens, an individual participant uses the opportunity to pursue a grievance over grades.

Bringing in a colleague who has not worked with a group to conduct an evaluation is a valuable means of evaluating a course when something is going wrong. Handled supportively, this can help the Course Tutor to get things in perspective and back on track during a course after listening to participants through the objective mediation of a third party. A similar strategy undertaken at the end of a course can also be extremely valuable and provide useful feedback for future planning and teaching.

Whenever formal evaluation takes place, however, we always try to ensure that we are not taken by surprise at any of the findings. As we tutor a course we like to keep a finger on the pulse through informal feedback sessions on a day-to-day basis, and we encourage our participants to talk to us about anything that might be worrying them.

SELF-EVALUATION

It is also important for participants to take a self-evaluative stance at the end of a course. A questionnaire based on Gibbs & Habeshaw (1989:217) can be a useful means of doing this. Usually, such questionnaires are for the private consumption of participants and, however curious we might be about the degree of self-awareness which they display, we never ask to see them.

Another form of self-evaluation which we use at the end of a course is the 'Letter to Myself', described here:

Letter to Myself
Write a letter to yourself, reflecting on the course and what you have learned from it and mentioning the plans you have made for professional action after the course. Seal it in a self-addressed envelope and exchange letters with a fellow-participant. Agree to

> post the letters to each other on a fixed date exactly six months from now.

Participants report that this is an excellent way of 'bringing the course back' when they are caught up in their daily routines at home, and reminding them of some of the things they wish to do by the way of an action plan, or which are important to them. This kind of self-directed writing or inner dialogue is similar to diary writing, but this has an added dimension of self-appraisal. It is also a very valuable experience for tutors to participate in as part of their own self-development. Receiving a letter six months on is a helpful reminder to pause for breath and take stock.

GROUP DISBANDING

The disbanding of a group can be a difficult and emotional moment for all concerned. Too often, groups split up in an unplanned way, leaving a feeling of emptiness and incompleteness behind. For this reason, we often make use of 'closing' activities which help the group to disband in a way which acknowledges the feelings and responses of each individual group member.

A particular favourite of ours is the *round*. Here is one we use for closing a session or sequence of activity.

ACTIVITY   A Round for Closing

Participants (including the tutors) stand or sit in a circle, close to each other, with no spaces between people. They are invited to take a few moments, in silent contemplation, to think of anything they'd like to say *to the group* before it breaks up. Contributions should be short (10-15 seconds) starting with a volunteer, each participant, including the tutors, says his/her piece out loud, taking turns clockwise
or anticlockwise round the circle. Anyone not wishing to contribute may simply say "Pass". Nothing is recorded or written down. When the last participant has contributed, the tutor may thank the group and it is ready to disband.

We find that this activity brings a lot of warmth to a session. Comments are sometimes surprising, but rarely unpleasant. Participants are usually fascinated to hear what their peers have made of the social experience of working and learning together in a group. Those who choose to pass may do so because they have nothing further to contribute, or because they are feeling emotional.

We also use rounds for many other purposes during the life of a group, and we find that they have a number of benefits:

- every single group member has a right to contribute and time is shared equally (in this sense they are intensely democratic)
- the configuration (a closed circle) allows everyone to see and hear everyone else, and it emphasises the 'wholeness' of the group
- there is no obligation to disclose anything which participants would prefer to keep to themselves
- tutors become indistinguishable from other group members, both in terms of their physical position and of the right to contribute
- a 'round' can be assembled, run through and concluded relatively quickly, even with a large group.

Occasionally, we have participants who dislike 'rounds', feeling them to be manipulative or too stressful, but we have always found that the benefits outweigh the drawbacks.

There are many other activities we have found useful as means of evaluating and/or closing a course 'Suitcases', for example, (see Chapter 3) and other data from agenda-setting activities can be 'exhumed' and used as a starting point for evaluation. A good example is to 'pack up' a suitcase at the end of the course with what's been learned, what's been memorable, what questions remain, other 'gains' from the course. A 'waste bin' can also be created for participants to deposit what they thought was of little use to them on the programme. Sometimes we have to 'roll' closure and evaluation into a single activity (Rounds can also be used for this purpose). The biggest problem we face, particularly on intensive courses when there is so much to cram into such a short time, is ensuring that there is adequate time for this kind of activity. Without it, a course is not really complete.

10.2 Feedback Issues in Process-Oriented Training

'If the assignment is the only way of assessment, then the usual way of lecturing on histories, theories, structures, prescriptive and fashionable knowledge, combined with more reading on one's own of relevant literature, should be more efficient and helpful than the present classroom processing which should be (at least to me) much more valuable, practical and motivating. Is it ever possible to solve the paradox?' (Ou Yang)

10.2.1 Questions

In this section we address fundamental questions about assessment and evaluation on any educational programme within the context of the types of training experience we discuss in other parts of the book:

- **WHY?** What are the aims and goals of assessment and evaluation on a training programme? What is their origin?
- **WHAT?** What exactly are we assessing and evaluating in a training programme?
- **WHEN?** When is it appropriate to apply assessment and evaluation procedures on a training programme?
- **WHO?** Who does the assessment and evaluation? For whom?
- **HOW?** What are appropriate procedures for assessment and evaluation on a training programme?

These are questions which may well be ones which you wrestle with as trainers, either on pre-service or in-service programmes. At different times, different questions will be more important than others. Many issues are raised by each of the questions, notably issues associated with assignments on courses, formative and summative assessment and evaluation, internal and external standards, self- and peer-evaluation, group and individual assessment and giving and receiving feedback. Rather than answer the questions in a linear fashion, we shall focus on these and some of the other issues which seem to be of most relevance, and allow the responses to the questions to emerge from the discussion. We shall summarise these at the end of the section for readers who might want to jump over the discussion, and also as a way of tying up our points.

WE ALL NEED FEEDBACK

We begin with the optimistic notion that all course and programme participants want to gain something from their efforts in contributing to the programme: they want feedback. Certification is the most overt and concrete recognition of these efforts and of the standards that have been attained on a course. But even on non-award-bearing training programmes participants want to be able to feel that they have progressed as a result of their attendance at a course or developed on a longer-term programme of training. This need raises two issues:

- how to find ways of enabling participants to demonstrate to themselves, their peers and trainers that they have progressed;
- how trainers, peers and individuals give feedback - how responses to training tasks and activities are offered and processed.

Since much of what is learnt on training courses concerns skills and processes rather than pure content, how the participants themselves give feedback, respond to assessment tasks and evaluate outcomes are key issues; they are an integral part of the experience of being trained and need to be addressed openly through the process of the course itself. This notion of **openness** in assessment and evaluation is a crucial element in the collaborative and participatory goals we set ourselves in the process of professional learning. We feel strongly that one important indicator of quality in training is the extent to which the assessment and evaluation systems are transparent and open. These themes underpin the discussion which follows.

STANDARDS AND CRITERIA

Award-bearing training courses (Postgraduate, Undergraduate, Certificate and Diploma) always feature a system of assessment. Participants must be seen to merit their qualification by passing, at the required standard, a series of assignments within the regulations of the programme. Much depends on who sets the standards, and by what criteria they are 'measured' or judged, and the modes of work adopted - whether written (the most common), oral or in practice (common for teaching and training qualifications). What is clear to us as tutors is that we are responsible for feedback whether or not the standards have been attained. So, who needs feedback?

PARTICIPANTS AND FEEDBACK

First and foremost, participants need and demand feedback, especially on award-bearing courses. We all need goals and targets to aim for, and training courses should both set standards and enable participants to set their own standards. Challenge is central to development, and is also a powerful motivator. A key issue here is the source of the goal and the challenge - is it set by the participant, or is it set by someone else? Is the standard set *internally* - by course participants - or is it subject to external reference points?

From time to time, we encounter participants who seem only to be motivated by the reward of a certificate. They are happy to submit to external criteria and standards, as long as they fulfil them. They may ignore or reject internally mediated standards, perhaps because they demand self-evaluation and a degree of honest introspection that may scare them. The problems begin, however, when they don't meet the external standards. Suddenly the criteria for success become important, and there can be requests for explicit statements of criteria. We have encountered 'bargaining', even threats. These are unfortunate occurrences, and although they are thankfully rare, they do merit some urgent reflection on our part. We need to create a system of assessment and evaluation which minimises the chance of such occurrences; below. We offer some tentative solutions to this thorny problem in Section 10., as we endeavour to move away from normative procedures, and search for modes of assessment which connect integrally with the processes of training.

A second indicator of quality on a training course is the extent to which participants are able to develop and articulate their internal criteria for success and progress, and the extent to which these criteria develop out of the programme itself, as part of the process. Any training programme which involves extensive periods of group interaction, self-directed tasks, practical tasks, and an acknowledgement that development is not necessarily linear and constant, needs a feedback system which enables everyone to assess their position at any stage on a programme. While many programmes require standard assessment tasks and attainment, the longer-lasting messages are those gained from direct personal experience of assessment and evaluation processes. Regardless of external criteria, people invariably pass judgement on what they or others do on the basis of their internal criteria. The development of these criteria in the training process is a major, and oft-neglected goal.

OUTSIDERS' EVALUATION AND FEEDBACK
We are also very aware that stakeholders from outside the training room want evidence of progress and quality. Sponsors, partner institutions and other interested parties want to know whether their investment is turning out to be worthwhile. They deserve and need feedback and we, in turn, need their feedback.

Feedback on training programmes is a means of communicating among the interested parties about all aspects of a programme. Feedback doesn't set standards or criteria - it provides **information** about the nature of the standards, the value of the criteria, and the quality of participants' **experience** on the programme. In running training courses, we are particularly interested in how we might give feedback, and in the types of task or product which we feel are appropriate for participants to give feedback on in training courses for education professionals. It is to these issues that we now turn.

GRADING

The requirement to award grades for course assignments is a perennial source of difficulty for us. Giving feedback, written and oral, presents us with far fewer problems than assigning a grade. Grades have an air of finality, of a world of secrecy, of decisions taken behind closed doors, of a significance far beyond the simplicity of the letter or number, of a power to judge. They are immensely symbolic, surrounded by mystery, apparently definitive, and yet open to debate and interpretation in different contexts. They are understood and interpreted differently by participants from different backgrounds and cultures. A 'C' may be seen as satisfactory in one context or educational culture, and as a relative failure in another. Grading thus poses immense emotional pressures on all parties.

We deal with these pressures and the associated difficulties in several ways. These are not definitive responses to the problems. We have been wrong as often as right in this area of our courses.

1. Open discussion with participants of the meaning of grades in the context of qualifications, and within the context of professional development. Participants can find grades quite helpful if they know about the criteria and background which informs them. They are markers of progress, and, accompanied by useful feedback, can assist in the setting of new targets or revising goals.
2. Use of a grading system to match the development of a course. On our Masters programmes, for example, we see the standard of work and thinking required increasing as a course unfolds, so that the appropriate standard at the beginning is somewhat lower than at the end of the programme. Courses are supposed to help people develop and progress, in other words to *reach* an agreed standard. Certainly, some participants are already close to or at the required *exit* standard when they enter the course, particularly in terms of their ability to think and write, and their advanced knowledge and skills can be appropriately rewarded, as can excellence in any given assignment, with judicious use of the grading system.

We see this working rather like this:

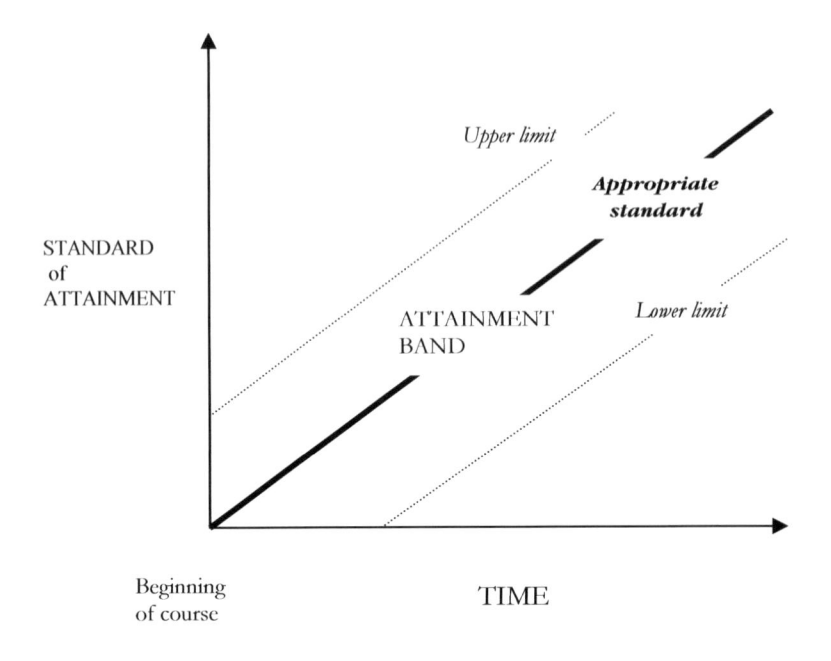

Figure 10.1 'Progressive' assessment in training programmes

As the course progresses, there is a gradual increase in the general levels of attainment expected. The appropriate standard thus increases. Participants perform within the upper and lower limits of attainment throughout.

3. Involvement of participants in self-assessment. Surprisingly, this is less popular with participants than we might reasonably expect. We have tried the following procedure:

When participants hand in an assignment, they accompany it with a signed, sealed envelope containing the grade they think the work merits. When the work has been assessed, the tutor puts their grade into an envelope. The envelopes are opened in tutorial, and the outcomes discussed.

For some participants, the system worked very well. However, in cases where the participant's grade was higher than that given by the tutor, there was sometimes dispute and even unpleasantness. But the contrary also happened: participants are actually more likely to be hard on themselves and underestimate their performance, and here we felt able to boost their self-esteem. In such cases, grading can have very positive effects.

We eventually abandoned the system (perhaps we should try again) but we did learn along the way that participants need a great deal of guidance and training in self-assessment. Self-assessment is new territory for the vast majority of course participants - it is part of a participant-centred regime, and cannot simply be thrust upon them overnight. They need the security of what they are used to at the outset - a trainer's assessment of their work. If this is accompanied by appropriate and useful feedback, it can prove to be a liberating experience, the first step towards autonomy and reliable self-assessment.

We have also invited participants to self-assess oral presentations and 'micro-training'. With these, they are more at ease, perhaps because the criteria have been collaboratively worked out and agreed in advance. Somehow, and this is to some extent a mystery, it is less threatening to self-assess a 'performance'. Written work carries with it such powerful overtones of academia, and all of us have a 'history' of our previous educational experiences. The work of trainers must be to lay some of the ghosts of this experience, and to move towards a more professionally enhancing system of assessment, which has an element of participation within it, and which can be seen to be contributing to development. Stephen Rowland's (1993) 'Inquiring Tutor' has been a valuable source for us in grappling with these issues.

SUMMATIVE FEEDBACK

Our assessment of assignment work on award-bearing coursers usually involves giving individual participants both formative and summative feedback. Summative feedback during a course consists of a series of way-stages in the development of a participant. Its main purpose is to offer participants a justification of the grade they have been given. Over the course as a whole, it provides an indication of progress to participants who, with this as guidance, can 'locate' themselves in professional terms. It may enable them to say, for example, 'I can write training materials, and trainers' notes which could be used, with modification'; 'I can participate actively in the design and delivery of a training course', and so on. In one-to-one sessions with tutors, participants can be encouraged to make these statements on the basis of achievement in various parts of a course. If the participant has also set personal goals, these can also be related to tutors' summative comments.

However, summative assessment is ultimately no more or less than a convention of award bearing programmes, and the comments are only valid for limited periods. People change and develop in unpredictable ways; the messages in a course component may take years to digest, and it may only be 5 years after a programme that *real* summative feedback can be given, usually by the participant to us.

A way of inviting participants into the process is to encourage explicit discussion of criteria for success in written assignments both at the outset of a programme, accompanied by clear statements of what assignments entail, and during the programme, at the time when each assignment is set. This is in addition to explicit statements about how written work is handled by the tutors during their assessment processes.

GROUP AND INDIVIDUAL ASSESSMENT

Under normal circumstances, assessment focuses on the individual. After all, it is the individual who completes the programme successfully, who learns, and who develops. We acknowledge this, but we also believe that there is value in identifying an element of the course which can be collectively assessed. Typically, this may be a shared presentation of a piece of material, or a course design. We mentioned in Chapter 5 that there are great benefits in working with others, particularly when giving and receiving feedback. Group collaboration on certain types of assignment can also have advantages.

- It can lead to the growth of teamwork and professional responsibility. The tradition of isolated academics and teachers working on problems is fading as the importance of teamwork in training and teaching is growing. The approach also ties in well with the group mode that is established in the 'reflecting' and 'meaning-making' stages of the training cycle (as discussed in Chapter 2). Seen this way, the course is a group experience which prepares participants for individual action. Many of the problems we face, and many of the tasks we have to accomplish professionally are simply too big for individuals to attempt alone. By building teamwork into training programmes, novel though it may be for some participants, and by linking it to assessment, we are, in effect, giving it an official 'stamp of approval'. This can lead to difficulties in a group, as not all will necessarily be committed to collective effort or able to handle the pressures of working with peers. For this reason, we need

to introduce the practice slowly and to build up to the collectively assessed assignment, as well as to provide ample opportunities to discuss the procedures involved and the principles behind them.
- Collaborative products are usually richer and deeper than those produced by an individual. Thus individuals have the opportunity to contribute to the learning of others and to learn from their peers.
- Self-evaluation can be carried out within a supportive team context and is therefore likely to be more realistic than individual evaluation. Teachers and trainers are notoriously hard on themselves, quite possibly a legacy of years of destructive assessment.
- We build in a review task to each collaborative assignment. The task invites the group, either collectively, or individually, to reflect upon the group process, to evaluate its effectiveness and contribution to their own thinking and development.

An example review task appears in Appendix III.

The group share the grade we award (if the work is graded), and know that the grade depends on their effectiveness as a team, on their coherence of thought and action, on their ability to communicate with each other, and on how realistically they assess their own work on the assignment. We also build in the opportunity for participants to reflect on the task itself and the experience of working as a team.

TYPES OF ASSIGNMENT

On award-bearing programmes, written assignments are the typical means by which participants are assessed. We have outlined how important we consider the writing process to be from the point of view of professional development, and have examined some of the ways in which we deal with written assignments on training courses. Here we shall look at different types of 'assignment' on training courses, and discuss their role in the development of participants' professional competence.

Trainers and teachers need to be able to perform a number of professional tasks, including some or all of the following:
- working with participant groups as a teacher or trainer
- writing programmes and materials
- articulating and presenting ideas orally or in writing
- giving and receiving feedback
- assessing performance (self and others)

- participating in the evaluation of programmes
- working individually or in a team on professional tasks of various kinds
- continuing their own development

For us there should be a clear link between these professional tasks and the types of task that are included in training programmes for the purposes of facilitating and, ultimately, assessing professional learning. This can be done either formally, as part of an assessment scheme or informally, as part of the natural process of the course. Related in-course tasks and assignments may include:

- giving oral presentations, with full use of visual support (OHP, video where appropriate, posters, etc),
- taking an active part in evaluations of work in progress,
- working in teams and reporting orally on this,
- carrying out investigations of teaching and training contexts and reporting on these orally and in writing, in different formats.

It is natural for experienced training course participants to want to 'hold the floor' whenever they can. Being on someone else's course is likely to inhibit them and even to frustrate them. So we provide as many opportunities as we can for participants to lead sessions, and to present the results of discussions, reading, investigations and project work. Provided that the opportunity for self- and group-assessment and evaluation of both process and product are an integral part of these procedures, we see them as usefully developmental. Training tasks should simulate or replicate the full range of professional activities in which participants require competence and confidence. This means setting up new criteria for assessment and finding appropriate ways of assessing what participants do.

SUMMARY

We have covered some of the issues related to the touchy subjects of assessment, evaluation and feedback in training. We are the first to admit that we have not solved to our own satisfaction the conundrum of matching a commitment to participant centredness with the need to work with externally imposed assessment criteria on award-bearing courses. However, we believe that sensitive feedback is the key to ensuring that participants maintain a developmental perspective even when they are immediately preoccupied with basic issues of passing and failing.

References
Gibbs, G. and T. Habeshaw (1989) Preparing To Teach. Bristol: TES.
Rowland, S. (1993) The Inquiring Tutor. London: Falmer.

CHAPTER 11
INSIDE A TRAINING COURSE 2
Methodology and Materials in Teacher Training
A Course for Trainers

This chapter describes the experience of teaching and learning on one of three 'professional' components of a Masters course we run for teacher trainers. Participants on this particular course come from a wide variety of contexts and backgrounds internationally, with a wide range of experience as trainers in initial and in-service programmes. Methodology and Materials aims to build trainers' knowledge, skills and awareness of all aspects of working with teacher training groups. We also make it a priority to focus on the **process** of the course as the training group experiences it. We regard this as a vital aspect a programme for trainers who are involved themselves in complex educational processes in their normal working environments. The course thus provides an opportunity to gain experience in reflecting on process aspects of courses for trainers and teachers that we have discussed in earlier chapters. The account we present illustrates many of the processes outlined in Chapters 3 – 10. It also adds to the repertoire of training activities which we have outlined in the book so far.

The Training Experience
The account follows the main stages of the course and describes selected events at each stage, highlighting aspects of both content and process of these training events. Tony ran the course described in the account with a group of 12 participants from 8 countries. The account consists of Tony's report on his experience of running the course (in italic), extracts from participants' evaluations and diaries, and a commentary and discussion of the rationale for different elements of the training process.

COURSE PLAN
I planned for the programme to go through 5 stages, as follows:
Stage 1: *Agenda-setting and awareness raising on training methodologies and materials (3 weeks)*
Stage 2: *Micro-training 1 (2 weeks)*
Stage 3: *Processing of Micro-training 1 and in-depth study of issues arising (2 weeks)*
Stage 4: *Micro-training 2 (2 weeks)*

Stage 5: *Processing of Micro-training 2, written assignment and follow-up (1 week)*

Commentary
The account that follows is structured around these main stages. Even on a process-oriented course, participants need to know what the main stages of will be, and Tony communicated these to participants in the first session. It is also essential that tutors know what direction a course will take. It doesn't need to be written down in detail, particularly as there are likely to be changes as a course proceeds, but an outline is very helpful for all concerned.

11.1 STAGE 1 - Openings: agenda-setting and awareness-raising

We report the first eight hours of this course, with a focus on how Tony attempted to start the course by working from participants' previous knowledge and experience. This was intended to raise awareness of key issues in the content and process of training, as well as to help participants begin to assess their own training skills, knowledge and awareness.

The main aims of this first stage were thus to:

1. Enable participants to address the issue of 'training methodology' and to demystify it sufficiently to enable participants to 'tame' it, as Maliki put it in his diary, reproduced below.

   > *'Methodology was an alien word to me, It only belonged to the elite educator. I was so worried about this that I asked my consultant to send me to a short training course in this area prior to the course. In the first term this horrendous term was introduced and frequently discussed, and it became a bit tame to me.' (Maliki)*

2. Discuss various issues involved in running training sessions to raise awareness prior to the sequence of micro-training activity which formed the central part of the course.

In an earlier part of the Masters programme, participants had already gained some experience in presenting new ideas to their colleagues in a peer training setting. Although the focus was on the *content* of these presentations, all participants had given considerable thought as to how they would run the sessions during which they introduced their colleagues to new ideas in selected ELT topic areas. From these sessions, we derived some 'messages' for trainers, as follows, which we agreed to take

Inside A Training Course 2

forward into the Professional component of the programme. Some examples follow:
- *How tightly framed do 'thinking questions' for trainees need to be?*
- *How to achieve smooth transitions between activities?*
- *How explicit to make the rationale for each activity?*
- *How much 'signposting' does there need to be in training sessions?*
- *How to bring trainee discussion to a halt?*

SESSION 1: Agenda Setting (2 hours)
I began Week 1 with a brief introduction to the structure of the programme, as outlined above, and then continued the 2-hour session with an exploratory discussion session which was based on the list of questions and issues which appear in Activity 1 on page:
At this stage in the course, I wanted the group to focus on central issues which had arisen from the sessions in the previous term, and also to begin to open up the agenda of training methodology, and the role of training materials. Participants were invited to look at the question list and do these activities. Participants were also invited to complete a grid after each of these initial activities, as a means of reviewing various types of training activity.

ACTIVITY 1
Questions and Issues in Teacher Training Methodology
1. Individually, look through each of the questions which follows and identify the main issue in each question from a trainer's perspective.
2. Add any further questions of your own.
3. Identify your 5 main questions
4. Then share your findings in a group of 3, ready to report back to the group in plenary.
- *How do we learn to teach?*
- *How for does our knowledge of teaching and learning contribute to our ideas about training?*
- *What training methodologies do you think are of most assistance to trainers?*
- *In what ways can training materials contribute to the process of learning to teach?*
- *What are a trainer's roles in training sessions?*
- *What kinds of relationship can be forged in training between the classroom and training?*
- *How can we relate practice and theory in training?*
- *What sorts of skill do you think training requires?*

- *What sorts of knowledge does a trainer need to conduct training sessions?*

Review

Complete the grid provided (below) to assist you in thinking about different types of training activity. Store this record for reference later in the course.

Name of Activity	Training Purpose of Activity	Feelings during and after the activity	Trainer role in the activity	Other Comments

Commentary

This type of opening activity sequence firstly enables the participants to have some individual thinking time with the questions. As they look through the questions individuals, they encounter some of the terminology of training methodology in questions which they find themselves responding. In our experience, individuals also find it helpful to include any of their own questions, both to provide them with the opportunity to include their own concerns for consideration in the programme, and also to 'test the water' of the group's current thinking, and find out if the group is 'on their wavelength'. By identifying the 5 main questions from the list, individuals were forced to prioritise their concerns. Subsequent sharing of responses in small groups enabled each participant to articulate in a relatively safe environment some of their thoughts about training before airing them in the larger forum of the plenary. The group discussion is an opportunity for participants to mobilise their 'training vocabulary' and to work towards the long process of agreeing terms for describing and analysing training experiences. This work we believe should begin in the early stages of any training course, as it gradually creates the basis for group discussion of key training issues. It further enables the training teams for the micro-training part of the programme to start their collaboration with a shared agenda. All the training activities in Stage 1 were recorded on the grid as a source of review and thinking about different types of training activity at the end of the stage.

After the group discussion, I chose to focus the plenary with the question **'As trainers, what do we need to know, be able to do and be aware of in training sessions?'** *The discussion which* *followed was referred back to this question if I felt that it was 'drifting' off the point. Following intensive discussion in groups, the following extra questions were added to the list on the handout:*

- What are the 'messages' that are transmitted by methodologies?
- Is training trainers different from training teachers?
- Is it necessary for the trainer to be familiar with the materials a trainee is going to use in the classroom?
- Does the trainer need to practice what the trainees teach?
- Does the trainer only teach methodology?
- How to help trainees become fully aware of their teaching principles?

The group decided that the question on 'learning to teach' was the most fundamental, and that the others were all important in their influence on trainers' choice of training methodology in training sessions. The group also agreed that 'methods' (or 'techniques') were a part of the more general category of 'methodology'.

I closed the session with a summary of issues which focused on the knowledge - of various aspects of both teaching and training - skills of training and awareness of trainers, drawing particularly from the question on 'messages' in training. The question of 'levels' was raised, and we spent some time examining different 'levels' in the training room - of classroom, of training room, and the level at which the group was working the trainer training setting.

Finally I gave the participants the self-study questionnaire 'Developing as a Trainer', reproduced in Appendix IV, aimed at helping them further refine their own agendas for investigating teacher training processes. Responses to the questionnaire were to be taken up in Session 3 later in the week.

Commentary

A plenary session can take many forms, depending on how closely it follows the questions or issues it is based on. In this case, Tony decided to use a focus question for the discussion, so that participants addressed any remarks they had with reference to the question. This makes for a more 'open' airing of views and allows for the unexpected to happen. The fact that participants may not be responding to a particular question may deflate any expectations of 'a right answer', at the same time encouraging participants with non-standard or unusual views to make contributions. This particular group was well able to cope with the uncertainty in this format.

The post-discussion summary is a singularly difficult trainer activity. If the trainer listens too hard to what is being said, the essence of what is said may be lost. Conversely, being too attentive and responsive to the point of being interventionist may prevent the trainer from hearing enough. Summaries are, then, inevitably partial, but nonetheless important for bringing a sense of closure, as well as providing an opportunity for making some points of principle, or linking discussion to theoretical material and reading.

SESSION 2 Good Training Activities (2 hours)

Session 2 was designed to enable participants to place the issues raised in the first session in the training room context by considering what they thought were the qualities of 'good' training activities. This was to help participants to further explore their own and each others' thinking on training issues, for example preferred ways of working in the training room, in the context of a focused, collaborative task. In this session, I divided participants into groups and set the task to complete within one hour, in order to leave time for some reflection and feedback at the end of the session. I monitored the work of the groups, added comments and ideas as the work progressed, and listened to what the groups were saying to build up a mental picture of their concerns both in terms of the group process triggered by the activity, and the task itself.

The task appears below.

ACTIVITY 2   What Makes a 'Good' Training Session?
Aims:
1. To establish individually and as a group the main characteristics of 'good' training sessions.
2. To experience working collaboratively.
3. To raise issues relating to training methodology to be followed up during the Term.

Task
1. Form a group of 3 or 4.
2. Brainstorm the characteristics of **'good' training sessions**.

Stage 1: Generate a list of characteristics. At this stage, anything goes. Don't challenge anything. You might want to write the characteristics on slips of paper before you announce them to your colleagues. Try to exhaust every possibility.
Stage 2: Now go through your list and look for overlaps, need for clarification of ideas and so on. Aim to refine your list. Eliminate what the group thinks are 'wild ideas'.

> Stage 3: Assemble your definitive, and agreed, list as a recipe for a 'training session stew'.
> 3. Put your 'stew' onto an A3 poster, for display and discussion. Be as 'visual' and creative as you can with your posters.
> 4. Presentation and discussion of posters:
> - look for similarities, themes etc.
> - clarify terms
> - give feedback and comments
>
> *What messages about training sessions have been generated by this activity?*
>
> **Reflection (complete your grid)**
> 1. Reflect on the experience of working in a brainstorming group - what are your feelings? What have you learned about groups and group work in training?
> 2. What have you learned about training sessions and participants' views of training sessions from your participation in this session (and your current reflection on the session)?
> 3. What would you like to follow up on and learn more about as a result of this activity? What intrigues you?

The finished products ('training activity stews') were displayed on the training room wall, and I invited the participants to circulate in their working groups to examine each others' posters, and note similarities and differences. (An example of a 'stew' produced by a training group appears in Appendix II.)

As they examined the posters on the walls, I then asked the group to frame questions and issues about training activities which came to mind as a result of the activity and each others' posters. The outcome of the post-'walkabout' discussion was recorded by a group member as a set of issues emerging from the activity. The note-taker also spontaneously added three thinking questions as she wished to practice formulating them.

I ended the session with a question asking the group to focus on what they individually thought a trainer brought to training sessions. This was in preparation for the next session which aimed to identify some of the group's perceptions of good training.

Commentary

Walkabout activities following group discussion are a valuable way of varying the ways in which a group responds to an activity and its products (if any). It gives the participants time to examine closely what others have done and also to formulate their own responses to the products. It also gives a group a chance to stretch its legs and move into a less formal mode of activity.

Inside A Training Course 2

Issues and Questions on Good Training Activities
1. The common theme of good interpersonal relationships
2. Do we always need 'material' in a training session?
3. 'Well-facilitated' = well-managed activities
4. Sharing perceptions is connected with feedback, and is an outcome of the 'cooking'.
5. Input comes from different sources, in different shapes and sizes.
6. Refreshment in training: food/drink or reviewing.
7. The trainer should not be too 'persuasive'. 'Telling' might contradict the other trainer messages unless signalled. How far should trainers impose their ideas on trainees?
8. Significant change is time-consuming.
9. Explicit methodology: aims to get the principle behind what we do and why we do it as trainers. In training it is useful to tell trainees what you are doing in terms of principles; in teaching, by way of contrast, it is perhaps rather an unnecessary procedure. But how explicit to be?
10. <u>Thinking Questions</u>
Can we think of a training session in terms of content and process?
Does input = content or process?
Are we going for depth or breadth in training?

The aim of inviting the group to raise the issues after the activity was to see first of all what they had derived from the activity itself. It was also to see how far their thinking about training had shifted since the first session. The rather general issues raised by the first session were now becoming more specific. For example, the group were homing in on issues such as the role and nature of 'input', away from the relatively global difference between teaching and training, and they were certainly becoming more focused on the training agenda, from a trainer's perspective. This is evidence to us that thinking does develop and become more refined, but that we need to provide participants time and opportunities to articulate concepts in different ways, to gain confidence as well as beginning to internalise them. Opportunities for talk, structured and unstructured, based on activities and their outcomes, are valuable means of nurturing this process.

SESSION 3 What do trainers do? (4 hours)
This session was intended first of all to build on the previous session and also to enable the participants to examine their own training styles and approaches in a non-threatening way. A spin-off was to help them begin to build a personal agenda for development in the coming micro-training sessions. Activity centred on the following worksheet:

199

ACTIVITY 3   Trainer Contributions To Training
AIMS:
1. To examine the qualities and attributes of the 'ideal' trainer
2. To consider the trainer's contribution to teacher training sessions
3. To examine your personal perceptions of trainer roles and contributions and to assist you in identifying particular areas for your own development.

TASKS
1. Do the 'Developing As A Trainer' sequence.
2. List the qualities and attributes that you believe a trainer should bring to a TT course in order to make a strong contribution to the experience for the participants. (You may wish to distinguish between initial training and INSET for the purposes of this task, but it is not essential.)
Followed by 9-card diamond activity (based on Easen 1985), and reflection.
3. In the light of your insights from 1 and 2 above, and your current perceptions as to trainers' roles and purposes, particularly in view of your initial perceptions as regards training activities and sessions ('stew') what do you think constitutes TRAINER INPUT? What is the relative value of trainer input to a programme, when compared with other types of input (reading, school visits, for example). **You may wish to discuss the notion of input before you do this activity.**

SELF-DEVELOPMENT ACTIVITIES
1. List areas in which you would like to develop as a trainer. Note potential benefits and risks involved. Identify ways in which you think the course tutors and course mates could assist you in your work on these areas.
2. Identify areas of trainers' roles and work which you think you could focus on during the micro-training sessions. Identify ways in which you think course mates and tutors could assist you.
3. 'Grid' every training activity you participate in and try in particular to identify purposes of activities (trainers' working principles or reasons for using a particular activity) and training sequences, as well as your personal response to each activity.

Step 1
I asked the participants to record their responses to the 'Developing As A Trainer' questionnaire in pairs, and noted their responses to the final part for reference later.

Step 2
Individually, the group members then listed the qualities and attributes they believed a trainer should bring to teacher training courses.

They then went into the '9-card Diamond' activity in groups of three. First they 'declared' their lists of qualities by reading each one out in turn and placing it on the table they were sitting around. They clarified any items which needed clarification and then arranged them in categories, agreed by the group. Finally, they arranged the 9 most important qualities agreed by the group from all members' contributions (the 9-card diamond). The group's four poster contributions 'GOOD TRAINING IS...' were as follows:

A short plenary session resulted in a further set of thinking and discussion questions which helped to deepen the first set we generated in Session 2. Discussion in the plenary focused on issues generated by the 9-card diamond posters, and question 3 on the handout, which was augmented by the following question:

Can we think of training sessions in terms of CONTENT and PROCESS or THEORY and PRACTICE?

THE POSTERS
Here is one of the posters produced. *(1 – most; 5 – least important)*

```
                    1. the conviction
                       that teaching
                       is a worthwhile
                       profession

         2. sensitivity and intuition          2. building on and from
                                                  trainer's and trainees'
                                                  experience

3. opportunities for     3. setting up an effective     3. understanding
   reflection               planning, delivery &           trainees'
                            evaluation cycle               well enough to
                                                           pitch input at the
                                                           right level

         4. good presentation              4. balance of theory
            and feedback stage                and practice

                    5. relevant take-away
                       materials
```

In plenary discussion, with reference to the 4 'Good training is ..' posters, we noted that there are three broad areas of interest to trainers:

WHAT (the topic or content)
HOW (the training activities and processes)
and
'FACTOR X' ('making the training sessions work as shared experiences for learning'). The group speculated that 'Factor X' might be an interpersonal dimension shared by trainers, the nature of which might be particular to adult learning.

I took this set of material away at the end of the session and wrote it up for the group with a set of focus questions and responses to guide them through the first phase of the micro-training. These were to be taken up, either directly or indirectly, at the end of the first stage of the micro-training. The second part of the handout appears on page 189. It is presented in full because it illustrates an important trainer task at junctures like the one the group had reached, in which they were beginning to conceptualise the training process. The trainer's task at these points is to act as a 'scribe' and recorder and to present material generated in discussion back to the group as a resource for further discussion and refinement. The thinking questions are designed for further review and reflection on the part of the group.

I also set the group a reading task, based on a set of articles on training methodology, which was to be to be discussed in Stage 3 of the course, between the two micro-training sessions. The task, similar to ones we describe in Chapter 9 is reproduced in Appendix IV.

Commentary

The 9-card diamond is, we find, a very good way of 'pushing' a group to make choices and to prioritise them. A forced choice of this sort seems to bring out what is significant for a group at the time it is responded to. Sometimes, we take the initiative and extend the notes made during a discussion in order to invite further thinking and conceptualisation of issues as Tony did on this occasion. It is also a way of making a contribution that can be considered in the participant's own time – this type of thinking demands time. Very often a group is tired after an intensive and discussion-rich session like the one based on the 9-card diamond, and they are not ready for any 'input' at the end of a session. The notes and the follow-up reading take the place of a trainer's summary.

Inside A Training Course 2

*SOME QUESTIONS AND THOUGHTS FOR TRAINERS
A possible set of questions and related issues for a trainer could relate to CONTENT (what?), METHODOLOGY (how?) and PEOPLE (who?). The main questions and the responses they elicited in our session are reproduced below

WHAT?

> "I need to know my stuff in order to feel confident with my training group. I need a good knowledge base in my subject area."

> "I need efficient ways of finding out about my subject, of storing the information and retrieving it when I need it. I suppose I can't know everything (none of us can) but I do need to know where to find what

HOW?

> "I need a range of effective techniques and procedures for introducing my trainees to new ideas and evaluating existing ones."

> "I need to be able to choose an appropriate activity for a specific purpose:
> e.g. When is it appropriate to give a talk/lecture?
> When is it appropriate to do a brainstorm?"

WHO?

> "I need to be able to relate to my trainees as individuals and as a group, and to help them to benefit from this experience."

> "I need to be aware of my own influence in training sessions, as a person, as a contributor and as a trainer."

Thinking Questions
What are your reactions to these questions and issues? Would you add any for yourself? Which are of the greatest relevance to you - personally and professionally - at this stage in the course?

The next set of sessions on training materials and their features drew on and extended the issues raised in the first 3 sessions, and provided further preparation for the first cycle of micro-training. A participant commented as follows after the initial sessions on the 'theoretical' aspects of training introduced and discussed:

> '... in Methodology and Materials sessions, we were provided basic issues that help us think and contemplate further. This course encompasses other disciplines such as Psychology, Management and more if we want to split hairs.' (Endalkachew)

11.2 STAGE 2: Micro-training - Cycle 1

We have outlined our approach to micro-training in Chapter 3 and this case study will provide a specific and in-depth account of the process. We have found that careful preparation and briefing of participants before this activity helps to settle nerves and dispel some of the inevitable apprehension participants feel before they 'train' their peers.

I made the following arrangements were made for the micro-training sessions.

- *The group divided into 6 working pairs of trainers who were responsible for planning and delivering a 1-hour training session together. Teamwork was preferred (a) because it enabled us to economise with time, but more importantly (b) to give each participant the opportunity to work closely with another professional with whom to share ideas on the training session and the inevitable ups and downs of the process. Training teams chose their own topic and were at liberty to create a context - pre or in-service. The rest of the group, including tutors, acted as the training group. We also agreed ground-rules for the sessions.*

- *Each team also acted as leaders of the post-session discussion for another training team, deciding, with my assistance, what the agenda for the discussion would be. This pair also acted as partners for giving feedback in private, after the session. I made myself available for the feedback sessions if the participants felt they needed an extra perspective. In practice this sometimes proved unnecessary.*

- *All the phases of the training were to be written up by the teams and 'banked' with me for future reference and feedback. (Participants were encouraged to develop their materials as the basis of a written assignment to be completed after the course component had finished.) The full specification for the assignment appears in Appendix IV.*

Over the next two weeks, the group experienced 6 training sessions, which, including the post-training discussions, each lasted 2 hours.

We have selected one team's training session in order to illustrate what can happen in a micro-training session.

Micro-Training Session Outline
The presenting team took the group, including myself, through a training sequence on 'Vocabulary Development Activities' with an audience of Secondary school in-service teachers in mind. The sequence of activities we experienced was, in the words of the presenters:

- Learning experience (Ways of remembering words - aim to draw from participants the implication of how vocabulary is learned or remembered and hence how vocabulary can be taught. This activity aimed 'to link the participants' own experience of learning vocabulary and what they actually do in their own language classroom.)
- Focus on previous teaching experience and basic techniques of vocabulary teaching. (Techniques of vocabulary teaching - aim to enable participants to look back at their past experience in teaching English vocabulary and share their experience with a partner. The activity is a brief summary of the main techniques of vocabulary teaching. It is also used as a shift from the discussion about teaching methods to model teaching.')
- Model teaching and reflection on the main principles of each task (Vocabulary development tasks - aim to give some examples to show how to explore interesting ways to teach, consolidate and check new words. After each task there is a short discussion about the trainees' feelings towards the task and the purposes of the task.)
- Brief summary of main points by the trainers.

In the post session discussion, three points were central to the group's discussion.
1. Pace and timing of the session. Several participants had felt 'rushed' during the session, and felt that they had had little time for reflection after the activities.
2. Sequence of activities. There was much discussion on whether or not exploration of previous teaching experience should come before new ideas for teaching. Some participants wondered why it was necessary to raise awareness among participants of their own vocabulary learning techniques.
3. Explicitness of the instructions for each activity and the perceived need among some participants for TRAINING level rationale for the activities during the session.

Inside A Training Course 2

The training team, in their written-up notes on the session, commented
'On the whole we were able to carry out what we had planned satisfactorily. It would have been better if we had given more time to trainees for their reflection on each task and discussion.'

I gave the training team the following written feedback, following a face-to-face session requested by the presenters. The feedback represents a summary of the face-to-face feedback discussion.

Micro-Training: Feedback
Many thanks for leading an active and well-conceived session. We appreciated the opportunity to experience a number of different vocabulary learning activities and enjoyed a 'different focus': learning instead of teaching. You worked well as a team and created an open and business-like atmosphere.

I liked:
- *your focus on developing learner skills, and your use of well-prepared teaching materials*
- *the way you used the 'principles' list as a focus and as a point of reference*
- *the patient and skilled way in which you dealt with M's and S's questions. You avoided derailment and yet met their needs and the group's needs*
- *a nice <u>range</u> of activities*
- *smooth transitions between the pair of you as you presented*
- *useful mini-summary at the end and links to potential follow-up session*
- *the interesting and novel sequence of materials working from teaching to learning*

Some points for you to think about and work on
1. Do you think it is helpful to be very explicit about the aims and content of a training session from the very outset? How might you introduce the session alternatively?
2. How much 'talking time' and feedback time do participants need after an activity?
3. Are there ways in which a presenter could resist the temptation to 'give the answer' after eliciting answers from the group?
4. In a discussion, is it better to sit or stand? What is the effect of each?
5. Have you further thoughts on
- *drawing principles out of activities*
- *the role and nature of input*
- *pacing of sessions*
- *giving instructions for activities*

Thanks once again - please come back to me with anything you'd like to discuss.

Inside A Training Course 2

The 'support team' also ran a feedback session and gave the presenters the following feedback:

> *Thank you for presenting us a very useful session. Your session opened up some important training issues:*
> - *it was well-presented, with a good start*
> - *you made effective use of visuals (OHP, board)*
> - *we appreciate your selection of materials*
> - *we hope the trainees benefited a lot from the vocabulary teaching techniques you used during the session*
> - *we cannot but appreciate your idea of involving us in reflecting on the activities*
> - *you managed to handle the trainees' questions well*
>
> *Some issues to consider*
> - *Pacing the Session – do you think you could have varied the pacing of the activities?*
> - *During the session we felt that we did not have enough time to reflect on the activities*
> - *We thought that you might have reduced the number of activities*
> - *Instructions*
> - *Could you have given clearer guidelines about timing for each activity?*

I also gave the following written feedback to the 'support team' who had led the discussion, following a brief face-to-face meeting:

> *Thanks for leading the group in the post-session discussion. As a participant I must admit to feeling that I was speaking too much - I know it's probably difficult to keep me quiet! Perhaps next time you need to work on your framing of questions and eliciting procedures in order to get discussion going in the group. Perhaps you adopted too low a profile? You are entitled to assert yourselves as chairs.*

All presenters experienced the same set of procedures during the micro-training sequence, as summarised in the flow chart on page 208.

The sense of unease that I had had at the beginning of the cycle of micro-training started to dissipate as the sessions unfolded. I noticed an increasing openness and frankness in the discussions following sessions, and a growing assurance among the presenters. A participant commented:

> As a result of the experience undergone during the micro-training sessions, I think my colleagues and I have grown closer in understanding of each other's practices, beliefs, values and attitudes. I could feel this esprit de corps building right from the beginning of the term ...(Elizabeth)

At the end of the sequence of sessions, the group moved to a review and consolidation stage.

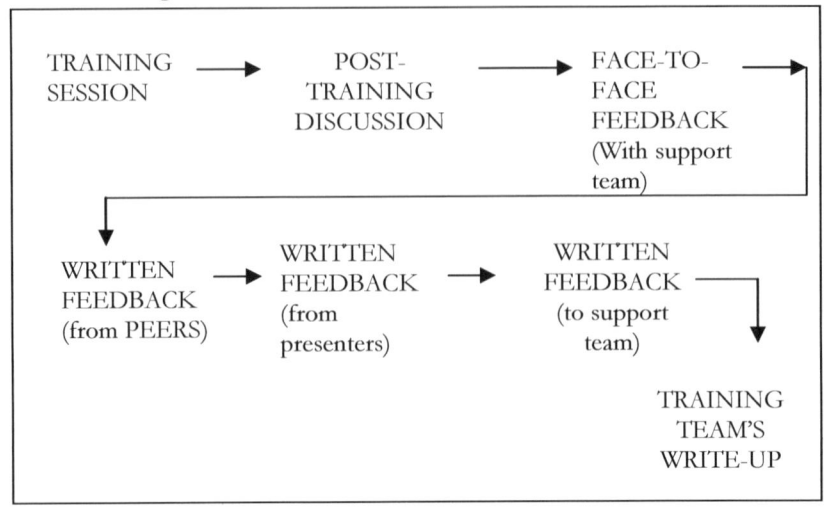

```
TRAINING  ──▶  POST-           ──▶  FACE-TO-        ──▶
SESSION        TRAINING             FACE
   │           DISCUSSION           FEEDBACK
   │                                (With support
   │                                team)
   ▼
WRITTEN   ──▶  WRITTEN         ──▶  WRITTEN
FEEDBACK       FEEDBACK             FEEDBACK        ──┐
(from PEERS)   (from                (to support       │
               presenters)          team)             │
                                                      ▼
                                             TRAINING
                                             TEAM'S
                                             WRITE-UP
```

Commentary

In activities such as 'micro-teaching' and 'micro-training', we prefer to participate as members of the training group during the session itself. We find that providing the training team with feedback from the perspective of a trainee is less threatening than observer feedback. We can actually ask questions and say things that observers are unable to – participation provides a perspective which persuades the trainer to consider their work from the point of view of a trainee. This, we feel, is ultimately what the effectiveness of training might most productively be judged against. It also seems to be less threatening to the individual to receive feedback from a participant than someone perceived to be superior and therefore potentially passing judgement. This process appears to have the effect of making the trainer see themselves from a different perspective and to encourage them further to see training experiences from the participants' point of view. This type of feedback appeals to the trainer's desire to meet participants' needs. A participant's question arises more naturally from the experience of 'being trained' and can have the effect of inviting a trainer to address aspects of their work in the training room that the questions of a detached observer.

Recording the process is very helpful to assist in review and further thinking about training issues. It is an artificial stage that a working trainer may not normally engage in – but in training it performs the important function of consolidation and helping a group move on from experience.

11.3 STAGE 3 - Review and Consolidation

There was now a 2-week period, with 12 hours' class contact, to review the first cycle of micro-training, to focus on central issues in training and to conceptualise these, finishing with an orientation towards the second cycle of micro-training. We shall highlight specific activities to show how an agenda developed from the micro-training experience, and how various training principles were formed.

Creating an agenda

Immediately following the final training session, I asked the group to work through the following activities:

Step 1. Divide the group into 4 sub-groups. Each group to identify what for them were key issues in the micro-training experience.

The group generated the following list:

- Instructions - clarity, focus, appropriacy
- Artificiality of situation
- Generating and maintaining an atmosphere suitable for the situation
- Time management
- Choice of training activities and relevance to aims of session
- Different perceptions by participants of the same activities
- Calculated risk-taking
- Tying up activities and session
- Objectives - think about at the outset of planning ('What do you want me to take away at the end of the session?')
- Reflection - after each activity? or after a sequence of activities?
- Affective element of activities in training - 'unloading feelings'

I then asked the group to refine the list by looking at a trainer's role, prompting the participants to clarify their ideas and where necessary to be more specific with regard to running training sessions. Together, we refined the list as follows:

Trainer's role and activities on a training programme
- Devising reflective tasks (At what stage do we discuss/reflect on methodology? Completing the training cycle effectively. In a

Inside A Training Course 2

> training session, do we need to complete all the stages of the learning cycle?)
> - Running plenary sessions (only for trainers to handle? skills required? pacing and timing of training sessions? questions in training and when to ask them?)
> - What's the place of lectures in training? What is the role of the trainer regarding input?
> - Feedback in training and micro-training
> - Significance of peer training in a programme: how often? to what extent?
> - Level shifting (what should trainees be conscious of during a session? who <u>are</u> we? Training room vs. classroom material? Should content/language be pitched at the level of participants?)

I then planned a sequence of activities to explore these questions, and to lead the group towards the second cycle of micro-training. The activity sequence was itself designed to be a further source of discussion about sequences of activity as well as training issues emerging from the micro-training experience.

ACTIVITY SEQUENCE
Step 1: Training Activities (with a grid)
(a) Warmer - 'Silly Walks' (adapted from Hadfield 1992) *(I decided to start the sequence of training activities as I might a genuine training sequence, with a warmer. It was my aim for the group to discuss warmers, and also to pick up from the activity training messages such as inhibition)*
(b) Activity: Micro-training stories - personal anecdotes from the participants on key moments in the micro-training cycle *(The aim with the narratives was to encourage individuals to concentrate on one incident or event in the experience as a source of understanding about training. It is based on the 'critical incident' work of Brookfield (1988))*
(c) Review of trainers' jobs, knowledge, skills and awareness, comparing with a checklist of trainer capacities from Burns (1994) *(This was a chance to revisit an earlier session in which we had examined what trainers can offer. It was also designed as the basis for a self-appraisal of training skills and awareness)*

Step 2: 'De-Gridding'
This began with group discussion of activities using notes from participants' grids. There was also discussion of the training principles embedded in activities (a), (b) and (c) - *(I was interested in their discussing which activities were suitable for particular stages in training, the sequence of activities themselves, the pace of different activities, and 'levels').*

Step 3: Further Reflection
We worked on the notion of reflection in training sessions with a focus on Boud et al's (1985) conceptualisation of reflection. There was a particular focus on the use of grids and other recording tools. There was an also examination of alternative activity types which encourage participants to reflect on past and shared training room experiences. *('Reflection' proved, as it always seems to, a somewhat elusive concept. Discussion of reflection enabled the group to develop their perceptions and also to voice doubts and worries.)*

Step 4: Issues for the Trainer
There were activities to work on training issues such as 'difficult customers', conflict, silence, feedback and so on. These emerged from a developed from Bentley (1994). *(It was extremely important for the group to engage with these interpersonal issues. Although they were initially reluctant to admit it, these were the ones that most worried them, and which they found it most difficult to find suitable responses to.)*

Step 5: Looking at Input
This was an examination of 'input' and 'lectures' with reference to Gibbs and Habeshaw (1989) leading to a discussion of the role and place of input in training sessions. *('Input' was an ongoing discussion item, and had caused some difficulty during the micro-training sessions – some participants had felt frustrated that they could not 'give the answer'. The activity did not settle matters but did succeed in assisting participants in refining their thinking.)*

Step 6: Theory Focus
This activity responded to the reading task on theory in training set earlier in the course. *(Like 'input', 'theory' was a contentious issue, and this activity enabled further debate of the issues. My contribution to the discussion was to remind participants of how 'theory' had been handled in their training sessions.)*

Step 7: Learning Cycle
I talked the group through a modified form of Kolb's (1984) learning cycle (Figure 2.1 in Chapter 2) with a particular reference to the stages through which the group had progressed during micro-training. *(Concrete illustrations of the stages are needed in order to assist a training group in identifying what stages they have been taken through and why.)*

Step 8: Individual action planning and agenda-setting for the second cycle of micro training. *(It was now time for the group to* *reorientate themselves with the practical training task, in preparation for the second round of micro-training activity.)*

SAMPLE ACTIVITIES

Here we focus on the activites at Step 1b and Step 6 of the sequence - the personal anecdotes and the discussion of lectures/input. These are specific illustrations of the types of activity that work well when discussing training activity, either in terms of real experience or in terms of more theoretical issues.

Sample Activity 1: MICRO-TRAINING STORIES (Step 1 - Activity (b))

I gave the following instruction to the group:

> Recall what for you was a key moment in the micro-training experience. (Close your eyes and try to visualise it if you can.) Now tell a partner your story; partner reflect and clarify the story, and help to identify themes. Swap roles and listen to your partner's story in the same way.
>
> Now give your story a title which 'captures' a training/trainer message. Write this on a slip of paper. Put your title with the collection on the board (Blutac provided) and try to guess the different messages in the titles. Group the messages if you can, and focus on this question:
>
> *What have you learnt about training and trainers' roles from this activity?*

The following titles *(italic)* and messages (CAPITALS) were generated:

> 1. *Back to the 50s* (INTRODUCTIONS)
> 2. *Oh! I missed something!* (REFLECTION)
> 3. *A session within a session* (TRAINING CYCLE)
> 4. *First impressions* (SIGNPOSTING/BEGINNINGS)
> 5. *Who am I?* (LEVELS/ROLES of PARTICIPANTS + CLARITY of INSTRUCTIONS)
> 6. *Oh! You embarrassed me* (TRAINEES' QUESTIONS)
> 7. *The verdict: Presenters found guilty* (DIRECTING FEEDBACK)
> 8. *The string* (EXPLOITING MESSAGES in TRAINING)
> 9. *Words words words* (THE CYCLE)
> 10. *If I were her or him* (DEVELOPMENT THROUGH REFLECTION ON PRACTICE)
> 11. *Unforgettable experience* (INPUT/TRAINER TALKING TIME)
> 12. *My dream comes true* (LEVELS/CYCLE - PRINCIPLES)

When we reviewed the activity after the group discussion, individuals made the following points:
- It was easy for some to make up a story, but not for others
- Participants selected from a wide spectrum of experience (what's significant for some may not be for others)
- Shared experience and insights are very valuable - trying to see another's point of view
- It is useful - helps to capture experiences which might otherwise be forgotten
- We can learn from others
- Understanding others' issues/problems can help foresight and planning
- Messages were highlighted from the group's agenda
- Reflection led to learning about listening to trainees and among trainees

Commentary

The story format is a helpful way of 'unloading' any negative feelings which may have survived from a challenging and possibly stressful training experience. The activity also exemplifies the process point that participants all experience events in very different ways for a variety of reasons. The outcome in this group was in the main cathartic and they declared themselves ready to continue exploring important conceptual and interpersonal issues in training following the activity. The discussion and disclosure in this type of activity requires a calm openness and trust; it also relies on individuals' confidence in themselves and each other. Again, the story format provides a useful vehicle for talking about sensitive issues.

Sample Activity 2: THE LECTURE and INPUT (Step 5)

This session focused on what was for many in the group a central issue. All had come to the course from previous training experiences and contexts which had relied heavily on trainers' lectures for input and content. Many members of the group used lectures themselves as a routine part of their own practice. Our own practice minimises the use of formal lectures (as discussed in Chapters 3 and 4), and this issue raised animated, often heated, discussion in the group (as it always seems to do).

In order to address this topic, I asked the group to read a section of 'Preparing to Teach' by Graham Gibbs and Trevor Habeshaw (1989), with a set of questions originally devised by Rod and then successively refined by both of us.

A group member recorded the discussion that resulted from the Gibbs and Habeshaw task and the readings. I added thinking questions later.

We have reproduced the notes in full as they are a good example of the sort of product that emerges from an intense debate. They are also an excellent example of the valuable contributions that group members can make to sessions as listener/note makers. We find that in a long course participants gain useful additional skills in this way, and also have the opportunity to listen carefully and practice framing thinking questions.

Lectures and Input: A Summary
1. Lectures: Some Points

- There are many factors to consider when giving lectures. Tutors have varied levels of ability in delivering lectures (the 'charisma' factor) - it is for example, difficult to maintain interest beyond 19 minutes (research is fairly conclusive on this)
- participants are generally <u>passive</u> in lectures, so it is vital that lecturers make the experience as interesting as possible. Therefore, vary lecture modes. (Although lecturers can always have 'off days'). Lecturers also need to be aware of audience reactions, although eye contact is not always maintained.
- Why not break away from tradition? Change modes and strategies (e.g. 'anti notes' - an idea of Rod's, and various ideas suggested by Gibbs and Habeshaw and Woodward (1992)). Talk to the audience rather than read from notes or prepared script. Keep information loads down. Enables eye contact and genuine communication with an audience.
- Is lecturing an efficient way of giving information? When to give information in T-T sessions? What sorts of areas on which to give information? Is lecturing a 'model'?

WHAT TO GIVE LECTURES ON?
- history of language teaching area
- provocative ideas on a topic
- general background orientation to an area
- summary of ideas discussed by a group

WHEN TO GIVE LECTURES?
- beginning of session
- after an activity
- to round up a session (tying up)

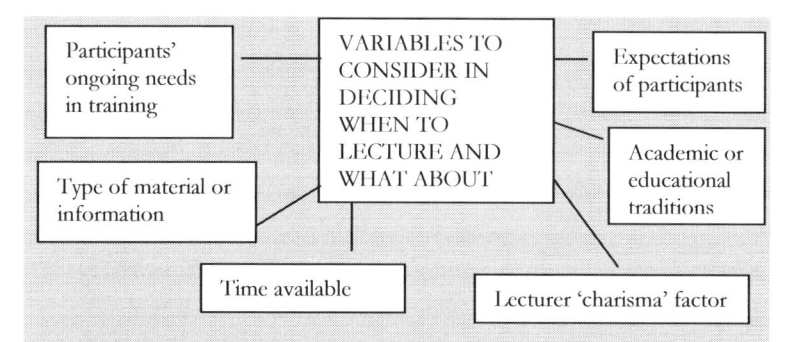

```
┌─────────────────┐   ┌─────────────────┐   ┌─────────────────┐
│ Participants'   │   │ VARIABLES TO    │   │ Expectations    │
│ ongoing needs   ├───┤ CONSIDER IN     ├───┤ of participants │
│ in training     │   │ DECIDING        │   └─────────────────┘
└─────────────────┘   │ WHEN TO         │   ┌─────────────────┐
┌─────────────────┐   │ LECTURE AND     │   │ Academic or     │
│ Type of material├───┤ WHAT ABOUT      ├───┤ educational     │
│ or information  │   └────────┬────────┘   │ traditions      │
└─────────────────┘            │            └─────────────────┘
         ┌─────────────────┐   │   ┌───────────────────────────┐
         │ Time available  ├───┴───┤ Lecturer 'charisma' factor│
         └─────────────────┘       └───────────────────────────┘
```

Thinking Questions
1. On Methodology courses, when are lectures appropriate?
2. Are there alternatives to lectures on 'content' areas such as language study?

Models of teacher education and their influence
- choice of various training modes depends on our personal models of teacher education. We need to consider
- types of knowledge and transfer in teacher education.
- is teacher education about skills, knowledge, attitudes or ideas and their transformation?
- to what extent is knowledge itself received or experiential?

Some Responses to the Issues
1. look at ways to improve lectures
2. Change delivery modes in Teacher training
3. Remember to be flexible and sensitive to participants' needs, wants and expectations
4. Learning to teach is about experience, which involves trial and error - lectures cannot deal directly with experience.
5. We need to think very carefully about the place of theory.

2. Input
Questions to consider about input
a. what? who gives? how? when?
b. what is the relationship between input and theory?

INPUT - SOURCES
- participants' experience
- rationale /theory
- trainer's articulation of rationale (may need 'learner training')
- demonstration
- activities/tasks
- materials

- feedback
- discussions
- process of training sessions

PRINCIPLES for GIVING INPUT
- a focus/starting point
- basis for discovery
- a stimulus (talks/lectures)
- an opportunity for learning

Notes: training sessions are always potential sources of input. Because of this potential, we have to try to make sessions challenging, interesting, provocative, dynamic.
(A restricted view of input equates it with lectures, whereas a broader view acknowledges all other sources)
Changing modes - people have various expectations. If we want to move away from training which is dependent on lectures, we have to move slowly, and be ready for friction and instability. As trainers we have to provide a framework of relationships to make this possible.

Thinking Questions

1. If training sessions are sources of input, what is the 'message' given by lecturing?
2. What levels of preparation are necessary for trainers in sessions in which most of the input comes from participants? How do trainers prepare under such conditions?
3. In training sessions that you run, can you see ways of enriching potential input sources?
4. What are the responsibilities of trainers in interactive sessions or activity-based sessions?
5. what is the value of TALK in training sessions?

3. Theory and Practice (With reference to the articles)
We saw several types of theory as follows:

Experiential Knowledge:	Personal theories of action
	'Practical theory'
	Implicit theory
Received Knowledge	Principles
	'Academic theory'

Both can be referred to as 'rationale'.
- Britten (1988), Ur (1992) and Ramani (1987) see a role for theory developed from practice
- Ellis(1990) seems to see a 2-way relationship

- Widdowson (1984) implies an 'academic theory' to practice relationship

An experiential model of training links theory to practice in 2 ways, and sees theory and practice in constant relationship, but with an accent on practice - teaching is PRACTICAL activity, first and foremost.

Thinking Questions
1. In your context, is the emphasis on theory or practice in training?
Is the relationship a reflection of the academic/professional hierarchy in your context?
2. In teaching, is theory open to change, growth and development?
3. What is the relationship between experiential knowledge and 'reflection in action' and implicit theory (Schön 1983, 1987)

A Final Note
"In much of your talking, thinking is half-murdered" Khalil Gibran

(Special thanks to Nuri for recording the session and writing up these notes)

Like so many debates within a training setting, this one was inconclusive. However, I felt at the end of the discussion (which lasted well over 2 hours) that the group had made some important breakthroughs in being able to articulate their ideas. Individual differences in training style were acknowledged and accepted by the group. What had been a polarised debate between 'those who lecture' and 'those who don't' had become a serious and focused discussion about how trainers can help trainees to articulate their emerging ideas in training and through so doing develop their principles. There were loose ends, naturally. In the notes, I decided to provide means to keep the discussion going and to keep the issue of context in mind by using thinking questions

11.4 STAGE 4 - Micro-training 2
Before we began the second cycle, I invited the group to share their remaining anxieties in an activity I call 'Message in a Bottle'. Each group member was asked to put a plea or question of doubt 'into a bottle' (drawn on paper) and cast it into the 'sea' (the classroom floor). The bottles then 'washed up' and were opened by passers-by. Messages were read out and the group gave supportive responses or advice or encouragement or said a kind word. The main messages were as follows:

Inside A Training Course 2

> ***Assertive Communication***
> ***Conflict Resolution: Guidance Needed***
> ***Incorporating Participants'***
> ***Body Language: How To Read?***
> ***Contributions. HELP!***
> ***Own Weaknesses and Gaps***
> ***Adult Learning Principles***
> ***How to Motivate a group?***
> ***Thinking on your feet***

A short open session was held in which we discussed each of the messages and what they might mean for further development as trainers.

The procedures for the second cycle were the same as for the first. Teams stayed together and did a second session. The only variation was that the order of presentation was reversed from the first cycle, to give those who had started the first cycle the chance to finish the second cycle.

I noticed in the second cycle that presenters were a lot more relaxed, and at ease with each other, that the teams were functioning much more efficiently and closely, and that the sessions themselves were 'looser' in structure, and yet more intensive. This was probably down to the presenters not trying to include too many activities, and to 'squeeze' more effectively the ones they used in order to develop methodological and other points.

An example of my reaction to a session in the second cycle appears below. It is my written feedback to the training team and the support team we featured in our account of the first cycle.

To the support team I wrote:

> Thanks for leading the discussion of N and S's session. You both have developed a very helpful way of framing questions. - direct but not threatening - and certainly spotted some key training areas for us to discuss. Good handling of the group, particularly when some pent-up emotions were coming out. You asserted yourselves confidently.

To the presenting team I wrote:
Microtraining 2 - feedback
Thank you both for providing us with a well-planned and smoothly executed training session on reading skills. You made good use of the material from Doff and kept us interested throughout. You made good use of the material from Doff and kept us interested throughout. Your attention to detail was appreciated.

Positive Points
1. A logical and developmental training sequence, working from experience through reflection to principles
2. Good linking and signposting of activities
3. Smooth teamwork - good to see you conferring and monitoring during the session - your attention to the process enabled us to contribute meaningfully and for you to adjust your plan to our needs as they emerged
4. Well-handled post-activity discussions which gave us plenty of opportunity to talk ideas and principles out
5. Nice idea to use the posters as a summary and reference point
6. Element of surprise in the first task got everyone interested
7. Your openness and good listening throughout the session - during your presentation and the post-session discussion

Action Points/Questions
1. Could you have linked the good 'warmer' directly to the session?
2. How much do we need to reveal to participants about the shape and direction of a session at the outset?
3. Do we always need to pitch activities at participants' levels? Any danger of role play as an activity in training sessions?
4. Can you suggest ways of developing the visual aspects of your presentation? (OHTs/OHP use/whiteboard)
5. Was it deliberate not to give us the 'takeaway' material during the session?
6. When giving instructions for an activity are there any 'dos' and don'ts'?

Again, thanks for leading the session. There is clear evidence of your development as trainers, especially in the 'looser' format you adopted, which enabled us to really get into the principles behind the practice. You are also developing distinctive trainer presences. Are you aware of their characteristics? Again, thanks! Well done!

11.5 STAGE 5 - Review
The final stage was slightly curtailed, but we did manage a review session in which the group addressed the following questions set by me:

- What have you become aware of as trainers during the second cycle?
- What questions and niggles do you have as a consequence of the second cycle?

These questions were discussed during the session, their outcomes noted by a group member, and with thinking questions added by myself for the final session, which focused on these and the final set of questions which looked back and looked forward to the next component of the course, namely training course design and management.

Micro-Training: Review

A. Awareness

Here are the areas in which the group members felt they had become more aware during the micro-training sessions:

GROUP A	GROUP B	GROUP C
1. teamwork/relationships
2. training cycle
3. role of questions
4. importance of feedback
5. implications for the classroom	1. training is not an ad hoc business
2. importance of trainees' personal experience
3. principles underlying past experiences
4. trainers should be academically and professionally competent
5. handling feedback	1. importance of setting the scene in sessions
2. importance of questions and instructions
3. taking risks is productive
4. training cycle in practice
5. sensitivity

Follow-up Tasks and Thinking Questions

1. Identify key development areas for yourself from the awareness lists. Draw up a plan for further professional development: what does your plan entail in terms of development?
2. How do the areas you have identified link to the practice and theory of training?
3. Can you regroup the material in terms of trainer attributes and skills?

B. Questions

Here is a digest of the questions you raised. Discuss them in groups.
1. Why a training cycle?
2. Is the cycle as 'neat' as portrayed?
3. What kind of 'learning is involved in training?
4. What is a 'plenary'? Is it a type of training activity?
5. How far do we adapt the training process for ITT situations?
6. Should we always stick to our session plan?
7. Is it always necessary to sum up at the end of a session?
8. Should we reveal the rationale behind training activities to participants? If so, when?
9. What next? Can we do this again?

> **C. Review**
> Go back over the 'Methodology and materials' questions raised at the beginning of the course.
> - Which do you now feel confident about answering?
> - Which do you want to work on further?
> - Which do you think inform course design for training?

Individual group members then spent a further 4 weeks on a coursework assignment writing up their training materials and reading in the professional literature to develop a rationale for the training activities, the sequences of activity they had chosen to use and their overall approach to training. This accompanied the final training materials and trainers' notes. The assignment was designed to assist the group in consolidating their learning and also to read in depth on the training topics covered in their assignments.

Final Thoughts

Reflecting on this training experience some time since it happened, with the benefit of having run other micro-training programmes and experiential hands-on work with both postgraduate groups and other professional groups, we see how our own practices had evolved up to that point in time and have evolved subsequently. Running experiential sessions with experienced and mature professionals is particularly challenging and rewarding; but it is not without its problems. For example, the intentions and messages of feedback can be misconstrued. A micro-training session can go badly wrong for one reason or another, and the training team needs support of many sorts. If a training group is not at ease with itself, the intense sharing and reliance on each other that micro-training and subsequent review and exploration demands may not be present, and the activity consequently impoverished. We have also, on a more positive note, seen a group become more comfortable with each other as a consequence of the micro-training experience. We have become more aware ourselves of the powerful emotional dimension of such activities as micro-training, and by extension, the emotional load of running process-oriented training sessions for all participants including the trainers. More than anything else, the micro-training experience cautions us to be more explicit in our own rationale to training groups at the outset and during the experience.

We leave it to the participants to have the final word on the experience. This is what two of them said:

> For me the main insight to come out of this component was a raised awareness of the difference between teaching and training. This was well illustrated by the two phases of micro-training. In the first phase of micro-training, my partner and I concentrated mainly on experiential activities but there was little scope for explaining the significance of what had just been experienced. By our second session, we were able to appreciate the role of input as a basis for reflection. This component produced a wealth of thinking questions. I am only now beginning to appreciate how much needs to be taken into account in planning a training session. (Mike)
>
> The micro-training was a very valuable experience from various angles. I learnt a lot from doing it myself, working with a partner and participating in others' sessions and feedback. I particularly enjoyed the fact that the training cycles were repeated so that we could build on the experience of the first. (Rose)
>
> Through training practice I have gained more confidence and through observing my colleagues' performances I have learnt a lot. Teamwork in micro-training brings colleagues closer than before. (Shukla)

References

Bentley, T. (1994) Facilitation. London: McGraw-Hill

Boud, D., R. Keogh and D. Walker (1985) (eds) Reflection: Turning experience into learning. London: Kogan-Page.

Britten, D. (1988) Three stages in teacher training. ELT Journal, 42/1.

Brookfield, S. (1988) Developing Critical Thinkers. Milton Keynes: Open University Press.

Burns, A. (1994) Suggestions for a short trainer course. The Teacher Trainer, 8/2.

Hadfield, J. (1992) Classroom Dynamics. Oxford: Oxford University Press.

Gibbs, G. and T. Habeshaw (1989) Preparing To Teach. Bristol: TES.

Kolb, D. (1984) Experiential Learning. Englewood Cliffs, NJ: Prentice-Hall. 3rd edition.

Ramani, E. (1987) Theorising for the classroom. ELT Journal, 41/1.

Schön, D.A. (1983) The Reflective Practitioner. San Francisco, CA: Jossey-Bass.

Schön, D.A. (1987) Educating the Reflective Practitioner. San Francisco, CA: Jossey-Bass.

Ur, P. (1992) Teacher learning. ELT Journal, 46/1.

Widdowson, H.G. (1984) The incentive value of teacher education. ELT Journal,
Woodward, T. (1992) Ways of Training. Harlow: Longman.

CHAPTER 12
DEVELOPING AS A TRAINER

In this concluding chapter we shall attempt to express what we see as the essence of our work and development as trainers which we have exemplified in this book. In Part A, we restate some of the main principles which guide us as trainers and in Part B we share our ideas on professional development in the field of training.

Part A - So what does it mean to be a trainer?
Most people involved in training teachers start out as teachers. Many continue to teach as well as train. There is no doubt that good teachers and good trainers share many of the same attributes, and that trainers are responsible for professional learning in the same way as teachers help their students to learn a subject or skill. Yet we have noticed that successful teachers are not all capable of making the transition to training. Just as a good linguist or native speaker of a language is not necessarily a good teacher of the language, a good language teacher may not be able to transcend the boundaries of her own classroom in order to perceive the wider issues which re involved in the professional preparation and development of teachers. Freeman (1996), drawing on Thomas (1987), conceptualises these three areas of work in a way which we find helpful:

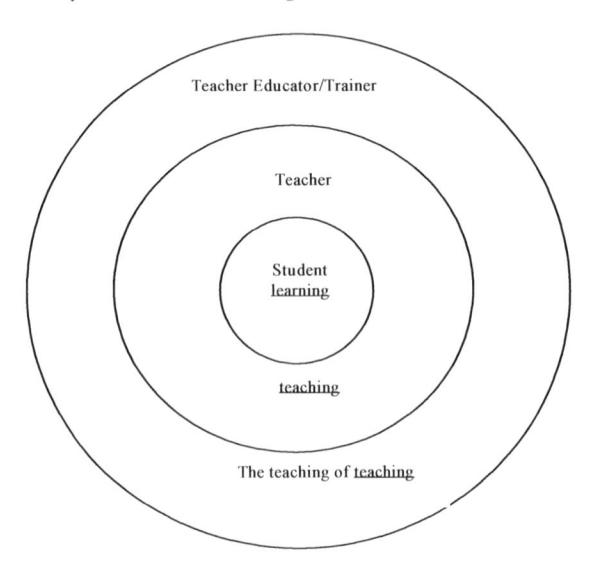

Figure 12.1 Levels of learning, teaching and training

This diagram puts the learner at the centre of our concerns (something which we believe trainers should never forget) and also neatly emphasises the interdependence of learning, teaching and teacher training. This in turn reminds us of the essentially **parasitical** nature of our existence as trainers and even more so (a fourth circle would be needed here!) as trainers of trainers. Seen in terms of our responsibilities as trainers, this means that our task is to facilitate the professional learning of those who train teachers and those who teach learners. If we do our job well, we will have a positive influence on others who train (a relatively small number) and indirectly on learners (an extremely large number). Awareness of this responsibility is both challenging and frightening. We have to be seen to 'know' what we are doing if we are to win the respect of those people whose professional learning we have been entrusted with, for however short a time. This means that our decisions have to be principled. What follows, therefore, is a restatement of the principles and beliefs we follow in our work.

1. About Groups

We have to be prepared for the fact that each group we work with is going to be different. It is comforting but also dangerous to emphasise the similarities between one group and the next. It can lead us to over generalize, to survive on 'old tricks' and to pull out and re-use old materials. Sometimes we do this, usually when we are pressed for time. We find that even those activities we know to be successful have to be adapted to the needs and interests of a particular group - the activities we have presented in this book are no exception. However, to understand the needs and interests of a group fully, we have to wipe the slate clean, to quieten down the noise of previous groups in our heads and to tune in completely to the new group. We have to be prepared to start of where *they* are and to make the journey of professional learning *with* them, hand in hand, rather than starting from where *we* are, exhorting them to come over and join us and follow us. This means that time spent on winning the trust of the group, on forming a fruitful working relationship with them, on building a 'learning community' in the training room, and, above all, on *listening* to them. How can we have anything useful to say to a group if we haven't listened to their interests, concerns, hopes and fears?

2. About Individuals

Professional development is also personal development. Each individual participant on a training course makes an investment of time and personal energy into the process of professional learning. Being a teacher, or trainer means for most of the time being alone in a room with a group of people for whose learning you are responsible. In this sense, professional training is an individual undertaking, and on every training course there are as many courses going on in the room as there are individual participants. As trainers we have to use every means at our disposal to understand each of these 'courses', as individual participants make their own sense of what is going on around them and within them.

We see these inner struggles and harmonies most clearly when the focus is on individual 'performance', in teaching practice, in micro-training or in individual assignments, for example. Issues can be aired in supervisory discussions or in tutorials. But we must also be on the lookout for different types of sign from individuals within groups - positive and negative body language, reticence, eagerness etc - and follow them up in one-to-one sessions whenever we feel it would be most helpful. We must also work constantly on our own interpersonal skills; the facilitation of individual learning requires added sensitivity since participants are often at their most vulnerable in one-to-one sessions (especially after the high level of emotional investment in an observed lesson or an individual presentation in the training room). It is in this area that the literature and practices of counselling (Egan (1983) and King (1983) for example) have made such valuable contributions to our own competence as trainers.

3. About Professional Learning

We have already emphasised the *individual* nature of professional learning, and the contributions which a group can make to it. We see our role as trainers in terms of supporting and facilitating the processes of awareness raising, reflecting and making meaning which we believe are also key stages in professional learning. To do this effectively, we also have to understand that we are working with *adults*, often with their own established styles and strategies, and that we can no more dictate what they ultimately learn on our courses than a teacher can force-feed a child with irregular verbs at school. As we make our own professional learning journeys with our participants we are constantly surprised by what they take from the experience. We don't always agree with the conclusions they come to, and will engage them in discussion if we think that there are flaws in their thinking. But we will not *impose* our thinking on theirs. We worry when we (as we sometimes do!) receive assignments which parrot our own views.

Learning and development are about *changes* in thinking, and ultimately, in actions, but token changes (to please the tutor or to achieve a good assignment grade) are rarely lasting changes. The challenge for us, as tutors, is to provoke and promote the kind of thinking and conceptualisation which reaches the level of values and beliefs, and which involves participants in a principles reappraisal of their practices. Learning at this level is truly their *own* learning, and it will have lasting value in their subsequent professional lives.

One final point, but a crucial one, here: we hope that we have made it clear in what we have written that professional learning is in many significant ways concerned with *processes* rather than just with *products*. Any products of our courses emerge as a consequence of the processes our participants have experienced - the processes of talk and interaction, of awareness raising, of different types of thinking, of reassessment and evaluating. It is our responsibility as trainers to ensure that these processes contribute to professional learning. That is why we find the framework provided by the learning cycle (Chapter 2) so valuable as a guide to course planning and implementation.

4. About Knowledge

As trainers, there are things we need to *know* about. We can't imagine working in our field without some knowledge, as we have discussed in this book, of, for example, group dynamics, of our own subject base in English Language and ELT Methodology, of the psychology and practices of adult learning (or andragogy), or of the professional literature in our field. But none of this knowledge is an end in itself. We have arrived at this knowledge through our own discovery of what is important to us as trainers, through the development of our own professional needs.

For the same reason, we do not see it as appropriate to 'peddle' knowledge on training courses in a gratuitous way. We accept that subject knowledge is a *sine qua non* on courses for English language teachers, and we work constantly at ways of developing our participants' knowledge bases when they are ready to extend them, and when we perceive shots of 'theory' are relevant. Teachers and trainers need to be seen as 'knowledgeable' in order to command respect from their learners and participants, but the best of them, in our experience, also know how to make this knowledge available when it is most needed without resorting to the kind of 'display' of knowledge which all to often results in complaints about 'irrelevant' theory, or in simply making participants feel inadequate.

5. About Self-awareness

We stated in Chapter 3 that we must be as open to learning from participants as they are to learning from us. If we can learn better to see the world through their eyes, then we will learn about them and will be better able to support their learning. In doing this, we learn more about ourselves, about our own prejudices and preferences, our strengths and weaknesses, our own hidden agendas and preconceived ideas. We also learn about the impact we have on trainees, the size of our 'presence' in the training room, the effect of our words on others and even the messages which our body language sends to participants.

> *When I saw you crouching down beside our group, I was shocked, to tell you the truth. I thought 'How can a lecturer or a teacher behave like this with his students? It could never happen in my country.'* (Abidine)

This kind of insight is invaluable to us as we think about our own professional behaviour and its significance to participants. We also need to listen to the voices in our own heads. We are sometimes aware of an 'alter ego' talking to us in training sessions, telling us to tread carefully, or to intervene, or even to stop bullshitting. The advice we get from this source is often the wisest! When we co-train, we learn about ourselves through working with each other. We also learn through the processes of training (e.g. the way each of us interacts with participants) and also through explicit feedback to each other.

We have also had to learn to be more aware of our own expectations of participants. Often we may feel frustrated if we fail to complete the activities we have planned for a particular session, of if a particular individual seems to be regressing rather than progressing in their learning. An ill-chosen comment in such circumstances can have a negative effect that is difficult to 'undo' later.

In supervisory discussions with participants we have to be aware of the images of good teaching which we carry with us and which may prevent us from being open to whatever a trainee has done in class, or may be trying to explain to us.

The types of self-awareness we have discussed here derive from openness to our participants and to our colleagues, as well as from internal dialogue and feedback to each other. It is sometimes difficult or painful to face and deal with. Without it, however, we can't be effective as trainers. It is the starting point of our own professional development, which we shall go on to discuss in more detail in the next section.

Part B - Our Own Development
Much of what we have written about in this book has concerned our work with training groups and individuals, as we have been involved in their development and learning. As we said in the Introduction, this work contributes directly to our own development, too. We learn so much from the process and from the participants themselves, a point we shall return to later. In this final section, we would like to share with you a few of those things - activities, encounters and ideas - which we have found give us a 'push' towards development and which we know will provide us with opportunities for development over the next few years of our professional lives. They are presented in no particular order.

1. New Courses, New Contexts
There is nothing better guaranteed to initiate new ideas and practices than working on a new course or programme, or with a new group. Running a short course is a prime example of this. In April 1997, for example, we ran a 1-week course for trainers working in INSET (a multinational group - 18 nationalities) under the auspices of the British Council. As we explored INSET principles and processes with this group, we found ourselves crystallising half-formed thoughts and working out new processes. An instance of the former occurred when we were working with the group in a discussion of different views of INSET. It became clear to us that working in two dimensions - thinking about INSET as either deficit or growth - told only part of the story. We became aware that there were two cross cutting dimensions: needs and professional focus.

By combining these we were able, as a consequence of the discussion to present the participants with a model as a follow-up. This framework (Figure 12.2) emerged from a discussion of needs diagnosis and approaches to INSET on short INSET courses. We followed it up with a session on change later in the course, referring to the framework.

One process idea which we refined on this particular course, and a way of exploiting the multinational composition of that group, was for individuals to interview other group members from different contexts, using a 'What Issues? Why? Who's Involved? When? and Where? of INSET' in their respective contexts. The information was then reported to a sub-group making a compilation for plenary discussion and further examination of possible frameworks for the organisation of INSET. The process provided opportunities to practice active

Developing As A Trainer

listening, experience sharing, empathising and group building, held as it was, on the second day of the 5-day course.

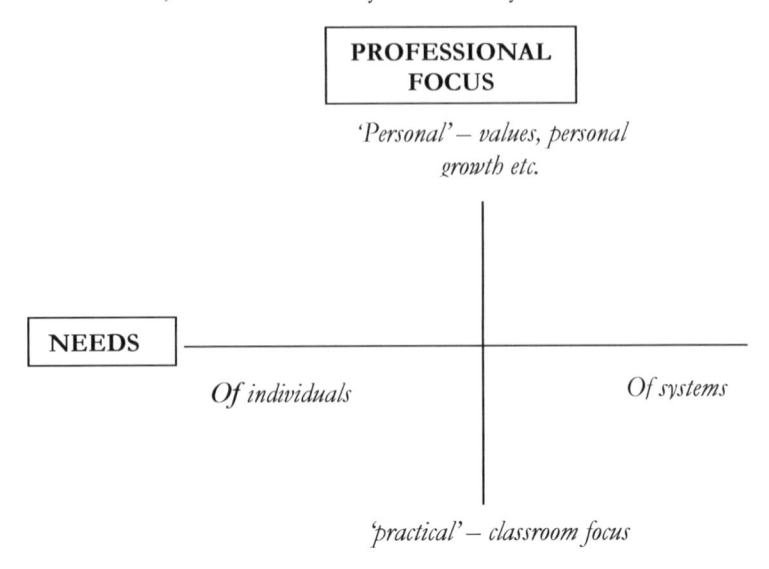

```
                    ┌──────────────┐
                    │ PROFESSIONAL │
                    │    FOCUS     │
                    └──────────────┘

                   'Personal' – values, personal
                           growth etc.
                               │
                               │
    ┌─────────┐                │
    │  NEEDS  │ ───────────────┼────────────────
    └─────────┘                │
           Of individuals      │        Of systems
                               │
                               │
                    'practical' – classroom focus
```

Figure 12.2 Dimensions of in-service training

Running courses as a process, based on the framework and activities we have presented in this book provides us with the challenge of the unexpected, compelling us to actively listen to a new group, to see where they need to go on their training journey. From new courses come new activities, new concepts and an enhanced understanding of process. We find that a lot of these new ideas are focused on helping participants process information, and experience. We see no end to this.

New courses also occasionally provide us with the opportunity to work together as a training team, to work in tandem with a group. This gives us unique opportunities to experience the training process as an 'insider' when one of us is leading and the other supporting, or taking a different role in a session. It also enables us the time to revisit each other's thinking, especially during the planning phase of a course, to 'tune in' as a prelude to tuning in to the course participants when we meet them.

Working in contexts which are new to us, and with unfamiliar cultures, is also a spur to development and change for us. Our work involves working with participants from many different cultures and contexts, each one a fine opportunity for learning. Going back to square 1 and starting afresh with people whose context we do not know is an immensely valuable opportunity to listen, to observe and to work our way into perspectives which are new to us. It is good to be 'taught' by our participants in these circumstances, and we find it a useful way to begin to enable them to articulate their thinking about teaching and training. While we inevitably draw from our 'stock' of materials and activities on these occasions with new groups in new contexts (these 'opening up' activities are a way for us to learn about a new context and the group, as a prelude to deeper training activity), we are always overwhelmed by the different responses to activities from different groups. New 'angles' are glimpsed, different issues are prioritised, groups process experiences in different ways. We have to remain flexible in order to respond to these twists and turns, and it is from the surprises and unexpected turnings that we learn and develop.

2. Our Mistakes and Wrong Turnings

We make mistakes. We get it wrong. We get into conflict with individuals and groups from time to time. We misunderstand. We might give the wrong message. So many things can, and do, go wrong in the training process. Perhaps the most difficult lessons for us to learn have been those we have had to face up to as a consequence of our own mistakes. We have discussed conflict in Chapter 3, but it's worth repeating that the successful resolution of conflict has often enabled us to reflect on our practices and our interpersonal skills. And that conflict unresolved has lingered like a ghost in later encounters of a similar type. We have been able to reach back into our memories of the unresolved conflict and prevent similar problems occurring when we have suspected they might be in the air. For example, individuals who believe that courses should cater solely for their needs deserve to be listened to so that we can respond with our point of view about individual needs versus group needs; at the outset of a course, the group has priority, particularly if the course is a long one. If, for some reason, we fail to listen to that individual we can easily end up in conflict.

Sometimes, we give wrong messages - our personal excitement about an issue may over-inflate its importance to a group. We might, as sessions progress, move onto another issue, but the group wants to keep working on the previous one. "But we thought you thought it was so crucial." Or we may write feedback on a piece of writing that, instead of encouraging, ends up deflating. We cannot always guard against these eventualities - but we forget to acknowledge them at our peril. And so we miss learning opportunities. Where we go wrong marks some of the most fertile territory for learning about training, participants and ourselves; as long as we remain open to our own failings.

3. New Groups, New Challenges
When running the same course over a number of years, procedures can become very 'cosy', and it is all too tempting to become complacent about the way in which we do things. New groups vary enormously, not only in the obvious ways - such as numbers, gender composition, culture, origins - but also in experience, personality and so on. We find that our 'set' course takes on new directions with new groups, that priorities vary and that different groups treat issues differently. We have to adjust our approach and style accordingly. These occasions are development opportunities. A simple example would be the organisation of micro-training as described in Chapters 5 and 11 with a large rather than a small group, and the range of different dynamics that this would create. Working out and managing the new process can contribute enormously to our own development, particularly of ways of handling content and varying ways of working with groups. From this work come new ideas and new insights into training and people.

4. New Ideas
We derive a great deal of pleasure from learning about our work through the ideas of others, particularly from books and articles. We also need to go outside the immediate confines of our work in search of new ideas, either for confirmation, inspiration or reassurance about what we are doing. Sometimes it seems as if we are deliberately drawn to particular sources, which make so much sense and create such an impact when we meet them, when we are 'ready' in the way we discuss in Chapter 3, as in our individual encounters with the writings of Carl Rogers; or more recently, with Michael Fullan's ideas about educational change, Donald Schön's writings on reflective practice or Guy Claxton's work on learning. Without these external sources of intellectual and emotional stimulation, we are certain that our own professional and personal development would have been stunted.

We continue to read and to explore, to try to create time for new books and ideas to enter our thinking. Reading enables us to venture outside our normal fields of interest and activity into valuable source areas such as mainstream management ideas, counselling and so on. These sources act as a spur to our thinking, and aid our conceptualisation of what we do in practice. We also find, as do many course participants, that our reading sources influence our writing in terms of precision, depth and style. In the Resources Section which follows this chapter, we list books and papers which we have found of value over the years.

5. Going Public
Both of us speak regularly at conferences and participate in other professional activity in publishing, examining and consultancy. In all these endeavours we find our principles challenged, open to the scrutiny of our colleagues and we value this immensely. Feedback from colleagues, or conference participants, debate with fellow examiners and editors all provide opportunities for us to reflect and readjust, to develop our thinking and refine our principles.

Similarly when we write about our work, there is great benefit in having to both condense and articulate our ideas and make them accessible to others. Going public in these ways is risky, but a risk that more than repays itself in terms of development opportunities. The act of focusing on an issue and developing it either in person or on paper is a valuable learning opportunity.

6. Personal Development
Training and teaching are both 'caring' activities, drawing on the types of skill, knowledge and awareness so important to other caring professions such as counselling, psychiatry, nursing and social work. We have noticed that practitioners in these professions often talk at length and in depth on how they see the personal and the professional so deeply intertwined that 'work' and 'personal life' are to some extent indistinguishable. For us, this is a major and continuing issue in our working and professional lives. At times, we find the personal and professional in conflict, both in terms of commitment and time, and also in our approach to issues at home or in the workplace. These can be times of turbulence and even unhappiness, in contrast to those times when we manage to maintain equilibrium in the balance between the two spheres.

We find that focusing on 'transition' - between work and home - is important. Learning to leave work at work, or to transform work issues into life issues, by putting them into context and into perspective, is also important. We have to learn and continue to learn to work with the tension between our inner selves and our professional selves. As we hinted in Chapter 4, this is very difficult, if not impossible, given the investment that we find we need to make of ourselves into our professional lives. We 'carry' troubles with us in the same way as we exude joy. We have found that the most difficult struggle that we face is to be ourselves, and yet not to allow any potential distraction from outside our immediate context -either personal or professional - to interfere with our focus on the actual moment we find ourselves in, whether with a group, an individual participant or a family member. It is a major area of sheer hard work to maintain the sort of focus we find we need in order to make the most of the moment.

The development opportunities in training and teaching are innumerable - from how to cope with stress (our own and others'), how to listen creatively, how to understand our own and others' personality, motivation and moods. These are all related to life skills - for us, professional life is a venue for developing life skills. These can enhance all aspects of our lives, and are an integral part of our development agenda. This happens consciously, as we attempt to acquire and refine skills, knowledge and awareness, and also unconsciously, in action, in the training room. The latter is where our work as a team is of such great value - being given supportive feedback or an ear for talk after a session is so useful. In an ideal world we would insist on post-session talk, possibly accompanied by a walk or a game of pool, for joint processing of perceptions and reflections. We can contribute to each other's development in these moments of relaxation and 'switching off', helping each other to process ideas and events. Like all personal development efforts, these are central to our continued development as teachers/trainers and as people.

Ultimately, developing as a trainer is about personal development and transformation of perspectives and behaviour. Without personal change and enhanced self-awareness, professional change and development is potentially shallow and empty. It is fairly rare for professional development to lead to personal development. Generally, it happens the other way round. Our most constant point of reference in our development and understanding of the process of learning is the knowledge that being a teacher or a trainer is first and foremost about who we are, rather than what we do. Herein lies the essence of developing as a trainer.

References

Egan (1997) The Skilled Helper. London: Brookes Cole.

Freeman, D. (1996) The 'unstudied problem': Research on teacher learning. In D. Freeman and J. Rodgers (eds) Teacher

Learning in Language Teaching. Cambridge: Cambridge University Press.

King, D. (1983) Counselling for teachers. ELT Journal, 37/4.

Thomas, A. (1987) Language teacher competence and language teacher education. In R. Bowers (ed) Language Teacher Education: An integrated programme for EFL teacher training. London: MEP.

Resources for Trainers

We decided not to include a conventional bibliography in this book. Instead, we offer some suggestions for resources which readers might find useful. These include both suggestions for training activities and more theoretical discussion of the issues we have raised.

Training Activities
The following are complete 'courses' which can be followed as they are presented or act as the inspiration for your own course.

Ur, P. (1996) A Course for Language Teachers. Cambridge: Cambridge University Press.
- a very comprehensive course for initial training

Tanner, R. and C. Green (1998) Tasks for Teacher Education. Harlow: Longman.
- consists of trainer's and trainee's book. The trainer's book is a useful guide to facilitation, and the trainee's book contains a range of activities.

Doff, A. (1988) Teach English. Cambridge: Cambridge University Press.
- the trainer's book has plenty to offer both in terms of planning sessions and rationale for training activities..

The following contain activities which can be used as they stand or adapted for your own purposes in training sessions. We have found them all to be very helpful in our work.

Brandes, D. and P. Ginnis (1996) A Guide to Student-Centred Learning. London: Nelson Thornes

Brandes, D. and P. Ginnis (1990) The Student-Centred School. Hemel Hempstead: Simon and Schuster.
- both contain a good selection of activities for awareness-raising and group development.

Brandes, D. and H. Phillips (1979) Gamesters' Handbook: 140 Games for Teachers and Group Leaders: No. 1. London: Stanley Thornes.

Edge, J. (1992) Cooperative Development Harlow: Longman

Edge, J. (2002) Continuing Cooperative Development.
- Edge's two books illustrate practical aspects of teacher-teacher work.

Phillips, H. and D. Brandes (2005) Gamesters' Handbook: No.2. London: Stanley Thornes.
- the gamesters' handbooks have a variety of activities for awareness-raising, group development and discussion.

Owen, N. (2001) The Magic of Metaphor. Crown House.
- a good collection of stories for use in training sessions.

Hadfield, J. (1992) Classroom Dynamics. Oxford: Oxford University Press.
- complete set of activities for group development.

Woodward, T. (2004) Ways of Working with Teachers. TW Publishing.
- variety of training activities (republication of 'Ways of Training' – Longman (1992))

Randall, M. with B. Thornton (2002) Advising and Supporting Teachers. Cambridge: Cambridge University Press.
- a good introduction to advisor training, with useful training activities.

Malderez, A. and C. Bodoszcky (1999) Mentor Courses. Cambridge: Cambridge University Press.
- a complete mentor-training course, with a wide range of activities.

Easen, P. (1985) Making School-centred INSET Work. Milton Keynes: Open University Press
- activity-based teacher development in schools, with discussion of process. Out-of-print, but worth getting hold of.

Wajnryb, R. (1992) Classroom Observation Tasks Cambridge: Cambridge University Press
- a valuable collection of activities to involve teachers and trainees in classroom observation.

Language Awareness

Arndt, V., P. Harvey and J. Nuttall (2000) Alive to Language. Cambridge: Cambridge University Press.

Bolitho, R. and B. Tomlinson (1995) Discover English. Oxford: Heinemann. 2nd Edition.
- two collections of language awareness activities for teachers and trainers.

About Training, Adult Learning and Associated Activities

This selection discusses and explains various aspects of the work of a trainer and also how trainers and teachers learn.

Bentley, T. (1994) Facilitation. London: McGraw-Hill.
- comprehensive account of the work of facilitators. Presents a 'strong' version of facilitation.

Brookfield, S. (1986) Understanding and Facilitating Adult Learning. Milton Keynes: Open University Press.
- a full and readable account of adult learning principles and practices by a key figure in the development of adult learning in the USA and UK

Brookfield, S. (1988) Developing Critical Thinkers. Buckingham: Open University Press.
- valuable and readable text on critical thinking and awareness-raising for adults. Sub-title: 'Challenging Adults to Explore Alternative Ways of Thinking and Acting.

Brookfield, S. (1990) The Skillful Teacher. San Francisco, CA: Jossey-Bass.
- readable autobiographical account of Brookfield's development as an adult educator.

Brookfield, S. (1995) Becoming A Critically Reflective Practitioner. San Francisco, CA: Jossey-Bass.
- challenging discussion of professional development.

Baldwin, J. and H. Williams (1988) Active Learning: A Trainer's Guide. Oxford: Blackwell
-very readable first hand personalised account of issues facing trainers in running training courses and sessions

Dillon, J.T. (1994) Using Discussion in Classrooms. Milton Keynes: Open University Press.
- practical and readable guide to using discussion-based activity in formal settings.

Fish, D. (1989) Learning Through Practice in Initial Teacher Training London: Kogan Page.
- helpful discussions of theoretical and practical issues entailed by work-based training.

Handal, G. and P. Lauvas (1987) Promoting Reflective Teaching: Supervision in Action. Milton Keynes: Open University Press.
- in depth look at the supervisory work of teacher educators.

Head, K. and P. Taylor (1997) Readings in Teacher Development. Oxford: Heinemann.
- a wealth of thought-provoking material here for any educationalist.

Jacques, D. (1993) Learning in Groups. London: Kogan Page. 2nd edition.
- excellent 'standard text' on students' and tutors' experiences of working in groups with good theoretical chapters on learning and groups. Also has a selection of activities.

McGill, I. and L. Beaty (2002) Action Learning: A practitioner's guide. London: Kogan-Page. 2nd edition.
- based on the procedures of action learning sets.

Moon, J (1999) Reflection in Learning and Professional Development. London: Kogan-Page.

Moon, J. (2001) Short Courses and Workshops. London: Kogan-Page.

Moon, J. (2004) A Handbook of Reflective and Experiential Learning. London: RoutledgeFalmer.

- Moon's books cover all aspects of 'reflective' and 'experiential' practice, and both theoretical and practical aspects.

Roberts, J. (1998) Language Teacher Education. London: Arnold.
- good discussion of the theory behind teacher education with case study illustrations.

Rowland, S. (1993) The Inquiring Tutor. London: Falmer
- provocative and readable personal account of the work of an adult educator, with illustration and discussion of many issues in the training process.

Schön, D. (1983) The Reflective Practitioner. San Francisco, CA: Jossey-Bass.

Schön, D. (1987) Educating The Reflective Practitioner. San Francisco, CA: Jossey-Bass.
- Schön's two books are essential reading for anyone involved in professional development.

Practitioner Research

Altrichter, H., P. Posch and B. Somekh (1993) Teachers Investigate Their Work. London: Routledge.
- a practical and easy-to-follow guide to classroom reseach and associated topics

Burns, A. (1998) Collaborative Action Research for Teachers. Cambridge: Cambridge University Press.
- clear, readable and practical book for teachers and teacher educators.

Rea-Dickens, P. and K. Germaine (1992) Evaluation. Oxford: Oxford University Press.

Weir, C. and J. Roberts (1994) Evaluation in ELT. Oxford: Blackwell.
- these two volumes cover most of the ground on evaluation issues.

Useful Papers

There are a vast number of papers on teacher training. We have chosen some personal 'favourites' from a rich and rewarding resource. From our experience we also know that articles can form a very effective reading 'base' for both short and long trainer development programmes.

Breen, M.P., C.N. Candlin, L. Dam and G. Gabrielson (1989) The evolution of a teacher training programme. In R.K. Johnson (ed) The Second Language Curriculum. Cambridge: Cambridge University Press.

Britten, D. (1988) Three stages in teacher training. ELT Journal, 42/2.

Brown, R.A. (2000) Cultural continuity and ELT teacher training. ELT Journal, 54/3.
Cullen, M. (1994) Incorporating a language improvement component in teacher education programmes. ELT Journal, 48/2.
Freeman, D. (1982) Observing Teachers: Three approaches to in-service training and development. TESOL Quarterly, 16/1.
Hayes, D. (1995) In-service teacher development: some principles. ELT Journal, 49/3.
Lamb M (1995)The Consequences of INSET. ELT Journal, 49/1.
Ramani, E. (1987) Theorizing from the classroom. ELT Journal, 41/3.
Sheal, P. (1989) Classroom observation: training the observers. ELT Journal, 43/2.
Underhill, A. (1992) The role of groups in developing teacher self-awareness. ELT Journal, 46/1.
Waters, A. (1988) Teacher training course design: a case study. ELT Journal, 42/2.
Williams, M. (1989) A developmental view of classroom observation. ELT Journal, 43/2.

Collections of Papers
Edge, J. and K. Richards (1993) (eds) Teachers Develop Teachers Research. Oxford: Heinemann.
- ground-breaking collection on teacher research as development.

Flowerdew, J., M. Brock and S. Hsia (1992) (eds) Perspectives on Second Language Teacher Education. City Polytechnic: Hong Kong.
- contains many interesting papers on teacher education, including teacher observation, teacher change, research and teacher education.

Claxton, G., T. Atkinson, M. Osborn and M. Wallace (eds) (1996) Liberating the Learner: Lessons for Professional Development in Education London: Routledge.
- many of these papers have a direct relevance to teacher education issues e.g. Claxton, John.

Boud, D., R.Keogh and D. Walker (eds) (1985) Reflection: Turning Experience Into Action. London: Kogan-Page.
- collection of articles on various aspects of 'reflection'. Not always easy to read but full of interesting insights and practical ideas.

Hargreaves, A. and M. Fullan (1992) (eds) Understanding Teacher Development London: Cassell.
- wide-ranging collection on aspects of teacher development. North American perspective.

Malderez, A. and P. Medgyes (1996) (eds) Changing Perspectives in Teacher Education. Oxford: Heinemann.
- covers all major aspects of teacher education.

McGrath, I. (1997) (ed) Learning To Train: Perspectives on the Development of Language Teacher Trainers. Hemel Hempstead: Prentice-Hall.
- interesting conference papers on trainer development.

Richards, J.C. and D. Nunan (1990) (eds) Second Language Teacher Education. Cambridge: Cambridge University Press.
- 'standard' collection of papers on teacher education.

Trappes-Lomax, H. and I. McGrath (1999) (eds) Theory in Language Teacher Education. Harlow: Longman.
- intriguing papers on theoretical aspects of teacher education.

Trappes-Lomax, H. and G. Ferguson (2002) (eds) Language In Language Teacher Education. Amsterdam: John Benjamins.
- comprehensive set of papers on language issues in teacher education.

Weil, S.W. and I. McGill (1989) (eds) Making Sense of Experiential Learning: Diversity in Theory and Practice. Buckingham: Open University Press.
- collection of papers from an early conference on experiential learning. Worth persevering with.

We also recommend 'The Teacher Trainer' which regularly features articles of interest.

Other Inspirational Work
Claxton, G. (1989) Being A Teacher. London: Cassell.
Claxton, G. (1990) Teaching To Learn. London: Cassell.
Claxton, G. (1999) Wise Up. London: Bloomsbury.
- Claxton writes with clarity and wit about learning, teaching and education.

Fullan, M. (1993) Change Forces London: Falmer Press
- Fullan writes passionately about the need to reform education.

Rogers, C. (1983) Freedom To Learn for the Eighties. Columbus, OH: Merrill.
- still a classic for educators everywhere.

APPENDIX I

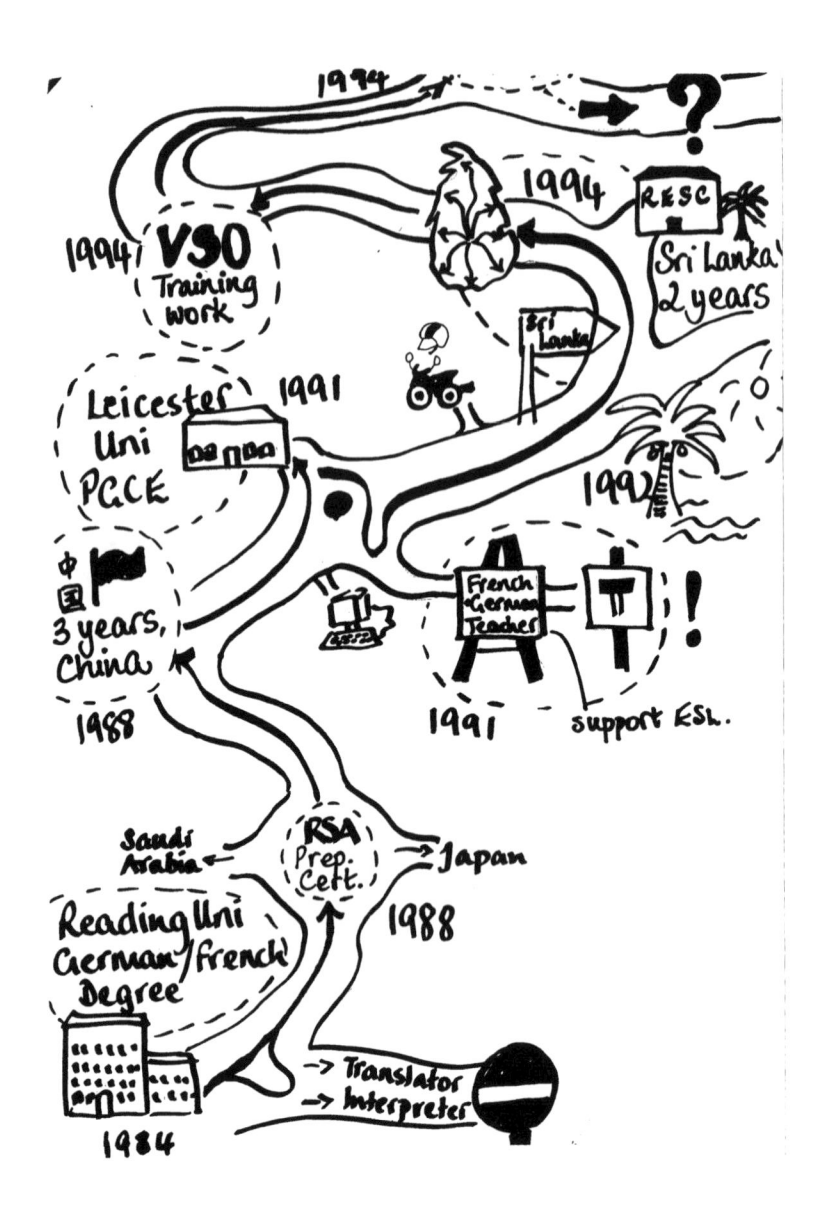

Sample of 'Career Road'

APPENDIX I

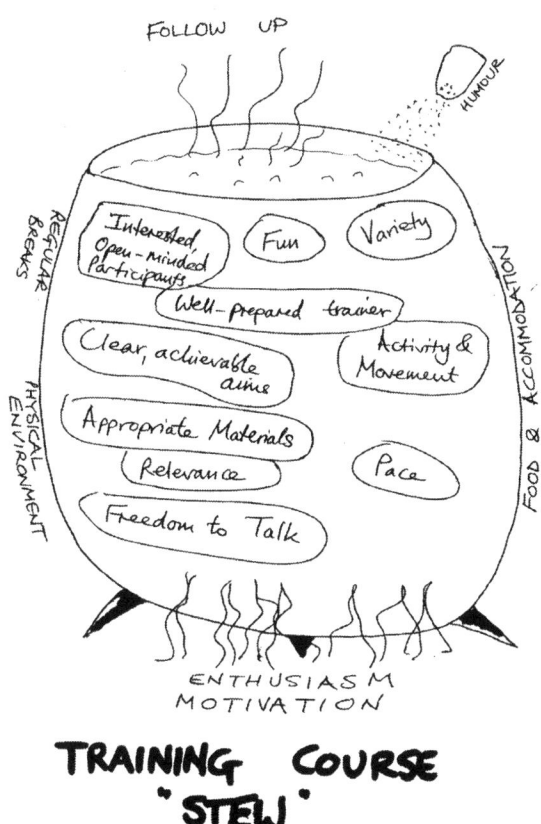

Ingredients of a Successful Training Course: Sample of a 'Stew' produced by participants

APPENDIX II
Characteristics of Adaptors and Innovators
[Based on Kirton (1989)]

The Adaptor	The Innovator
Characterised by precision, reliability, efficiency, methodicalness, prudence, discipline, conformity	Seen as undisciplined, thinking tangentially, approaching tasks from unusual angles
Concerned with resolving residual problems thrown up by existing ways of doing things	Searches for problems and alternative solutions, cutting across existing practices.
Seeks solutions to problems in tried and tested ways	Manipulates problems, and questions underlying assumptions
Reduces problems by improvement and greater efficiency, with maximum continuity and safety	A catalyst in settled groups, irreverent of consensual views. Abrasive and dissonant
Seen as safe, sound, conforming, dependable	Seen as unsound, impractical, shocking
Liable to make goals of means	Goal-oriented; treats means with little regard
Seems impervious to boredom: able to maintain high accuracy in long spells of detailed work	Only capable of detailed work in short bursts
Is an authority within given structures	Takes control in unstructured situations
Challenges rules rarely, cautiously, when assured of strong support	Often challenges rules; has little respect for the past
Tends to high self doubt. Reacts to criticism by closer outward conformity. Vulnerable to social pressure and authority. Compliant.	Appears to have low self-doubt when generating ideas. Does not need consensus
Is essential to the functioning of the institution all the time, but occasionally needs to be dug out of his immediate system	Ideal in unscheduled crises, or better to help avoid them if well controlled
When collaborating with innovators Supplies stability, order and continuity to the partnership	*When collaborating with adaptors* supplies task orientations and break with the past and tradition
Is sensitive to people; maintains group cohesion and co-operation	Appears insensitive to people; threat to group cohesion and co-operation
Provides a safe base for the innovator's more risky operations	Provides the dynamics to bring about radical change

APPENDIX II

KEY
Your Score and Tendency

14-22	Strong Adaptor	39-47	Moderate Innovator
23-30	Moderate Adaptor	48-56	Strong Innovator
	31-38	Rough Balance	

APPENDIX III

SKILLS FOR TEACHER EDUCATION
Weekly Review 1

Preparation

Take some time to go back through your notes and papers from last week's work on the module. Look through your learning log.
Make a note of significant material, experiences and thoughts/feelings during the week.
Think about

- How the tutors managed the work of the week in and out of the training sessions
- The role of trainer talk in the training sessions
- How trainers gave feedback to the group and individuals
- The role of reading in the training process
- The purposes of discussion in the training room

See what connections you can make to Module 2 issues such as learning and teaching from your experience during this week's work.
Identify what were, for you, key learning or awareness moments in the week's work.

Reflective Writing

Write a review entitled 'The Training Experience' drawing on the material above, reflecting on the experience of Week 1.

Write approx 500-750 words.

APPENDIX III

SAMPLE of COMMENTS on STUDENTS' WRITTEN WORK
We give written summative feedback under three headings, as illustrated in the sample below.

Content
You have made the most of the opportunity to review an initiative in your home context. This has enabled you to re-examine the foundations of action research and to assess the project in which you were involved. There is a strong sense of context throughout- this would have been enhanced by more explicit reference to the conditions under which participating teachers work so that readers can see more clearly why so many were happy to pass on the work to others when the project ended. However, your criticisms of the project are well made and supported with very appropriate references both to the literature and participants' voices. Your review of the literature on action research has identified key issues which you use intelligently to support your suggestions for an alternative approach. These needed a little more fleshing out despite the length of the paper. For example, the section on 'personal questions' is rather 'loose' and vague. There is, on the whole, clear evidence that you not only appreciate the issues entailed by a research stance towards teaching, but that you have also considered their relevance to you and colleagues in your context.

Presentation
Neatly word-processed and set out with helpful headings and sub-headings which, together with effective signposting and summarising, make for an enjoyable read. You need to work on the precision of some of your statements, and think about the impact of rhetorical questions on a reader. Proofread to avoid unnecessary grammatical slips.

Overall
This is work of a high standard, demonstrating wide and effective reading, a clear professional focus and above all, independent judgement and thinking.

APPENDIX III

Orientation Week Activities
Evaluation/Self-Evaluation

A. Evaluation

Here is a list of the orientation week activities. Please decide on their relative value to you by grading them each on a scale 1-5 (1 for lowest vale and 5 for highest value).

In the 'comments' box, note any highlights, low points, memorable aspects, things you wish you'd done more/less of, and any other comments.

Make an overall evaluation in the space provided, add any suggestions you have for future orientation weeks and any other comments you have.

	Value (1-5)	Comments
Orientation/Briefing (Monday)		
Professional Development (Tuesday/Wednesday)		
Professional Presentations (Thursday)		
Feedback/Evaluation (Friday)		

Overall Evaluation

Suggestions

Other Comments

APPENDIX III

B. Self-Evaluation

Here are some questions to help you evaluate your own contributions to the orientation week. Write your responses and comments. Please feel free to take up points in tutorial.

1. **Your Contributions To Activities**
   a. Did you contribute enough?
   b. Did you feel comfortable?
   c. Were you able to concentrate all the time?
   d. Did you ever feel lost, frustrated or annoyed?

2. **Obtaining Information**
   a. Did you ask enough questions?
   b. Were you able to get satisfactory answers to your questions?
   c. Did you feel you were able to ask for help when you needed it?

3. **Relationships**
   a. Did you feel able to get on with your colleagues and tutors?
   b. Were you able to help colleagues and tutors?

4. **Preparation**
   a. Did you feel that you did enough to prepare yourself for the course?

APPENDIX III

SAMPLE OF 'ONE YEAR LATER' QUESTIONNAIRE

This questionnaire is sent to participants a year or more after they have completed their Masters programme. We find the feedback extremely useful as by then former students will have had a chance to put into practice what they have learnt.

Dear Friend

It may have been a long time since we were in touch. We hope this finds you well.

We're contacting you because we'd like to know how you've been getting on since you did your Masters with us. We'd be grateful if you could spare a few minutes to let us have your reflections on your academic and personal experience when you were here at the College. This will help us gain a different perspective on our programmes and also to enable us to develop the programme and perhaps identify any current needs internationally.

Thanks very much for your time and trouble
With very best wishes

Please answer the questions below. (Continue overleaf if there isn't enough space)

1. What job/work are you doing at present? Briefly describe your main professional tasks and, if possible, how the course prepared you for these.

2. What have been the most valuable and useful benefits of your Masters course in your work and life since completing?

3. Looking back, was there any topic or area 'missing' from your course, or was there an aspect that you'd wished you'd spent more time on?

4. What are your strongest memories of your time the College and of your course?

5. Any other comments you'd like to make on your Masters programme at Marjon? (Continue overleaf if you wish)

Thanks for your time and trouble!

APPENDIX IV

METHODOLOGY and MATERIALS in TEACHER TRAINING
Issues In Teacher Training : Reading

As an integral part of our first cycle of work on teacher training methodology and materials, it is essential to consolidate our understanding of the issues through reading of selected articles. The reading task is as follows:

- during Weeks 6-9 inclusive, read each of the articles provided (There are two packs of articles circulating in the group, as well as there being copies of each article in the group collection. You will also be able to find the articles in the Library. A full list is provided below.) You may want to form a reading syndicate to ease the burden of reading.

While you are reading, focus on the following questions:
1. What is the *main training focus* of the article in each case?
2. What is the author's stance on the relationship between *theory and practice* in teacher training? (either implied or stated)
3. In your view, do you think that the author of each article is in sympathy with classroom or 'theoretical' issues?
4. What is the author's conception of *'professional competence'* (implied or stated)?
5. What are the *implications* of each article for designing and conducting training sessions?
6. What are *your reactions* to each article? Do you find yourself in agreement or disagreement with the author of each?

In order to help you collect your responses to each article, and also to focus on the essence of the issues, draw up a table in which to record your responses. Use the following headings:

Main focus	**Theory/practice**	**Prof. Competence**
Implications	**Reactions**	**Other Comments**

Be ready to discuss the articles during the sessions in Weeks 9-12 of the course.

Articles

Britten, D. (1988) 3 stages in teacher training. *ELT Journal*, 42/1.
Ellis, R. (1985) Activities and procedures for teacher preparation. In J.C. Richards and D. Nunan (eds) (1990) *Second Language Teacher Education* Cambridge: Cambridge University Press.
Ramani, E. (1987) Theorizing from the classroom. *ELT Journal*, 41/3.
Ur, P. (1992) Teacher learning. *ELT Journal*, 46/1.
Widdowson, H.G. (1984) The incentive value of theory in teacher education. *ELT Journal*, 38/2.

APPENDIX IV

SAMPLE ASSIGNMENT SPECIFICATION
TEACHER TRAINING PROCEDURES and MATERIALS

Your task is to devise a training session (or series of linked sessions) for either (a) a group of experienced English teachers or (b) a group of initial trainees

The training session should consist of 3-4 hours of training room activity. The session can cover any area of ELT or teacher development you consider relevant to the needs of the target group, or from a set syllabus.

Some possible examples to get you thinking

- *Teaching of reading/ writing/ speaking/ listening skills*
- *Teaching of grammar/ vocabulary*
- *Integration of skills e.g. project work*
- *Developing learner autonomy*
- *Motivation in the ELT classroom*
- *Using drama or role play*
- *Language awareness for teachers*
- *Exploratory teaching*
- *Action research for teachers*

Etc. (Your suggestions are welcome)

Your paper should include the following
  (a) a brief introduction
  (b) a brief outline of the context in which the training sessions will take place, including a brief profile of participants
  (c) a rationale in which you explain and justify your training approach and the training activities, with reference to the professional literature
  (d) clear details of all training activities, including 'ready-to-use' handouts for the training group
  (e) detailed trainer's notes on how to use the materials
  (f) an annotated bibliography on the topic of the sessions for the participants
  (g) a further review section in which you *either* discuss the potential difficulties that using the materials may create for trainers or participants *or* discuss the experience of producing the materials and the design process *or* report on the experience of using the materials with a group, suggesting changes and modifications

APPENDIX IV

Developing as a Trainer

Please complete the questionnaire as indicated.

Section 1
What are your perceptions of a trainer's role?
For each of the listed features of a teacher's work, identify a parallel and related feature for a trainer. (You will note that this task involves generalising. You do not need to be specific and detailed in your responses at this stage.) Use the spaces after 9 and 10 to add further features of your own if you wish.

Teacher	Trainer
	(choose initial or in-service)
1. responsible for (usually) school-aged learners and their learning	
2. operates mainly in the classroom & has direct contact with learners	
3. makes teaching decisions	
4. corrects learners' errors	
5. familiar with the subject syllabus & course books	
6. day-to-day work is largely <u>practical</u> in nature	
7. often subject-focused	
8. trained by trainers	
9.	
10.	

It will help to discuss your perceptions with a colleague, focusing on the differences you have perceived between the roles of teachers and trainers. Do you find yourself more content-focused in your views about training than process-focused? What are the implications for your practice as a trainer?

Section 2
In which of the following roles have you seen trainers at work? Which roles have you played yourself? (**Underline your choices. Add more if you wish.**)

253

APPENDIX IV

supervisor	resource manager	facilitator	expert
assessor	lecturer	counsellor	teacher
observer	adviser	listener	model
summariser	personal tutor	researcher	timekeeper
inspector	monitor	....	....

Look again at the roles you have ticked. Are there any implications for the roles of trainees/course participants?

Now place the roles you have identified at an appropriate point on this continuum.

⬅—————————————————➡

subject-matter people-oriented
oriented roles roles

Section 3
What's involved in becoming a trainer in contexts you are familiar with? *Underline the relevant choices. Add any others involved in your experience?*

taking a course	knowing your subject in more depth
observing other trainer	seeking higher status
higher academic qualification	personal qualities
a desire to develop yourself professionally	patronage/influence of superiors

Self-Development Activity
WHAT IS YOUR REASON FOR BECOMING A TRAINER? What's involved for you personally from the list above? How far do you think this reflects your own stance on training? For you, what is most important in becoming a trainer - knowledge of the subject area in which you are training people; use and development of interpersonal skills; something more personal?

Printed in Great Britain
by Amazon